EXTENDED-REACH DRILLING

Solutions and Applications

Robello Samuel

DISCLAIMER. While both authors and publisher have used their best efforts in preparing and producing the book, they make no representations or warranties with respect to the accuracy or completeness of the contents of this book and specifically disclaim any implied warranties of merchantability or fitness for a particular purpose. No warranty may be created or extended by marketing or sales representatives or in print or online sales and marketing materials. The advice and strategies contained herein are the opinions of the authors and may not be suitable for your situation. You should consult with the proper professional where appropriate. Neither the publisher nor the authors shall be held liable for any loss of profit or any other commercial damages, including but not limited to special, incidental, consequential, or any other damage.

This publication or any part thereof may not be copied, reproduced, stored in a physical or electronic retrieval system, or transmitted in any form by any means, electronic, mechanical, photocopying, scanning, recording, or otherwise, except as permitted under Section 107 or 108 of the 1976 United States Copyright Act, without either: (1) the prior written permission of the publisher, or (2) authorization through payment of the appropriate per-copy fee to the Copyright Clearance Center, 222 Rosewood Drive, Danvers, Massachusetts, 01923, (978) 750-8400, fax (978) 646-8600, or at www.copyright.com.

Extended Reach Drilling - Solutions and Applications

Copyright © 2016 Halliburton. All rights reserved.

First printing August 2016.

Published in the United States of America by Halliburton.

Library of Congress Cataloging-in-Publication Data
Samuel, Robello.
Includes bibliographical references and index.

Printed in Canada by Friesens Corporation.

ISBN 978-0-9864417-1-4

Contents

CHAPTER 1: **INTRODUCTION** 1
    Extended-Reach Drilling (ERD) 2
    Exented-Reach Drillling (ERD) Envelope 7
    Designer Wells...7
    Ultra-Extended-Reach Wells 8
    Extreme-Extended-Reach Wells 9

CHAPTER 2: **ROCK MECHANICS IN WELL CONSTRUCTION** 13
    Loading/Unloading Characteristics...13
    Fracture Toughness 19
    Near-Wellbore Stress Field...20
    Failure Criteria..25
    Wellbore Stability During Drilling...31
    Wellbore Stability, Eccentricity Effects, and Casing Loading.........................36

CHAPTER 3: **FORMATION PRESSURES** 41
    Pressures...42
    Origin of Abnormal Pressure...45
    Abnormal Pressure Indicators During Drilling 50
    Differential Pressure Decrease Due to Background Gas................................53
    Pore-Pressure Estimation..54
    Pore-Pressure Calculation...58

CHAPTER 4: **WELL DESIGN** 71
    Well Profiles and Terminology 72
    Types of Wells...76
    Selecting the ERD Well Type...80
    Risk Management Process...82
    Survey Management...83

Contents - continued

BHA and Drillstring Desing 84
Hydraulics Management 84
Torque and Drag Management 84
Vibration Management 85
Design Control 86

CHAPTER 5: **WELL PATHS** 89
Factors Influencing ERD Well Path Design 89
Basic Well Path Designs 91
Catenary Design 95
Transition Curves 104
Clothoid Curve 105
Curvature Bridging 109
Trajectory Calculations 110
Curvature and Torsion 112
Quantification of Borehole Complexity 112
Wellbore Indices 114
Samuel's Wellbore Energy Index 116
Total Strain Energy Change 116

CHAPTER 6: **DRILLING HYDRAULICS** 127
Hydraulics and Wellbore-Pressure Management 128
Mud Consideration 130
Impact of Hole Cleaning and Cuttings Transport on ECD Management ... 133
Problems Related to Drilling Fluid 136

CHAPTER 7: **DRILLSTRING MECHANICS** 151
Drillstring Design 152

Contents - continued

Torque and Drag	154
Trip Speed and Pipe Rotation	155
BHA Modeling	157
Rig Capabilities	160
Drillstring Considerations	162
Drillstring Dynamics	163
Deconvolution of Vibrational Data	169
Tool-Failure Prediction	172
Drillstring Buckling	173
CHAPTER 8: WELL CONTROL	**177**
Fundamentals of Primary Well Control	178
Maintaining Primary Well Control	180
Kick Detection	182
Regaining Primary Well Control	187
CHAPTER 9: CASING DESIGN	**197**
Properties of Casing	197
Combined Stress Effects	205
Connections	210
Radial Safety Factor	214
Loads on Casing Strings	218
Pressure Load Cases	231
Mechanical Loads	246
Thermal Loads and Temperature Effects	250
CHAPTER 10: CASING WEAR	**253**
Casing Wear and Hole Erosion	253

Contents - continued

Estimation 255

Studies 256

Casing-Wear Model 258

Torque-and-Drag Model – Soft String vs. Stiff String 260

Casing-Wear Factors 261

Influencing Parameters 262

Foreword

Eric Carre, Executive Vice President, Global Business Lines

I am pleased to introduce the book '*Extended Reach Drilling-Solutions and Applications*' by Dr. Robello Samuel. This is Dr. Samuel's third book in the series on Drilling Solutions, addressing the technical challenges associated with Extended Reach Drilling and the successful delivery of complex wellbores.

This publication offers drilling professionals practical considerations and novel methods supported by deep technical understanding. Over time, our industry has evolved to address the challenges of hydrocarbon development from a variety of reservoirs and geologies. Extended Reach Drilling (ERD) has become an increasingly important technology for the development of unconventionals and to produce reservoirs with challenging access.

The next decade of hydrocarbon development will demand greater efficiencies and in-depth technical knowledge as we deal with the increasing complexity of drilling operations. We believe a collaborative approach, engineered solutions, and flawless execution remain the keys to success.

Preface

As the world is becoming more digital, it makes us wonder why another hard bound book? The answer is that we still have not lost the touch in reading from the hard bound book. It is my sincere hope that this book provides insight into extended reach drilling (ERD) so that it can be used effectively in such operations. Some of the work is edited from previously published Halliburton books (*Drilling Engineering, An Engineering Approach to Horizontal Drilling, Horizontal Drilling – Solutions and Applications, and Petroleum Well Construction*) and Halliburton authored SPE papers for which different authors have contributed and are noted in the acknowledgements section as well as in the references. Relevant material has been added wherever necessary in the appropriate chapters.

Every possible effort has been taken to acknowledge and give appropriate credits to the contributors. Should there be any omission, I sincerely apologize for the mistake, and suitable correction will be made at the first possible update.

Dr. Robello Samuel

Drilling Engineering

Horizontal Drilling

About Dr. Samuel

Dr. Robello Samuel is a Halliburton Technology Fellow. Having been with Halliburton since 1998, he helps lead well-engineering applications and is responsible for research in new drilling technologies. He makes decisions and recommendations that are authoritative and that have a far-reaching impact on the company's research and scientific activities, and he serves as a corporate resource, providing technical direction and advice to management in long-range planning for new or projected areas of drilling. He has more than 30 years of multi-disciplinary experience in oil and gas operations, management, consulting, software development, and teaching. His special areas of oilfield expertise include onshore and offshore well engineering, cost estimation, and drilling supervision.

Dr. Samuel has written or coauthored more than 160 journal articles, conference papers, and technical articles. He is regarded as one of the world's most influential contributors to advancement of research and practice in drilling engineering. Dr. Samuel has been the recipient of numerous awards, including the SPE Regional Drilling Engineering Award, SPE International Drilling Engineering Award, SPE Distinguished member, and the "CEO for A Day (Halliburton)" award. He presently serves as a review chairman on several journals and professional committees. He has taught on the faculty of various Universities and holds an adjunct professor appointment (concurrently) for the past 13 years, at the University of Houston.

Dr. Samuel serves regularly as a keynote speaker at major conferences and corporate forums. He is presently serving on several Editorial Review Committees, notably: on the Board of Directors in Research Partnership to Secure Energy for America (RPSEA), an Advisory committee member at Ocean Energy Safety Institute (OESI) program, an Evaluator for Accreditation Board for Engineering and Technology, Inc. (ABET), and a representative at Society of Petroleum Engineer's Research and development advisory board.

Dr. Samuel, a Society of Petroleum Engineer Distinguished Lecturer, holds B.S. and M.S. degrees in mechanical engineering from The University of Madurai and College of Engineering, Guindy. He also holds M.S. and Ph.D. degrees in petroleum engineering from Tulsa University.

Dr. Samuel's unique blend of skills with broad experience as a field engineer, thinker, thought leader, innovator, researcher, and an educator has given him the ability to author twelve drilling books and a forthcoming book, Applied Drilling Engineering Optimization. He can be reached via e-mail at robello.samuel@halliburton.com / robellos@hotmail.com, or phone at (832) 275-8810.

Acknowledgments

We would like to express our gratitude to all those who were involved in the editing and production of this book. We would especially like to thank Akshay Sagar who initiated this endeavor so that engineers can use this book as an aid to their work. Special recognition and thanks are due to Eddison Fu who coordinated the work on a tight schedule and brought all the chapters into production.

We gratefully acknowledge the contributors who have invested their time in preparing the contents and text.

Wael El Deftar, Halliburton.

Adolfo Gonzales, Halliburton

Aniket Kumar, Halliburton

Michael J. Economides and Larry Moran (Deceased), Larry T. Watters, CSI Technologies, Shari Dunn-Norman, University of Missouri-Rolla and Stefan Miska, University of Tulsa, Lance D. Underwood, Stealth Mode Startup Co. Michael L. Payne, BP,W.E. Hottman, Andrew A. Mills, John W. Minear, K. Joe Goodwin, Hernando Jerez, Robert Mitchell and Mike Stephens, Robert Beirute, Beirute Consulting LLC. Richard Jones, Kash Oil & Gas Inc. Randolf R. Wagner, Apache Corporation, Dan R. Collins, James R. Longbottom, Iain Dowell,.

Finally, we would like to extend a special thanks to Kristie Landwair from TekSpert Consulting, LLC for copyediting, Debbie Markley from Wordsmith Communications for proofing, and Regina Bean from Clearpoint Creative for preparing the layout and design of the book.

CHAPTER **ONE**

Introduction

Directional-drilling limitations result from the interaction of the wellbore with the constraints of the drilling rig, drilling fluid, and drilling equipment. One limitation is how rapidly the angle can be built or the direction changed. This boundary is now being expanded with the increased application and advancement of short- and intermediate-radius drilling technology. Another limitation is the maximum drilling depth of directional wells. This limitation is linked with the tension and torque loads that deep directional drilling imposes above the loads in deep vertical wells. Deep directional drilling is limited by the tension and torque capacities of the drillpipe and rig equipment.

Analogous to short-radius and deep directional drilling, there are also limitations as to how long or complex a departure can be drilled. This section will discuss these additional boundaries of directional-drilling technology. Technologies for, and operations of, extended-reach drilling and so-called "designer well drilling" are rapidly expanding, and both will become more significant in the future.

Extended-Reach Drilling (ERD)

Various definitions exist for extended-reach-drilling (ERD)-class wells. One common definition is a departure of at least twice the true vertical depth (TVD) of the well (a reach-to-TVD ratio of two or more). This definition separates conventional directional wells from wells that could require ERD technology. However, since state-of-the-art ERD can involve wells with reach-to-TVD ratios of four to five or even higher, it should be recognized that distinct classes of ERD wells do exist, as shown in **Fig. 1.1**. These definitions are listed as follows:

- Reach-to-TVD Ratio < 2   → Conventional Directional Drilling (Non-ERD)

- Reach-to-TVD Ratio = 2 to 3 → Extended-Reach Drilling

- Reach-to-TVD Ratio > 3   → Ultra-Extended-Reach Drilling (u-ERD)

- Reach-to-TVD Ratio > 15   → Extreme Extended-Reach Drilling (x-ERD)

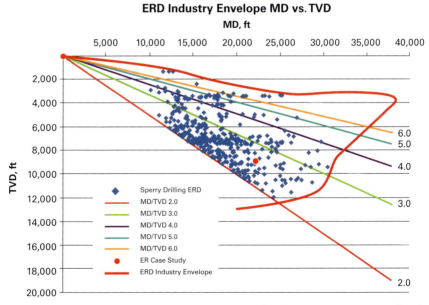

Fig. 1.1 – ERD industry envelope of measured depth (MD) vs. true vertical depth (TVD).

These classifications are somewhat arbitrary, and drilling a well with a reach-to-TVD ratio of less than two can be quite challenging depending on the formations involved and the type of rig available.

According to PetroWiki, some of the notable extended-reach wells include:

- Exxon Neftegas Limited, Sakhalin Island Russia, (MD/TVD = 3.9 to 6.9)

- Maersk Oil Qatar in the Al Shaheen field, Qatar (MD/TVD = 11.1)

- BP on the Wytch Farm project, England (MD/TVD = 6.9 to 6.6)

- Total in Argentina, Cullen Norte #1 (MD/TVD = 6.7)

- ExxonMobil in the Santa Ynez Unit, offshore California, USA (MD/TVD = 5.36)

Engineers must understand the technical interactions between the rig and equipment in addition to the well being attempted so that constraints and risks can be identified and resolutions can be sought as early as possible. Various technologies must be applied for the successful planning and execution of an ERD well. These technologies include:

- Optimized directional trajectory design

- Refined mechanical wellbore-stability estimates for mud-weight windows

- Properly engineered drilling fluids for optimization of chemical wellbore stability, cased-hole and openhole lubricity, and cuttings transport and suspension

- Calibrated torque-and-drag models to allow for projection of field loads and diagnosis of deviations from predictions during field execution

- Sizing of rig components to provide adequate rotary, hydraulic, hoisting, solids control, and power capabilities

- Properly designed drillstring that minimizes drillpipe pressure loss (allowing for higher flow rates for given surface-pressure limitations)

- Other technologies, such as:
  - Soft-torque top drives
  - Special running systems and techniques for casings, liners, and completion strings
  - Rotary-steerable directional-drilling systems

The unique issues associated with ERD wells largely stem from the high inclination of the well required to reach the objective departures. Tangent "sail" angles in some ERD wells have been 80° or higher, while "average" angles from surface to total depth (TD) have been 70° or higher. Some "ERD" wells have, in fact, been drilled as extremely long horizontal wells, where the bulk of the well has been drilled horizontally (defined as an inclination of 88° or more).

At such high inclinations, the transport of cuttings from the well is more difficult than in vertical wells. As a result, higher flow rates, tighter control of drilling-fluid rheology, and the use of nonconventional mechanical means to assist hole cleaning must be used. Such mechanical means might include high drillstring rotation (off-bottom)or the use of specially bladed drillpipe to mechanically stir cuttings beds. High rotary speeds and backreaming help clean the hole but can increase drilling shocks and cause fatigue or backoff of motor housings. Therefore, such practices should be viewed as secondary hole-cleaning methods and used only if the primary hole cleaning method is inadequate. A common method of removing cuttings beds is the use of low-viscosity sweeps that scour the cuttings off the low side of the hole; high-viscosity sweeps are then made that carry the dislodged cuttings to the surface. The fundamental driver of hole cleaning, however, is flow rate, and high flow rates are strongly recommended throughout high-inclination sections if ERD allows. Flow rates of 1,000 to 1,100 gal/min in a 12¼-in. hole and 500 to 600 gal/min in an 8½-in. hole are not uncommon. For this reason, the rig's pump and piping capacities with regard to flow rate, pressure, and drillstring design are critical.

Other implications of high inclination include the greater likelihood of mechanical wellbore instability and, hence, the need for careful

mud-weight planning. Since more formation is exposed for longer periods, chemical stability also becomes more critical.

Aside from hydraulics and formation stability, another potential ERD constraint is the ability to sustain drilling torque and run tubulars in the well. Both of these processes are impacted by optimizing the well trajectory and field control of variations from this directional plan. In terms of design optimization, the ERD trajectory will be subject to similar geologic constraints. Additionally, the trajectory should be designed to minimize the induced torque during drilling and to maximize the available weight while casing is run. Satisfaction of these objectives varies depending on the TVD and departure of the target and the frictional behaviors of the various hole sections and the location of those sections.

One observation from several studies (Banks et al. 1992; Dawson and Paslay 1984), however, is that multiple build rates should be used to initiate inclination into the well gradually. Increasing the build rates in several steps minimizes near-surface doglegs and the associated torque and drag.

The final tangent angle and shape of the trajectory through the reservoir can be determined on the basis of several considerations. If the well design is close to the limit of wireline intervention capabilities (65° to 70°), it may be best to keep the kick-off point (KOP) high and limit the inclination so that wireline operations are feasible. If the well angle is more severe and the inclination will already exceed wireline operating limits, it may be appropriate to slightly deepen the KOP to increase formation stability and allow for a more gradual build section. In such cases, although a higher final inclination angle will result, the higher inclination may, in fact, be optimal, since it inhibits buckling of the drillstring and coiled tubing, which could be critical controlling factors in severe ERD wells.

In addition to an optimized trajectory plan suited for the specific well application, directional drilling must be performed well in the field to minimize unexpected doglegs and variations from the plan. Such doglegs will increase drilling torque, make tubular running more difficult, and provide potential trouble spots for excessive casing wear, which can

lead to failures. These serious detriments have been recognized previously (Sheppard et al. 1987; Mueller et al. 1991), and a specific measure is available for defining how closely the well is or has been drilled according to plan. This measure is known as tortuosity, which is the sum of all the increments of curvature along the section of interest subtracted from the planned curvature and divided by the footage drilled. In the well-planning phase, specific tortuosity guidelines should be generated for each section of the well based on torque-and-drag modeling. Tortuosity limitations should generally be the most stringent in the upper portion of the well and in the build section, where high drillstring tension causes high-side loading, which results in torque and drag, keyseating, and worn tool joints and casing. Reducing tortuosity requires an integrated engineering approach, as described:

- The rotary-drilling directional tendency of bottomhole assemblies (BHAs) should be tracked, quantified, and refined to yield rotary behaviors that are as close as possible to planned build rates. This process minimizes the use of oriented drilling as a means of inclination control.

- When steering is required, it should be executed in a controlled manner. For example, doglegs can be minimized by sliding for only part of a joint, or a single joint or stand; then, rotary drilling can be used for the remaining footage. This process can then be repeated as required to offset the build, drop, or turn behavior of the rotary BHA that is causing the problem.

- Sliding repeatedly in short intervals is greatly preferred over executing one continuous, long sliding section, which will cause a significant and sharp dogleg.

A systematic analysis and planning of BHAs, as well as careful field execution, will enable good control of well tortuosity and will ensure that pre-drill torque-and-drag projections are not exceeded. Projecting requirements for ERD wells, properly sizing the drilling rig and equipment, and optimizing the trajectory are all subject to detailed, site-specific engineering. The key to success is to recognize those technologies that are critical and those tradeoffs that must be examined to engineer the best possible approach for a given well.

Extended-Reach Drilling (ERD) Envelope

In the early 1980s, a well with a horizontal displacement of 1,500 m (~ 5,000 ft) from the surface location was considered to be an "extended-reach" well, while in recent years, over 12,000 m (~ 40,000 ft) of displacement has been achieved. Previously, the industry defined an extended-reach well as one in which the departure or displacement was greater than twice the TVD. "Designer" wells with negative sections or 3D complex trajectories are not well quantified using displacement/TVD criteria. Today, the industry uses the MD/TVD ratio to define ERD wells.

Fig. 1.1 shows the current industry envelope for extended-reach drilling. Gravity has a big impact on the drilling process; the shallower the well, the more complex the ERD operation. Several factors come into play, including available weight to drill with, tripping into and out of the hole, fracture gradients, equivalent circulating densities, and torque and drag.

The MD/TVD ratio is a measurement used to define the complexity of the ERD operation. ERD wells represent critical operating environments, and downhole components must be managed from the perspective of component specification, confidence, and reliability. One of the tools that has enabled the expansion of ERD applications is the rotary steerable system. Many of the challenges involved can be overcome with the right planning tools to simulate different BHAs and optimize the BHA based on modeling analysis.

Designer Wells

"Designer wells" are similar to ERD wells, but they may be even more complex because they involve multiple-target trajectories with substantial and potentially difficult azimuthal steering. Therefore, designer wells may require inclination control combined with strong azimuthal curvature to allow for the intersection of these offset targets (**Fig. 1.2**). Although the industry has no widely accepted definitions for what constitutes a designer well, some definitions have been proposed based on MD/TVD ratios. Such a distinct definition from the reach-to-TVD definition for ERD is necessary, because designer wells involve substantially drilled footages that may not necessarily increase well departure.

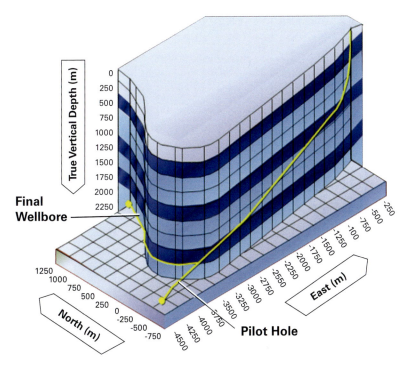

Fig. 1.2 – Designer ERD Well Path.

Ultra-Extended-Reach Wells

Extended-reach drilling (ERD) technology has been rapidly developed during the past two decades, and drilling ultra-extended-reach (u-ERD) wells, as well as extending their reach to greater depths, requires improved models. Wellbore friction is an important issue for ultra-long wells, and optimizing the design of the well path is an effective means to reduce torque and drag.

ERD wells not only provide solutions for restricted reservoir production, but also help eliminate additional platforms. ERD techniques and technologies have rapidly evolved, and step-out wells have incrementally increased since 1993 when the ERD program commenced, accessing offshore reserves under Poole Harbour from land-based wellsites (Robertson et al. 2005). Wytch Farm was at the forefront of extended-reach drilling. In 1997, Well M11 broke the 10-km (~ 33,000-ft) departure mile-

stone to set a new world record. In 2000, Well M16 established another world record at 10,727 m and a measured depth of 11,278 m (37,001 ft) (Robertson et al. 2005; Meader et al. 2000). Mason and Judzis (1998) indicated that it was possible to drill and complete u-ERD wells in the future.

Extreme-Extended-Reach Wells

Drilling extreme-extended-reach (x-ERD) wells and extending their reach to greater depths require both improved models and a comprehensive analysis. Wellbore friction is an important factor in drilling ultra-long wells, and optimizing the well-path design is an effective means for reducing torque and drag. This book describes a new well-path design that will enable extending the reach of a well to a greater depth. Usually, well trajectories are designed with constant curvature with well-defined arcs connecting the transition between the tangent sections. Even though the transition between the tangent and build sections or tangent and drop sections appears to be smooth, there will be some discontinuity that will result in high stresses on the tubulars, increase torque and drag, and result in poor hole cleaning and other problems. To avoid curvature and geometrical torsion discontinuities between sections, curvature-bridge curves or transition curves can be used.

References

Azar, J.J. and Samuel, R. 2010. *Drilling Engineering*. PennWell Publishers.

Samuel, R. 2014. *Horizontal Drilling Engineering*. Houston, Texas: SigmaQuadrant Publishers.

Hansford, J.E. and Lubinski, A. 1973. Cumulative Fatigue Damage of Drillpipe in Doglegs. SPE Reprint Series, 6a: 285–281.

Hogg, W.T. and Thorogood, J.L. 1990. Performance Optimization of Steerable Systems. *ASME PD* **27**: 49–58.

Jogi, P.N., Burgess, T.M., and Bowling, J.P. 1990. Predicting the Build/Drop Tendency of Rotary Drilling Assemblies. *Directional Drilling*, SPE Reprint Series No. 30.

Johancsik, C.A., Friesen, D.B., and Dawson, R. 1984. Torque and Drag in Directional Wells—Prediction and Measurement. *JPT*, **36**(06). SPE 11380.

Larson, P.A. and Azar, J.J. 1992. Three-Dimensional, Quasi-Static, Drill Ahead BHA Model for Wellbore Trajectory Prediction and Control. *PED, Drilling Technology, ASME* **40**.

Meader, T., Allen, F., and Riley, G. 2000. To the Limit and Beyond—The Secret of World-Class Extended-Reach Drilling Performance at Wytch Farm. Paper SPE 59204 presented at the IADC/SPE Drilling Conference, New Orleans, 23–25 February.

Mason, C.J. and Judzis, A. 1998. Extended-Reach Drilling—What is the Limit? Paper SPE 48943 presented at the SPE Annual Technical Conference and Exhibition, New Orleans, 27–30 September.

Murphey, C.E. and Cheatham Jr., J.B. 1965. Hole Deviation and Drillstring Behavior. Paper SPE 1259.

Nicholson, J.W. 1994. An Integrated Approach to Drilling Dynamics Planning Identification and Control. Paper SPE 27537 presented at the SPE/IADC Drilling Conference, Dallas, Texas, 15–18 February.

Odell, A. and Payne, M. 1995. Application of a Highly Variable Gauge Stabilizer at Wytch Farm to Extend the ERD Envelope. Paper SPE 30462 presented at the SPE Annual Technical Conference and Exhibition, Dallas, Texas, 22–25 October.

Payne, M.L. and Spanos, P.D. 1992. Advances in Dynamic Bottomhole Assembly Modeling and Dynamic Response Determination. Paper SPE 23905 presented at the SPE/IADC Drilling Conference, New Orleans, Louisiana, 18–21 February.

Payne, M.L., Abbassian, F.A., and Hatch, A.J. 1995. Drillstring Dynamic Problems and Solutions for Extended-Reach Drilling Operations. Paper presented at the ASME Energy-Sources Technology Conference, Houston, Texas, 29 Jan–1 Feb.

Rasmussen, B., Sorheim, E., Seiffert, O., Angeltvadt, O., and Gjedrem, T. 1991. World Record in Extended Reach Drilling, Well 33/9-C10, Statfjord Field, Norway. Paper SPE 21984 presented at the SPE/IADC Drilling Conference, Amsterdam, The Netherlands, 11–14 March.

Robertson, N., Hancock, S., and Mota, L. 2005. Effective Torque Management of Wytch Farm Extended-Reach Sidetrack Wells. Paper SPE 95430 presented at the SPE Annual Technical Conference and Exhibition, Dallas, Texas, 9–12 October.

Underwood, L. and Odell, A. 1994. A Systems Approach to Downhole Adjustable Stabilizer Design and Application. Paper SPE 27484 presented at the SPE/IADC Drilling Conference, Dallas, Texas, 15–18 February.

Williamson, J.S. and Lubinski, A. 1987. Predicting Bottomhole Assembly Performance. *SPEDE*, **2**(01), SPE 14764.

Wolff, C.J.M. and de Wardt, J.P. 1981. Borehole Position Uncertainty— Analysis of Measuring Methods and Derivation of Systematic Error Model. *JPT*, **33**(12): 2339–2350.

EXTENDED-REACH DRILLING

CHAPTER **TWO**

Rock Mechanics in Well Construction

Rock mechanics is an important part of extended-reach drilling. As the well is drilled, it undergoes a lot of changes, and the mechanical properties change due to loading/unloading characteristics, as well as cyclic loading, poroelasticity, viscoelasticity, and fracture toughness. A wellbore drilled through a rock formation introduces a new stress field at the wellbore proximity that may be great enough to cause failure. This chapter discusses this effect with respect to the geomechanics perspective.

Loading/Unloading Characteristics

Wellbore construction consists of loading and unloading the formation and cement sheath. Therefore, studying the characteristics of a complete loading and unloading cycle is important. Additionally, evaluating cement and formation samples for the effect of cyclic loading can be beneficial during wellbore construction.

The stress/strain relationship describes the way the formation's framework of granular material responds to the applied load. This relationship

indicates whether the material exhibits elastic or plastic, brittle or ductile, strain-softening or strain-hardening behavior during loading. The following characteristics of the formation are important to consider:

- Poroelasticity
- Viscoelasticity
- Thermoviscoelasticity
- Fracture toughness

Poroelasticity

Within the proximity of the wellbore, poroelasticity can be examined based on the effective-stress concept introduced by Terzaghi (1943) and Biot (1941). This concept suggests that pore pressure helps counteract the mechanical stress carried through grain-to-grain contact. The efficiency of the pore pressure, p_r, effect is measured by the poroelastic factor, α. This relationship is illustrated by Eq. 2-1.

$$\sigma' = \sigma - \alpha p_r \tag{2-1}$$

Where,

σ' is the effective stress, and

σ is the total (absolute) stress,

The poroelastic constant is represented by Eq. 2-2.

$$\alpha = 1 - \frac{c_{ma}}{c_b}, \quad 0 \leq \alpha \leq 1 \tag{2-2}$$

Where,

C_{ma} is the compressibility of the rock matrix.

The bulk compressibility, c_b, is given by Eq. 2-3.

$$c_b = \frac{3(1-2\nu)}{E} \tag{2-3}$$

Where,

v is Poisson's ratio, and

E is Young's modulus.

If the rock has no porosity, the rock-matrix compressibility, c_{ma}, is equal to c_b, and α becomes zero. Conversely, with high porosity, the matrix compressibility is small compared to the bulk compressibility, and α approaches unity. Although the poroelastic constant can be evaluated in the laboratory, the following technique explains physically how α can be evaluated from a given failure envelope obtained from dry samples.

Viscoelasticity

"Creep" is a viscoelastic property or time-dependent phenomenon that significantly contributes to many instability problems related to wellbore construction. Creep tests study rock deformation under constant stress as a function of time. The total displacement obtained from applying a constant stress is the sum of two components, as shown in Eq. 2-4.

$$\varepsilon_t = \varepsilon_e + \varepsilon(t) \tag{2-4}$$

Where,

ε_t is the total strain, and

ε_e is the elastic strain.

The creep function, $\varepsilon(t)$, characterizes the rheological properties of a rock. A general equation for the creep function can be very complex, and it is best described by experimental data for a given range of stress and temperature.

Thermoviscoelasticity

Some formations not only exhibit viscoelasticity, but they also depend on the temperature. Rock salt behaves as a thermoviscoelastic material and has a tendency to creep when subjected to stress. The creep strain rate is influenced by the formation temperature, mineralogical composition, presence of impurities, water content, and the extent to which differential

stresses are applied to the salt body (Baker et al. 1992). For example, the rock tachyhydrite ($CaCl_2 \bullet 2M_gCl_2 \bullet 12H_2O$), which is a type of salt formation, is very weak in comparison to halite and can develop a creep strain rate that is two orders of magnitude faster than halite for the same-state variables, temperature, and stress (Costa et al. 2010).

The viscous plasticity of the salt rock is responsible for wellbore closure as a function of time, creating significant difficulties for well construction (Costa and Poiate Jr. 2008). The wellbore closure process is not so fast that it could not cause severe operational issues. However, well closure may occur and eventually cause severe problems with casing failures in front of the salt (Rike et al. 1986). Casing collapse is most likely the main concern related to the development of the pre-salt areas, which demands the construction of wells with preserved structural integrity for at least 25 years (Beltrão et al. 2009). A typical axial creep deformation curve is illustrated in **Fig. 2.1**.

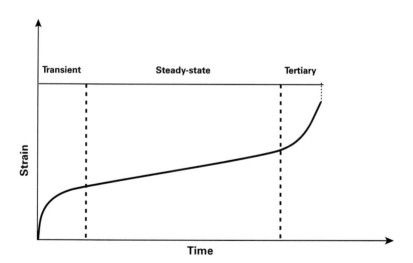

» Transient creep stage—normally found in drilling and is fully dissipated in a short period of time.

» Tertiary creep stage—microfracturing develops, leading to failure of the specimen.

Fig. 2.1 – Creep Deformation.

A typical creep curve for salt consists of two or three creep stages. Following the application of the stress difference, the strain rate is very high. This rate then decreases monotonically with time until a constant strain rate is observed. These two stages are called transient and steady-state creep stages, respectively. Depending on the level of temperature and the differential stress applied to the specimen, a third stage, called tertiary creep, may become evident. This is characterized by the acceleration of the creep strain rate caused by the specimen structure damage induced by the creep-strain accumulation with time. At the tertiary creep stage (the dilation phenomenon), an increase in volume through microfracturing develops, leading to failure of the specimen.

The creep rate in salt formations can be defined by two components, as described above. One component is known as the primary creep rate, $\bar{\dot{\varepsilon}}_p$, while the second component is known as the secondary creep rate, $\bar{\dot{\varepsilon}}_s$. The additive decomposition is given by Eq. 2-5.

$$\bar{\dot{\varepsilon}} = \bar{\dot{\varepsilon}}_p + \bar{\dot{\varepsilon}}_s \tag{2-5}$$

The primary creep effect is assumed dissipated during the drilling operation and is not considered in the production phase. In other words, the relationship of $\bar{\dot{\varepsilon}} = \bar{\dot{\varepsilon}}_s$ is assumed in this study. The law that describes the deformation mechanisms for the evaporate rocks was developed based on the following three mechanisms (Munson et al. 2004):

- Dislocation glide

- Dislocation climb

- Undefined mechanism

The largest contribution of any of the mechanisms depends on the temperature conditions and differential stress to which the salt is submitted. The double mechanism creep law is shown in Eq. 2-6.

$$\bar{\dot{\varepsilon}} = \bar{\dot{\varepsilon}}_0 \left(\frac{\sigma_{eff}}{\sigma_0}\right)^n e^{\left(\frac{Q}{RT_0} - \frac{Q}{RT}\right)} \tag{2-6}$$

Where,

$\bar{\dot{\varepsilon}}$ is the strain rate owing to creep at the steady-state condition,

$\bar{\dot{\varepsilon}}_0$ is the reference strain rate owing to creep (steady state),

σ_{eff} is the creep effective stress,

σ_o is the reference effective stress,

n is the exponent dependent on creep mechanism,

Q is the activation energy (kcal/mol),

$Q = 12$ kcal/mol,

R is the universal gas constant (kcal/mol.K);

$R = 1.9858E-03$; T_o is the reference temperature (K), and

T is the rock temperature (K).

Creep tests can be performed on salt samples retrieved from cores or during exploratory activities in the laboratory (using simulated field conditions). The creep tests are used to determine the creep constants needed in Eq. 2-6. Experimental data of halite, as shown in **Fig. 2.2**, are used to fit the equation in this study. From the interpolation of experimental data at test temperature, the following parameters can be determined:

- Reference temperature $T_o = 359.15$ K
- Reference effective stress $\sigma_{ov} = 10$ Mpa
- If creep effective stress $\sigma_{ef} <$ reference effective stress σ_o, then n = 3.36
- If creep effective stress $\sigma_{ef} >$ reference effective stress σ_o, then n = 7.55

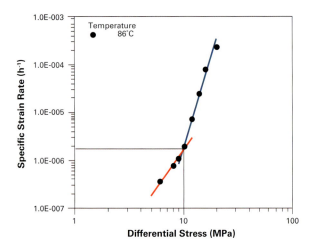

Fig. 2.2 – Experimental Data.

Fracture Toughness

Fracture toughness is a material property that reflects the rock resistance for an existing fracture to propagate for a given fracturing mode. For a radial or "penny-shaped" fracture to propagate, the following condition must be satisfied at the fracture tip:

$K_I \geq K_{IC}$

$$K_I = (p_f - \sigma_{H,min})\sqrt{\pi\, l} \qquad (2\text{-}7)$$

Where,

$\sigma_{H,min} = \sigma'_{H,min} + p_r$ and

p_f is the pressure inside the fracture.

When linear-elastic fracture mechanics are used, fracture toughness can be related to tensile strength, T (assuming static condition), as follows (Economides and Nolte 1987):

$$T = \frac{K_{IC}}{\sqrt{\pi\, l}} \qquad (2\text{-}8)$$

Where,

l is the half-length of an existing crack.

Other useful correlations between fracture toughness and tensile strength, T, Young's modulus, E, and compressive strength, C_o, are given by Whittaker et al. (1992):

$$K_{IC} = 0.27 + 0.107T \tag{2-9}$$

$$K_{IC} = 0.336 + 0.026E \tag{2-10}$$

$$K_{IC} = 0.708 + 0.006C_o \tag{2-11}$$

Where,

K_{IC} is in MPa $\sqrt{m}$,

E is in GPa, and

C_O is in MPa.

Near-Wellbore Stress Field

A wellbore drilled through a rock formation introduces a new stress field at the wellbore proximity that may be great enough to cause failure. Additionally, when a wellbore is actively loaded (pressure in the wellbore is less than the reservoir pressure) or passively loaded (pressure in the wellbore is higher than the reservoir pressure), another stress effect could cause formation failure. If we assume a homogeneous, isotropic, linearly elastic rock mass being stressed below its yield limit, a stress field expressed in polar coordinates as vertical, tangential, and radial is given by the Kirsch solution (Jaeger and Cook 1979), as shown in Eq. 2-12.

$$\sigma'_v = g \int_0^H \rho_b dH - \alpha p_r \tag{2-12}$$

Where,

ρ_b is the bulk density of the overburden layers, and

H is the depth.

$$\sigma'_{rr} = \frac{1}{2}\left(\sigma'_{H,max} + \sigma'_{H,min}\right)\left(1 - \frac{r_w^2}{r^2}\right) +$$

$$\frac{1}{2}\left(\sigma'_{H,max} - \sigma'_{H,min}\right)\left(1 - \frac{4r_w^2}{r^2} + \frac{3r_w^4}{r^4}\right)\cos 2\theta + \frac{r_w^2}{r^2}(p_w - p_r) \quad (2\text{-}13)$$

$$\sigma'_{\theta\theta} = \frac{1}{2}\left(\sigma'_{H,max} + \sigma'_{H,min}\right)\left(1 + \frac{r_w^2}{r^2}\right) -$$

$$\frac{1}{2}\left(\sigma'_{H,max} - \sigma'_{H,min}\right)\left(1 + \frac{3r_w^4}{r^4}\right)\cos 2\theta - \frac{r_w^2}{r^2}(p_w - p_r) \quad (2\text{-}14)$$

Where,

p_w is the well bottomhole pressure, and

p_r is the reservoir pressure.

$$\tau_{r\theta} = \frac{1}{2}\left(\sigma'_{H,max} - \sigma'_{H,min}\right)\left(1 + \frac{2r_w^2}{r^2} - \frac{3r_w^4}{r^4}\right)\sin 2\theta \quad (2\text{-}15)$$

Where,

the compressive stresses are positive and θ is the angle measured from the direction of $\sigma_{H,max}$.

At the wellbore, $r = r_w$, and, assuming that a mudcake differentiates the wellbore pressure, p_w, from the reservoir pressure, p_r, then:

$$\sigma'_{rr} = p_w - p_r \quad (2\text{-}16)$$

$$\sigma'_{\theta\theta} = \sigma'_{H,max} + \sigma'_{H,min} - 2\left(\sigma'_{H,max} - \sigma'_{H,min}\right)\cos 2\theta - \left(p_w - p_r\right) \quad (2\text{-}17)$$

and

$$\tau_{r\theta} = 0$$

If we consider two cases where $\theta = 0$ ($\sigma_{H,max}$) and $\theta = 90$ ($\sigma_{H,min}$), we get:

$$\sigma_{\theta=0} = 3\sigma'_{H,min} - \sigma'_{H,max} - p_w + p_r \qquad (2\text{-}18)$$

and

$$\sigma_{\theta=90} = 3\sigma'_{H,max} - \sigma'_{H,min} - p_w + p_r$$

To initiate a tensile failure, as is the case in hydraulic fracturing, $\sigma_{\theta=0}$ should become a negative value of the tensile strength ($\sigma_{\theta=0} = -T$). The breakdown pressure, p_{bd}, required for initiating a fracture can be readily calculated from Eq. 2-19.

$$p_{bd} = 3\sigma'_{H,min} - \sigma'_{H,max} + T + p_r \qquad (2\text{-}19)$$

Or, in terms of total stresses,

$$p_{bd} = 3\sigma_{H,min} - \sigma_{H,max} + T - p_r \qquad (2\text{-}20)$$

The stresses, $\sigma_{H,min}$, $\sigma_{H,max}$, and σ_v, should be determined in the field; however, if no field information is available, the following approximation can be used:

$$\sigma'_v = 1.1\,H - \alpha\,p_r \qquad (2\text{-}21)$$

Based on the assumption that the formation is elastic, tectonically relaxed, and constrained laterally, the effective minimum and maximum horizontal stresses can be estimated as follows:

$$\sigma'_{H,min} = \frac{v}{1-v}(\sigma'_v) \qquad (2\text{-}22)$$

and

$$\sigma'_{H,max} = \frac{\sigma'_v + \sigma'_{H,min}}{2} \qquad (2\text{-}23)$$

The previous solution is valid only for elastic rocks. However, when a wellbore is introduced to an intact formation, a plastic region is developed in the proximity of the wellbore, extending a few wellbore diameters before an in-situ elastic region prevails, as shown in **Fig. 2.3**. The plastic region can create many wellbore instability problems during drilling. In the pay zone,

as a result of production, the plastic region may propagate deeper into the reservoir, causing sand production. In fractured rocks, wellbore collapse may result unless a high drilling-fluid weight is used. The size of the plastic region must be known for such applications as wellbore stability, perforations, and sand production.

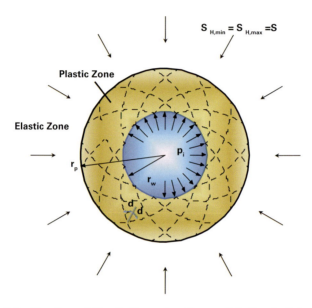

Fig. 2.3 – Plastic and Elastic Zones (as Assumed in Bray's Solution).

Bray (1967) assumed that fractures exist in the plastic zone with log spirals inclined at δ degrees, with the radial direction as shown in **Fig. 2.4** (Goodman 1980). If we apply the Mohr-Coulomb theory, the radius of the plastic zone, r_{pl}, is:

$$r_{pl} = r_w \left[\frac{2\sigma' - C_o + \left(1 + \frac{1+\sin\phi}{1-\sin\phi}\right) C_j \cot\phi_j}{\left(1 + \frac{1+\sin\phi}{1-\sin\phi}\right)\left((p_w - p_r) + C_j \cot\phi_j\right)} \right]^{1/Q} \quad (2\text{-}24)$$

Where,

$$Q = \frac{\tan\delta}{\tan(\delta - \phi_j)} - 1 \quad (2\text{-}25)$$

- C_j is the cohesion for jointed rocks (experimentally determined)
- ϕ_j is the internal friction angle for jointed rocks.

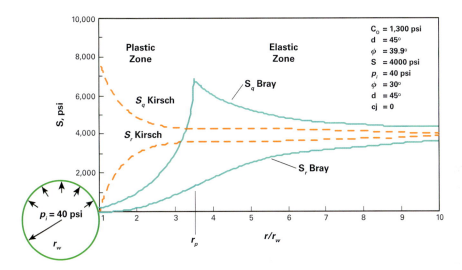

Fig. 2.4 – Kirsch and Bray Solutions (Goodman 1980).

In Eq. 2-24, $\sigma'_{H,min} = \sigma'_{H,max} = \sigma$ within the elastic and plastic zones. Bray's solution is given by:

$$\sigma'_r = \sigma' - r_{pl} \left[\frac{\left(\frac{1+\sin\phi}{1-\sin\phi}-1\right)\sigma' + C_o}{r^2\left(\frac{1+\sin\phi}{1-\sin\phi}+1\right)} \right] \quad (2\text{-}26)$$

$$\sigma'_{\theta\theta} = \sigma' - r_{pl} \left[\frac{\left(\frac{1+\sin\phi}{1-\sin\phi}-1\right)\sigma' + C_o}{r^2\left(\frac{1+\sin\phi}{1-\sin\phi}\right)+1} \right] \quad (2\text{-}27)$$

for the elastic zone, and

$$\sigma'_{rr} = \left((p_w - p_r) + C_j \cot\phi_j\right)\left(\frac{r}{r_w}\right)^Q - C_j \cot\phi_j \qquad (2\text{-}28)$$

$$\sigma'_{\theta\theta} = \left((p_w - p_r) + C_j \cot\phi_j\right)\frac{\tan\delta}{\tan(\delta - \phi_j)}\left(\frac{r}{r_w}\right)^Q - C_j \cot\phi_j \qquad (2\text{-}29)$$

for the plastic zone.

Failure Criteria

To understand a failure mechanism, we must apply a specific and compatible failure criterion. Granular material, such as sand, fails in shear, while, for soft material, such as clays, plastic compaction dominates the failure mechanism.

The following failure mechanisms can cause wellbore and near-wellbore instability problems:

- Shear failure without appreciable plastic deformation, such as a breakout
- Plastic deformation and compaction, which may cause pore collapse
- Tensile failure, causing the formation to part
- Cohesive failure, equivalent to erosion, which can cause fines migration and sand production
- Creep, which can cause a tight hole during drilling
- Pore collapse, which is a comprehensive failure of the infrastructure of the matrix framework that can occur during the latter phase of production

Many empirical criteria have been developed that predict rock failure. It is imperative to understand the physical interpretation of those criteria before they are applied for problems associated with wellbore construction. Such criteria are empirical, and engineers should carefully select the appropriate ones for a given problem. Generally, failure criteria are used to generate failure envelopes, usually separating stable and unstable zones. Although some engineers attempt to linearize the failure envelope, such linearization is artificial. The three criteria that are useful to wellbore and wellbore proximity failure are presented in the following sections.

Mohr-Coulomb Failure Criterion

The Mohr-Coulomb failure criterion relates the shearing resistance to the contact forces and friction, as well as the physical bonds (cohesion) that exist among the grains. A linear approximation is given by Eq. 2-30.

$$\tau = C + \sigma'_n \tan \phi \qquad (2\text{-}30)$$

Where,

τ is the shear stress,

C is the cohesive strength,

ϕ is the angle of internal friction, and

σ'_n is the effective normal stress acting on the grains.

Factors C and ϕ are coefficients for the linearization and should be determined experimentally.

A deviation from a straight line is very common during attempts to interpret other failure mechanisms with this criterion, which is solely based on shear failure. Therefore, this criterion should be applied only to situations for which it is valid. The failure envelope is determined from many Mohr circles. Each circle represents a triaxial test where a sample is subjected to lateral confinement ($\sigma_2 = \sigma_3$), and axial stress (σ_1) is increased until failure. The envelope of Mohr circles represents the basis of this failure criterion.

Sometimes, it is more convenient to express the Mohr-Coulomb linear envelope in terms of σ_1 and σ_3. This expression becomes:

$$\sigma'_1 = \frac{1+\sin\phi}{1-\sin\phi}\sigma'_3 + C_o \qquad (2\text{-}31)$$

$$C_o = 2\,C \tan\left(\frac{\pi}{4}+\frac{\phi}{2}\right) = 2\,C\,\frac{\cos\phi}{1-\sin\phi} \qquad (2\text{-}32)$$

Eq. 2-34 is also equivalent to Eq. 2-33.

$$\sigma_1' = C_o + \sigma_3' \tan^2\left(\frac{\pi}{4} + \frac{\phi}{2}\right) \qquad (2\text{-}33)$$

Once the failure envelope is determined, stability can be analyzed by calculations of the normal and shear stresses for a given situation, as shown by Eqs. 2-34 and 2-35.

$$\sigma_n' = \frac{\sigma_1 + \sigma_3}{2} - \alpha p_r \qquad (2\text{-}34)$$

and

$$\tau_{max} = \frac{\sigma_1 - \sigma_3}{2} \qquad (2\text{-}35)$$

These points are then plotted on the failure envelope, and the rock is evaluated for stability. If the failure envelope exhibits nonlinear behavior, the linearization attempt should be exercised for the stress range for which the given problem is applied.

Hoek-Brown Criterion

The Hoek-Brown criterion (Hoek and Brown 1980) is also empirical and applies more to naturally fractured reservoirs. The criterion states that:

$$\sigma_1' = \sigma_3' + \sqrt{I_m C_o \sigma_3' + I_s C_o^2} \qquad (2\text{-}36)$$

Where,

I_m is the frictional index, and

I_s is the intact index.

Both indices are material-dependent properties.

This criterion reasonably matches the brittle failure, but it gives poor results in ductile failure. Therefore, it is used for predicting failure in naturally fractured formations. The parameters, I_m, I_s, and C_o, are measured in the laboratory. For weak rock, I_m is less than 0.1 and I_s is less than 0.0001; however, for hard rock, I_m ranges from 5 to 15 and I_s is equal to 1.

Drucker-Prager Criterion (Extended Von Mises)

The Drucker-Prager criterion is based on the assumption that the octahedral shearing stress reaches a critical value, as shown in Eq. 2-37.

$$\alpha I_1 + \sqrt{J_2} - K = 0 \qquad (2\text{-}37)$$

Where,

$$J_2 = \frac{1}{6}\left[(\sigma_1' - \sigma_2')^2 + (\sigma_2' - \sigma_3')^2 + (\sigma_3' - \sigma_1')^2\right] \qquad (2\text{-}38)$$

and

$$I_1 = \sigma_1' + \sigma_2' + \sigma_3' \qquad (2\text{-}39)$$

which is the first invariant of stress tensors.

The material parameters, α and K, are related to the angle of internal friction, ϕ, and cohesion, C, for linear conditions, as follows:

$$\alpha = \frac{2\sin\phi}{\sqrt{3}(3 - \sin\phi)} \qquad (2\text{-}40)$$

and

$$K = \frac{6C\cos\phi}{\sqrt{3}(3 - \sin\phi)} \qquad (2\text{-}41)$$

A plot of $\sqrt{J_2}$ vs. I_1 at failure conditions enables the evaluation of a given problem related to rock failure. This criterion fits the high stress level.

Wang and Samuel Approach (Extended Von Mises)

For presalt and creeping formation failure, the criterion has to be modified, as illustrated in the following. The description and mathematical equation of each mechanism considered in the study are also presented (Wang and Samuel 2013).

Equilibrium is expressed by writing the principle of virtual work for the volume under consideration in its current configuration (Eq. 2-42).

$$\int_V \sigma : \delta\varepsilon \, dV = \int_S t \cdot \delta v dS + \int_V f \cdot \delta v dV \qquad (2\text{-}42)$$

Where,

δv is a virtual velocity field,

$\delta\varepsilon$ is the virtual rate of deformation,

t is the surface tractions per unit area, and

f is the body forces per unit volume.

This equation is then discretized using a Lagrangian formulation, with displacements as the nodal variables.

The constitutive equation for the solid is expressed as:

$$d\sigma = E{:}d\varepsilon \qquad (2\text{--}43)$$

Where,

σ is the stress,

ε is strain, and

E is the material stiffness.

The constitutive equation for salt behavior, which is based on the double-mechanism creep law, is developed in a subroutine written by Fortran; during simulation, the subroutine can interact with the nonlinear solver based on the implicit Newton-Raphson iteration method to update simulation results at the end of each iteration.

(1) At the end of the transient process, the displacement field $[\sigma_0]$ and stress field $[\delta_0]$ are solved, which are then passed into the production process as initial values.

$$[K][\delta_0] = [F] \tag{2-44}$$

$$[\sigma_0] = [D][B][\delta_0] \tag{2-45}$$

Where,

[K] is the stiffness matrix of the whole system,

[F] is the equivalent nodal force,

[D] is the elasticity matrix, and

[B] is the geometric stiffness matrix.

(2) Assume the stress field remains unchanged during each increment (within the interval from t to $t+\Delta t$, the stress is $[\sigma_t]$), then calculate the creep-strain increment, $[\Delta \varepsilon_t^c]$, during time interval, Δt.

$$[\Delta \varepsilon_t^c]_{\Delta t} = \Delta t [\dot{\varepsilon}_t] \tag{2-46}$$

Where,

$[\dot{\varepsilon}_t]$ is the creep rate at time t and

$$[\dot{\varepsilon}_t]^T = (\dot{\varepsilon}_1, \dot{\varepsilon}_2, \dot{\varepsilon}_3)$$

The components of $[\dot{\varepsilon}_t]$ can be expressed as follows:

$$\dot{\varepsilon}_1 = \frac{\bar{\dot{\varepsilon}}}{\sigma_{eff}} \left[\sigma_1 - \frac{1}{2}(\sigma_2 + \sigma_3) \right] \tag{2-47}$$

$$\dot{\varepsilon}_2 = \frac{\bar{\dot{\varepsilon}}}{\sigma_{eff}} \left[\sigma_2 - \frac{1}{2}(\sigma_1 + \sigma_3) \right] \tag{2-48}$$

$$\dot{\varepsilon}_3 = \frac{\bar{\dot{\varepsilon}}}{\sigma_{eff}} \left[\sigma_3 - \frac{1}{2}(\sigma_1 + \sigma_2) \right] \tag{2-49}$$

and

$$\sigma_{eff} = \frac{1}{\sqrt{2}} [(\sigma_1 - \sigma_2)^2 + (\sigma_2 - \sigma_3)^2 + (\sigma_3 - \sigma_1)^2 + 6(\tau_{12}^2 + \tau_{23}^2 + \tau_{13}^2)]^{\frac{1}{2}} \tag{2-50}$$

(3) The increment of nodal force, $[\Delta F_c(t)]$, in each increment can be expressed as:

$$[\Delta F_c(t)] = \int_\Omega [B]^T [D][\Delta \varepsilon_t^c] \, d\Omega \tag{2-51}$$

Eq. 2-51 above is applied to all the domain of salt formation.

(4) Solve the following equilibrium equation.

$$[K][\Delta \delta^c]_t = [\Delta F_c(t)] \tag{2-52}$$

Calculate the creep-induced increment of nodal displacement, $[\Delta \delta^c]_t$, during Δ_t, then the stress increment during this time interval can be expressed as:

$$[\Delta \sigma^c]_t = [D]([B][\Delta \delta^c]_t - [\Delta \varepsilon_t^c]) \tag{2-53}$$

(5) Add $[\Delta \delta^c]_t$ and $[\Delta \sigma^c]_t$ to displacement field, $[\delta_t]$, and stress field, $[\sigma_t]$, at time, t, then calculate stress, $[\sigma_{t+\Delta t}]$, and displacement, $[\delta_{t+\Delta t}]$, at the end of this time interval.

$$[\sigma_{t+\Delta t}] = [\sigma_t] + [\Delta \sigma^c]_t \tag{2-54}$$

$$[\delta_{t+\Delta t}] = [\delta_t] + [\Delta \delta^c]_t \tag{2-55}$$

Check the total simulated time (in this study, the end of simulation is after 500 days of production). If the total simulated time equals 500, then terminate the calculation; if the total simulated time is less than 500, then continue the calculation from steps (2) through (5).

Wellbore Stability During Drilling

Most wellbore-stability problems occur as the long tangent section is drilled. Unfortunately, clay/shale properties range from very soft to very hard and from highly laminated to highly intact. Several mechanisms cause wellbore-instability problems (**Fig. 2.5**); chemical and mechanical effects will be discussed in this section.

EXTENDED-REACH DRILLING

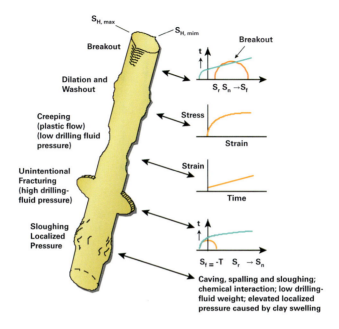

Fig. 2.5 – Possible Wellbore Instability Problem During Drilling.

Wellbore Instability:

- Breakout
- Dilation and washout
- Creeping
- Unintentional fracturing
- Sloughing

Chemical Effects:

- Clay swelling (hydration) and migration
- Ion exchanging
- Cementation deterioration
- Near-wellbore damage

Mechanical Effects:

- Tensile failure
- Shear failure
- Drilling-fluid weight

Chemical Effects

Ion-exchanging clays, such as illite, mica, smectite, chlorite, mixed-layer clays, and zeolites, can cause many wellbore-instability problems. The following failure mechanisms during wellbore construction can be related to chemical causes.

Clay Swelling (Hydration) and Migration

Most shale formations contain water-sensitive clay materials, such as smectite, illite, and mixed-layer clays, which absorb water that induces an elevated localized pressure. This pressure reduces the effective stress around the wellbore, which causes the shale matrix to swell, disintegrate, and collapse (Dusseault and Gray 1992).

Ion Exchanging

Brines, such as KCl, can control clay swelling, but illite, chlorite, smectite, and mixed-layer clays can change the brine through ion-exchanging mechanisms and swell afterward.

Cementation Deterioration

When examining sand formations, engineers must study the degree and type of cementation. Mineralogical analysis, thin-section petrography, and fluid compatibility are viable testing methods for evaluating sand production.

Near-Wellbore Damage

Near-wellbore formation damage can occur because of paraffin deposits, scale deposits, fines migration caused by kaolinite and illite clays, asphaltene precipitation, sand production, emulsions induced by iron, formation of oil emulsions by acid in combination with soluble iron,

iron-compound precipitation, and even emulsions formed from fracturing fluids during stimulation.

Mechanical Effects

Tensile and shear-failure mechanisms should be considered for wellbore-stability evaluation during drilling.

Tensile Failure

The effective stress at the wellbore exceeds the tensile strength of the formation and causes tensile failure. Therefore, an induced fracture can result because of drilling-fluid loss if:

$$p_w \geq p_r + \sigma'_{\theta\theta} + T \qquad (2\text{-}56)$$

For an elastic medium, this is given by Eq. 2-57 (Haimson and Fairhurst 1967).

$$p_w = 3\sigma'_{H,min} - \sigma'_{H,max} + T + p_r \qquad (2\text{-}57)$$

However, if a natural fracture exists, then the tensile strength, T, should be assumed to be zero.

Shear Failure

Once a wellbore is drilled and a stress concentration field is established, the rock will either withstand the stress field or yield, resulting in a near-wellbore breakout zone that causes spalling, sloughing, and hole enlargement. An appropriate failure criterion should be used for evaluating this type of failure.

Drilling-Fluid Weight

Drilling-fluid weight should be calculated as a means of preventing the initiation of tensile and shear (plastic) failures. In some cases, the drilling-fluid weight should prevent creeping in viscoplastic formations, such as salt rock. Drilling-fluid weight is an important consideration for treating wellbore-instability problems and is limited by two boundaries.

- The upper boundary is the pressure that causes tensile failure and drilling-fluid loss. This pressure can be determined in the field based on Eq. 2-45.

- The lower boundary is the pressure required to provide confining stress, which is removed during drilling. The confining stress prevents shear failure, the creation of a plastic zone, and plastic flow (creep).

The upper boundary is estimated from the in-situ stress field, and the tensile strength is measured in the laboratory. While the lower boundary is estimated from the in-situ stress field, mechanical properties of the formation are estimated from the described failure criteria that best models a given formation. The Mohr-Coulomb failure criterion, which is a two-dimensional model, can be used for determining the drilling-fluid weight required to prevent shear failure (Eq. 2-31).

Near the wellbore, stress, σ'_3, can be represented as σ'_{rr}.

However, the term, σ'_1, can be represented by the tangential stress, $\sigma'_{\theta\theta}$, which is described by Eqs. 2-18 and 2-19. Of the two equations, 2-19 represents the point at which the wellbore will be exposed to the most tangential stress. This stress should be considered for drilling-fluid-weight calculations. Therefore, the term, σ'_1, is given by:

$$\sigma'_1 = 3\sigma'_{H,max} - \sigma'_{H,min} \tag{2-58}$$

By substituting these results in Eq. 2-31, we get:

$$3\sigma'_{H,max} - \sigma'_{H,min} = \frac{1+\sin\phi}{1-\sin\phi}(p_w - p_r) + C_o \tag{2-59}$$

or

$$p_w = \frac{3\sigma'_{H,max} - \sigma'_{H,min} - C_o}{\frac{1+\sin\phi}{1-\sin\phi}} + p_r \tag{2-60}$$

If we assume that $\sigma'_{H,max} = \sigma'_{H,min} = \sigma'$, then:

$$p_w = \frac{2\sigma' - C_o}{\frac{1+\sin\phi}{1-\sin\phi}} + p_r \qquad (2\text{-}61)$$

The drilling-fluid weight should be calculated based on p_w, as given in Eqs. 2-60 or 2-61.

A different model can be used based on the radius of the plastic zone created as a result of drilling a wellbore, as given by Eq. 2-24.

To prevent the generation of a plastic zone, r_{pl} must equal r_w. Substituting this condition in Eq. 2-24, we get:

$$2\sigma' - C_o = \left(1 + \frac{1+\sin\phi}{1-\sin\phi}\right)(p_w - p_r) \qquad (2\text{-}62)$$

Then,

$$p_w = \frac{2\sigma' - C_o}{1 + \frac{1+\sin\phi}{1-\sin\phi}} + p_r \qquad (2\text{-}63)$$

The drilling-fluid weight should be determined based on p_w. A comparison of Eqs. 2-62 and 2-63 suggests that the two models will provide different results for the drilling-fluid weight. The following example demonstrates the use of these models to determine the drilling-fluid weight constraints that should be considered for the prevention of wellbore instability.

Wellbore Stability, Eccentricity Effects, and Casing Loading

Casing eccentricity has been considered problematic during the design and operations of primary cementing, particularly in extended-reach wells. Engineering calculations based on the assumption of concentric annuli may lead to erroneous or, at least, inaccurate results. In very soft and unconsolidated formations, where hole enlargement and washout are typical problems while drilling and cementing, it is necessary to use enough centralizers on the casing to maintain the casing at the center of the wellbore. If the hole is washed out and there are not enough centralizers placed on the casing,

casing eccentricity is inevitable (Matsuzawa et al. 2006). The deflection of the casing in the borehole is directly related to the casing eccentricity through Eq. 2-64.

$$\varepsilon = \frac{e}{r_0 - r_i} \qquad (2\text{-}64)$$

Where,

  ε is the casing eccentricity,

  e is the deflection of the casing from the center of the borehole (distance between the center of the hole and the center of the casing),

  r_0 is the radius of the borehole, and

  r_i is the outside radius of the casing.

The stress distribution around casing during drilling and production is shown in **Figs. 6** and **7**. (Wang and Samuel 2013). The results show that the maximum stress in the casing occurs along the direction of deflection, which is closer to the wellbore. As eccentricity increases, the maximum stress increases during both drilling and production.

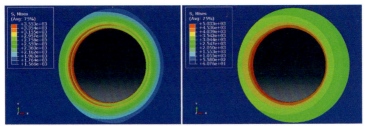
Stress Distribution around Casing when Eccentricity=0.25.

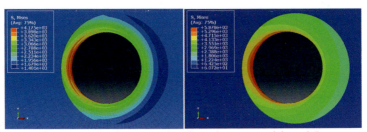
Stress distribution around casing when eccentricity = 0.5.

Fig. 2.6 – Eccentricity Effects.

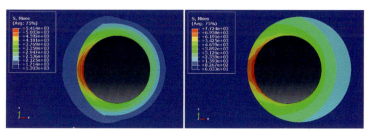

Stress distribution around casing when eccentricity = 0.75.

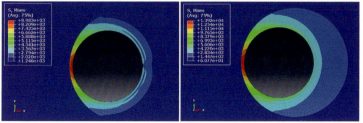

Stress distribution around casing when eccentricity = 1.0.

Fig. 2.7 – Eccentricity Effects.

References

Beltrão, R.L.C., Sombra, C.L., Lage, J.R., Netto, F., and Henriques, C.C.D. 2009. Challenges and New Technologies for the Development of the Pre-Salt Cluster, Santos Basin, Brazil. Paper OTC-19880 presented at the Offshore Technology Conference, Houston, Texas, 4–7 May.

Biot, M.A. 1941. Generalized Theory of Three-Dimensional Consolidation. *J. Applied Physics*, **12**: 155–164.

Bray, J. 1967. A Study of Jointed and Fractured Rock—Part II. *Felsmechanik and Ingenieurgeologic*, (4).

Costa, A.M., Poiate Jr., E, Amaral, C.S., Goncalves, C.J.C, Falcao, J.L., and Pereira, A. 2010. Geomechanics Applied to the Well Design Through Salt Layers in Brazil–A History of Success. Paper 10-239 presented at the 44th U.S. Rock Mechanics Symposium and 5th U.S.-Canada Rock Mechanics Symposium, Salt Lake City, Utah, 27–30, June.

Daneshy, A.A., et al. 1986. In-Situ Stress Measurements During Drilling. *JPT*, 891–898.

Dusseault, M.B. and Gray, K.E. 1992. Mechanisms of Stress-Induced Wellbore Damage. Paper SPE 23825 presented at the SPE Formation Damage Control Symposium, Lafayette, Louisiana, 26–27 February.

Economides, M.J. and Nolte, G.N. 1987. *Reservoir Stimulation*. Schlumberger Educational Services.

Haimson, B.C. and Fairhurst, C. 1967. Initiation and Extension of Hydraulic Fracture in Rocks. *SPEJ*, **7**.

Hoek, E. and Brown, E.T. 1980. Empirical Strength Criterion for Rock Masses. *J. Geotech. Eng. Div. ASCE* **106 (GT9)**, 1013–1035.

Hubbert, K.M. and Willis, D.G. 1957. Mechanics of Hydraulic Fracturing. *Petro. Trans.*, AIME **210**: 153–166.

Jaeger, J.C. and Cook, N.W. 1979. *Fundamentals of Rock Mechanics*. New York: Chapman and Hall.

Matsuzawa, M., Umezu, S., Yamamoto, K. 2006. Evaluation of Experiment Program 2004: Natural Hydrate Exploration Campaign in the Nankai Trough Offshore Japan. Paper SPE 98960 presented at the IADC/SPE Drilling Conference, Miami, Florida, 21–23 February.

McLeod, H.O. 1983. The Effect of Perforating Conditions on Well Performance. *JPT*, **35**(01).

Munson, D.E. 2004. M-D Constitutive Model Parameters Defined For Gulf Coast Salt Domes and Structures. Paper 04-549 presented at Gulf Rocks 2004, the 6th North America Rock Mechanics Symposium (NARMS), Houston, Texas, 5–9 June.

Rike, E.A., Bryant, G.A., and Williams, S.D. 1986. Success in Prevention of Casing Failures Opposite Salts, Little Knife Field, North Dakota. *SPEDE*, 131–40.

Roegiers, J.C. and Zhao, X.L. 1991. Rock Fracture Tests in Simulated Downhole Conditions. Paper ARMA-91-221 presented at the 32nd U.S. Symposium on Rock Mechanics (USRMS), Norman, Oklahoma, 10–12 July.

Soliman, M.Y. 1993. Interpretation of Pressure Behavior of Fractured Deviated and Horizontal Wells. Paper SPE 21062 presented at the SPE Latin America Petroleum Engineering Conference, Rio de Janeiro, Brazil, 14–19 October.

Terzaghi, K. 1943. *Theoretical Soil Mechanics*. New York: Wiley.

Thiercelin, M. and Roegiers, J.C. 1986. Toughness Determination with the Modified Ring Test. Paper ARMA-86-0615 presented at the 27th U.S. Symposium on Rock Mechanics (USRMS), Tuscaloosa, Alabama, 23–25 June.

Wang, H. and Samuel, R. 2013. Geomechanical Modeling of Wellbore Stability in Salt Formations. Paper SPE 166144 presented at the SPE Annual Technical Conference and Exhibition held in New Orleans, Louisiana, 30 September–2 October.

Whittaker, B.N. et al. 1992. *Rock Fracture Mechanics Principles, Design, and Application*. New York: Elsevier.

CHAPTER **THREE**

Formation Pressures

The accurate prediction of formation pressures, such as pore pressure and fracture pressure, is not only important during the planning of an ERD well, but also during drilling and completion. These predictions provide the boundary conditions for planning the drilling fluids, casing, cementing, and completion programs. Pore pressure plays a vital role in the casing-seat location, whereas fracture pressure limits the density of mud and cement that can be used. Thus, methods for estimating a formation's pore pressure can be classified as:

1. Pre-drilling

2. During drilling

3. Post-drilling

This chapter describes the basics of the formation pressures, as well as some predictive methods that are needed for well engineering.

The terms "overburden gradient" and "pore-pressure gradient," are frequently

called the "overburden" and "pore pressure," respectively, with the specific meaning inferred from the associated unit of measure.

Pressures

It is customary to express stress in conventional units of force per unit area (e.g., psi or kPa), as well as in units that are equivalent to the unit used for the drilling fluid density. This is accomplished by considering the stress gradient, which equals the stress at a given depth per unit of vertical depth. Gradients are expressed strictly in units of force per unit area, per unit of vertical depth (e.g., psi/ft or kPa/m), but they can be expressed equivalently in "density" units (e.g., lb/gal, g/cm^3, or specific gravity).

The different types of pressures used include:

- Overburden pressure
- Formation pressure
- Fracture pressure

Overburden Pressure

Overburden pressure is created by the weight of the overlying rocks and fluid, and, thus, depends on the density of the sedimentary rocks and fluids in the pore spaces. Traditionally, an average overburden pressure gradient of 1.0 psi/ft is assumed. In deepwater environments, this pressure can vary according to water depth. Again, the overburden stress is the vertical stress caused by the weight of the overlying formations and fluids.

Because overburden calculations are key to most pore-pressure prediction methods, it is important to perform these calculations as carefully and consistently as possible. In general, the overburden stress at any depth depends on the cumulative weight of the overlying materials. In theory, we can obtain the overburden by numerically integrating the density vs. the depth information of the overlying material. In practice, however, we do not often have complete information regarding the bulk density of the sediments at the prediction site.

Formation Pressure

Hydrostatic pressure at a particular depth is the pressure exerted by the weight of the water column, which is equal to 0.433 psi/ft based on fresh water at ambient conditions. This is also called the "normal pressure" or "normal-pressure gradient" (**Fig. 3.1**). The three types of formation pressure conditions include:

- Normal pressure: Hydrostatic pressure of a column of pore water, from the current depth to the surface

- Subnormal pressure: Condition in which the pore pressure is less than the normal pore pressure

- Abnormal pressure: Condition in which the pore pressure exceeds the normal pressure; the terms "abnormal pressure" and "overpressure" are sometimes used interchangeably

    – Overburden stress: Vertical stress caused by the weight of the overlying formations and fluids

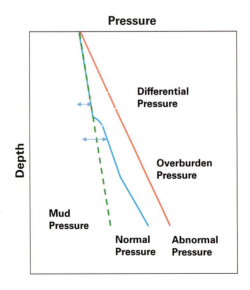

Fig. 3.1 – Normal, Abnormal, and Differential Pressures.

The rate of penetration (ROP) is critical as different sections of the well are drilled, which also depends on the differential pressure (**Fig. 3.2**) (i.e., the difference between the wellbore pressure and the formation pressure). Thus, the accurate estimation of the formation is imperative in order to optimize the drilling parameters so that the rate of penetration is maximized.

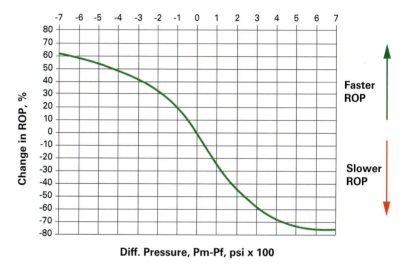

Fig. 3.2 – ROP vs. Differential Pressures (Vidrine and Benit 1969).

Further, several lab studies have demonstrated this effect. As the well is drilled with an extended-reach well-path design, the true vertical depth change is very narrow; therefore, the effect of bit types also plays a major part in consideration of the formation matrix, which is further related to the formation pressure.

The effect of the drillability of roller-cone bits and polycrystalline diamond compact bits (PDCs) with respect to overbalance is shown in **Figs. 3.3** and **3.4**, respectively.

FORMATION PRESSURES

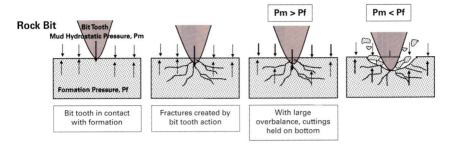

Fig. 3.3 – Formation Drillability vs. Differential Pressures for Rollercone Bit.

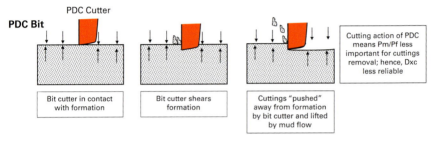

Fig. 3.4 – Formation Drillability vs. Differential Pressures for PDC Bit.

Origin of Abnormal Pressure

Undercompaction (Compaction Disequilibrium)

- Trapped pore fluid squeezed by the overburden stress

Fluid Expansion

- Trapped pore fluid constrained from an increase in volume
    - Heating (aquathermal pressuring)
    - Clay diagenesis
    - Hydrocarbon maturation
    - Charging from other overpressured zones
    - Up-dip transfer of reservoir pressures (lateral transfer)

Tectonics

- Trapped pore fluid squeezed by tectonic stresses

Fracture Pressure

Fracture pressure is the pressure at which the formation breaks down, resulting in a fracture of the formation. This fracturing may result from the wellbore hydraulic pressure exceeding the formation strength, which can lead to lost circulation; pressures exceeding 1 psi/ft of depth can overcome the overburden gradient.

Overburden Pressure

The overburden pressure can be given as:

$$P_o = \frac{weight(rock \text{ matrix} + fluid)}{Area} \tag{3-1}$$

which can be given in general form as:

$$P_o = \sum_{i=0} C\rho_{ma}^i \Delta L_i \tag{3-2}$$

Where,

ρ^i_{ma} is the average density within the ith interval,

ΔL_i is the interval length over which r_i is calculated, and

C is the unit conversion constant.

Considering the porosity of the formation, overburden pressure can be expressed by Eq. 3-3.

$$P_o = D\left[(1-\phi)\rho_{ma} + \phi\rho_f\right] \tag{3-3}$$

Where,

D is the vertical height of the geologic column in ft or m,

ϕ is the porosity of the formation expressed as a fraction,

ρ_{ma} is the density of the rock matrix in lb/ft³ or kg/dm³, and

ρ_f is the density of fluid in lb/ft³ or kg/dm³.

Average porosity can be given as:

$$\phi = \phi_0 e^{-KD} \qquad (3\text{-}4)$$

Where,

ϕ_0 is the surface porosity,

K is the decline constant, and

D is the depth in ft or m.

Using the porosity equation, overburden can be expressed as below:

For offshore wells, the Eq. 3-4 should be split into two parts:

1. Surface to seawater bottom:

$$\sigma_{ob} = g \left[\int_0^D \rho_{ma}(1-\phi) + \rho_f \phi \right] dD \qquad (3\text{-}5)$$

2. Seafloor to the depth of interest:

$$\sigma_{ob} = g \int_0^{Dw} \rho_{sw} dD + g \int_{Dw}^D \left[\rho_g - (\rho_g - \rho_f)\phi_0 e^{-K} \right] \qquad (3\text{-}6)$$

Integrating the previous Eq. 3-6 and substituting $D = D\text{-}D_w$ yields:

$$\sigma_{ob} = g\rho_{sw} D_w + g\rho_g D_s - \frac{(\rho_g - \rho_f)g\phi_0}{K}\left(1 - e^{-KD}\right) \qquad (3\text{-}7)$$

Where,

ρ_{sw} is the seawater density, and

D_w is the seawater depth.

Formation Pressure

Geological settings can often make it very difficult to quantify the various interrelated causes that may result in an abnormal formation pressure. However, there are several well-defined reasons that can cause abnormal pressure, some of which are listed below.

Undercompaction (Compaction/Disequilibrium)

- Trapped pore fluid squeezed by the overburden stress

Fluid Expansion

- Trapped pore fluid constrained from an increase in volume
  - Heating (aquathermal pressuring)
  - Clay diagenesis
  - Hydrocarbon maturation
  - Charging from other overpressured zones
  - Up-dip transfer of reservoir pressures (lateral transfer)
  - Tectonics
- Trapped pore fluid squeezed by tectonic stresses
- Faults
- Shale diapirism
- Sandstone dikes
  - Osmotic phenomena
  - Diagenesis phenomena
  - Salt deposition
  - Permafrost environment

Undercompaction

Fig. 3.5 illustrates the condition of abnormal pressure due to compaction disequilibrium. It can be seen that water expulsion is impeded in the low-permeability zone, which results in a shift in the pressure line. The weight of the overlying sediment is supported by the pore fluid.

A decrease in porosity is necessarily accompanied by an increase in bulk density. Under normal compaction, porosity will decrease with depth. The percentage of fluid decreases with depth unless undercompaction is occurring.

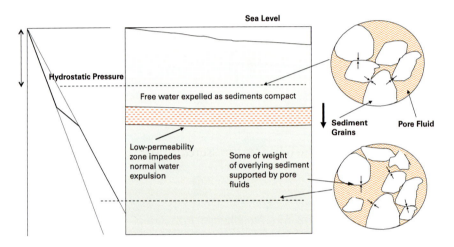

Fig. 3.5 – Abnormal Pressure – Disequilibrium.

Aquathermal Pressuring

In this case, the abonomal pressure results from an increase in pore-fluid temperature. As the fluid expands, greater pressure is necessary to make the water fit inside the pore space, which results in excess pressure and, thus, abnormal pressure, as shown in **Fig. 3.6**.

Other Origins

- *Faults and fractures*: Conduits for pressures from deeper zones or seals against fluid movement

- *Poor drilling practices in an offset well*: Insufficient sealing of permeable zones (e.g., leakage via poor cement around a casing string or across a permeable zone)
- *Topography*: Well elevation relative to the potentiometric surface
- *Structure*: Centroids

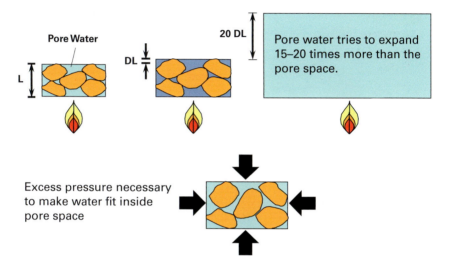

Fig. 3.6 – Aquathermal Pressuring.

Abnormal Pressure Indicators During Drilling

Mud gas: Gas-cut mud provides a warning signal of potential change in the formation pressure. Gas shows during drilling can be a good indicator that abnormal pressure has been encountered or is going to be encountered (**Fig. 3.7**).

The exact cause of any background gas should be isolated. The background gas observed during the following operations may aid in additional evaluation (**Fig. 3.8**).

- Drill gas (background gas)
- Connection gas

FORMATION PRESSURES

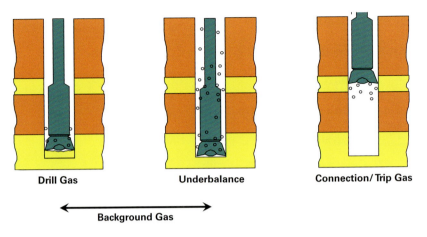

Fig. 3.7 – Background Gas.

- Trip gas
- Pump-off gas
- Gas from shales
- Gas entering from drilled zones due to insufficient mud-weight control

Background Gas

- Mud properties   – Permeability
- Pump rate   – Porosity
- ROP   – Gas composition
- Mud weight   – ECD

Connection/Trip Gas

- Pump shutdown time – Permeability
- Swabbing   – Porosity
- Mud weight   – ECD

EXTENDED-REACH DRILLING

Rate of Penetration (ROP)

The rate of penetration is another indicator of abnormal pressure.

- Normalized ROP (d-exponent and other methods)

Cuttings/Cavings and Hole Instability

- Cavings size and shape, splintery, rotor-shaped
- Torque, drag, hole washout

Variations in shape, size, and volume of drilled cuttings can provide an indication of abnormal pressures. At the transition zone, the pressure increase causes a decrease in overbalance, which may result in longer, thinner, and more numerous cuttings. Physical and chemical measurements also provide such indications, as do measurements of bulk density and the moisture content of the cuttings.

Formation Temperature

Formation temperature is usually inferred from the downhole circulating temperature or flowline temperature. Continuous monitoring of mud temperature into the wellbore and flowline temperature out of the wellbore may indicate a change in the formation pressure (**Fig. 3.9**). A sudden increase in the flowline temperature above the normal trend may indicate an abnormal pressure or may result from other changes in drilling practices. The cause of this temperature increase must be determined, as the trend can provide valuable information.

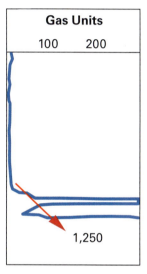

Fig. 3.8 – Background Gas Unit Change.

Mud Properties

- Background chlorides
- Trip chlorides

FORMATION PRESSURES

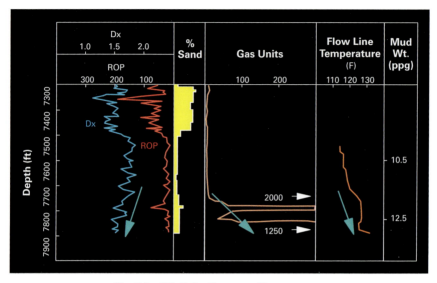

Fig. 3.9 – Wellsite Pressure Parameters.

Differential Pressure Decrease Due to Background Gas

To compensate for gas changes that do not result from the differential pressure:

$$G_n = G\left(\frac{ROP_n}{ROP}\right)\left(\frac{D_n}{D}\right)^2\left(\frac{Q}{Q_n}\right)\left(\frac{1}{E}\right) \qquad (3\text{-}8)$$

Where,

G_n represents the normalized total gas units,

G represents the measured gas units,

ROP_n is the reference ROP,

ROP is the actual ROP,

D_n is the reference bit diameter,

D is the actual hole size,

Q_n is the reference pump rate,

Q is the actual pump rate, and

E is the gas system efficiency.

Pore Pressure Estimation

The estimation of pore pressure is given by Eq. 3-9.

$$P_p = \sigma_{ob} - \sigma_z \tag{3-9}$$

Where,

P_p is the pore pressure (**Fig. 3.10**),

σ_{ob} is the vertical total stress or the overburden, and

σ_z represents Terzaghi's vertical effective stress.

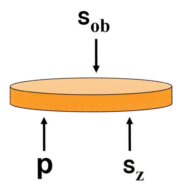

Fig. 3.10 – Effective Stress Law.

By dividing each of these stresses by the true vertical depth, the stresses can be expressed as gradients, which are dimensionally equivalent to the density. The resulting expression can be solved for the pore-pressure gradient to obtain the fundamental equation for pore-pressure prediction, as shown in Eq. 3-10.

$$PP = OBG - ES \tag{3-10}$$

Where,

> PP is the pore-pressure gradient,
>
> OBG is the overburden gradient, and
>
> ES is the effective stress gradient.

Various investigators, including Eaton, Bowers, Alixant, and others, have provided means for estimating the effective stress from porosity or directly from sonic velocity. These methods provide the basis for pore-pressure estimation from well logs or seismic velocities.

- Shale or claystone has a log response that can be quantitatively related to its state of effective stress. Sandstone and other sedimentary rocks may not undergo significant porosity reduction with burial.

The next two assumptions apply to resistivity-based pore-pressure prediction models.

- The resistivity of the connate water is relatively constant over an interval characterized by a particular lithology.

- The effective stress in the shale can be inferred from the porosity-dependent log response. Specifically, the effective stress is presumed to be adequately modeled using a technique introduced by Eaton (1972) for resistivity geopressure analyses.

Fracture-Gradient Prediction

The general equation for fracture gradient presumes that the force required to generate a fracture equals the minimum horizontal stress. This, of course, does not account for stress concentration effects around a wellbore or any tensile strength of intact rock; thus, it implicitly (and conservatively) assumes that a wellbore is likely to have intersected a preexisting fracture oriented in the most critical direction. In a tectonically relaxed sedimentary basin, the contribution of tectonic stresses is considered negligible.

It is further presumed that we know the ratio between the minimum horizontal effective stress and the vertical effective stress. The more commonly

used formulations were developed by Mathews and Kelly (1967) and Eaton (1968, 1997).

In Eaton's formulation (1968, 1997), the term, $\frac{\mu}{1-\mu}$, is substituted for the matrix stress coefficient, F_σ. Since both F_σ and Eaton's μ are empirically determined, it does not matter which formulation is used; however, it is more straightforward to use F_σ. Regardless, it is important to keep in mind that published values of either F_σ or μ were empirically derived, and these derivations may have used the unreasonable assumption that sediment bulk densities are the same at shallow depths as they are at greater depths.

The different methods presented include the following:

- The Hubert and Willis method
- The Mathews and Kelly method
- Eaton's method
- Christman's method

Hubert and Willis Method:

Fracture pressure is given as:

$$p_{ff} = \sigma_h + p_p \tag{3-11}$$

Considering the horizontal stress to be minimal, then Eq. 3-11 can be written as follows:

$$p_{ff} = \sigma_{min} + p_p \tag{3-12}$$

Further, if horizontal stress is assumed to be one-half (½) and one-third (⅓) of the overall stress, then the minimum and maximum horizontal stresses can be written as:

$$\sigma_{hmin} = \frac{1}{3}\sigma_z = \frac{1}{3}(\sigma_{ob} - p_p) \tag{3-13}$$

$$\sigma_{hmax} = \frac{1}{2}\sigma_z = \frac{1}{2}(\sigma_{ob} - p_p) \tag{3-14}$$

Using Eqs. 3-13 and 3-14, the fracture pressure can be written as:

$$p_{ff} = \frac{1}{3}(\sigma_{ob} + 2p_p) \tag{3-15}$$

$$p_{ff} = \frac{1}{2}(\sigma_{ob} + p_p) \tag{3-16}$$

Hence, the fracture gradient can be given as:

$$\frac{p_{ff\min}}{D} = \frac{1}{3}\left(\frac{\sigma_{ob} + 2p_p}{D}\right) \tag{3-17}$$

$$\frac{p_{ff\max}}{D} = \frac{1}{2}\left(\frac{\sigma_{ob} + p_p}{D}\right) \tag{3-18}$$

Mathews and Kelly Method:

In the Mathews and Kelly (1967) formulation, the proportionality constant is equal to a function of an empirically established "matrix stress coefficient," as shown in Eq. 3-19.

$$\sigma_{\min} = F_\sigma \sigma_z \tag{3-19}$$

Substituting Eq. 3-19 into Eq. 3-11, the fracture pressure can be written as:

$$p_{ff} = F_\sigma \sigma_z + p_p \tag{3-20}$$

Thus, the fracture gradient becomes:

$$\frac{p_{ff}}{D} = \frac{F_\sigma \sigma_z}{D} + \frac{p_p}{D} \tag{3-21}$$

Where,

F_σ denotes the matrix coefficient.

Eaton's Method:

In Eaton's formulation (1968, 1997), the term, $\frac{\mu}{1-\mu}$, is substituted for F_σ in Eq. 3-21.

$$\sigma_x = \sigma_y = \sigma_h = \frac{\mu}{1-\mu}\sigma_z \qquad (3\text{-}22)$$

Expressing Eq. 22 in terms of gradient gives:

$$\frac{p_{ff}}{D} = \left(\frac{\mu}{1-\mu}\right)\left(\frac{\sigma_{ob}-p_p}{D}\right) + \frac{p_p}{D} \qquad (3\text{-}23)$$

Since both F_σ and Eaton's μ are empirically determined, it does not matter which formulation is used; however, it is more straightforward to use F_σ. Regardless, it is important to keep in mind that published values of either F_σ or μ were empirically derived, and these derivations may have used the unreasonable assumption that sediment bulk densities are the same at shallow depths as they are at greater depths.

Christman's Method:

This method is a modified Eaton method for predicting the fracture gradient in offshore wells by accounting for the effect of water depth.

$$\frac{p_{ff}}{D} = \left(\frac{1}{D}\right)(\rho_w D_w + \rho_b D_f) \qquad (3\text{-}24)$$

Pore-Pressure Calculation

Estimation Theory and Assumptions

Pore-pressure analysis models are typically based on the following assumptions:

- Mechanical compaction is the dominant mechanism for porosity reduction in the sediments, and the effects of secondary mineralization are minimal or can be calibrated into models.

- Mechanical compaction depends on current and previous values of Terzaghi's effective stress, which equals the total stress minus the pore pressure.

- Compaction is basically a one-dimensional process. As a consequence, the vertical effective stress can be used by itself to define a sediment's compaction state.

FORMATION PRESSURES

- The total vertical stress or, equivalently, the overburden is known. This is usually calculated from density logs, regional correlations, or density/velocity transforms.

- Then, by the effective stress definition, the pore pressure is related to the above two variables as follows:

$$p_p = \sigma_z - \sigma_{ob} \qquad (3\text{-}25)$$

Where,

P_p is the pore pressure,

σ_{ob} is the vertical total stress, or the overburden, and

σ_z is Terzaghi's vertical effective stress.

By dividing each of these stresses by the true vertical depth, the stresses can be expressed as gradients, which are dimensionally equivalent to density. The resulting expression can be solved for the pore-pressure gradient to obtain the fundamental equation for pore-pressure prediction:

$$\frac{p_p}{D} = \frac{\sigma_z}{D} - \frac{\sigma_{ob}}{D} \qquad (3\text{-}26)$$

Where,

$\dfrac{p_p}{D}$ is the pore-pressure gradient,

$\dfrac{\sigma_{ob}}{D}$ is the overburden gradient, and

$\dfrac{\sigma_z}{D}$ is the effective-stress gradient.

Projected Pore Pressures

Using offset well data and knowledge of the geologic structure, it is possible to project pore pressures to the proposed well location. This requires an assumption regarding the fluid content of the pore space, as well as the assumption that there is adequate hydraulic conductivity between the well

locations. The pore pressure in the proposed well location, according to assumptions, will be different from the pore pressure in the offset location by an amount equal to the pressure exerted by the column of fluid between the elevations of correlating formations in the wells.

$$p_1 = p_2 + \rho_f \lambda (D_2 - D_1) \qquad (3\text{-}27)$$

Where,

p_1 is the pore pressure projected to the well of interest in appropriate pressure units,

p_2 is the known pore pressure in an offset well in appropriate pressure units,

ρ_f represents the density of the pore fluid in appropriate units,

λ denotes the unit conversion factor (e.g., 0.433 for pressure in psi and depth) in ft,

D_1 is the correlation depth from well of interest in appropriate length units, and

D_2 is the correlation depth of an offset well in appropriate-length units.

It is important to note that the pore pressures referred to above are in pressure units, which are not equivalent mud densities or pressure gradients. Known pore-pressure gradients in offset wells are converted into pressures prior to the application of this formula.

Basic 1-D Pore-Pressure Estimation Process

The conventional pore-pressure analysis is based on Terzaghi's effective stress principle, which states that the vertical stress (σ_{ob}) is equal to the sum of the effective vertical stress (σ_z) and the formation pore pressure (p_p) as follows:

$$\sigma_{ob} = \sigma_z + p_p \qquad (3\text{-}28)$$

The basic steps in performing a conventional 1-D pore pressure analysis

are outlined below:

1. Calculate the total vertical stress (S_v) from the rock density.
2. Estimate the vertical effective stress (σ_e) from log measurements or seismic (LWD-WL, Vel).
3. Determine the pore pressure, using the calculation, $p_p = \sigma_{ob} - \sigma_z$.

The analysis is then calibrated to additional information as it becomes available.

- mdt/rft
- Shut-in drill pipe pressure (SIDPP)
- Splintered cavings
- Exceptional connection gas
- Hole fill
- Excess drillstring drag

Pore Pressure from Seismic Interval Velocities – Eaton

The pre-spud pore-pressure analysis uses a method attributed to Eaton (1972) and is applied to the seismic interval velocity. With normal compaction, the interval velocity, especially in shale, tends to increase with increasing depth, indicating a reduction in porosity. Deviations from the trend of increasing shale velocity imply that compaction is being inhibited because pore fluids cannot flow out of the sediment. Since a normal-compaction trend line is required for this method, and because the velocity at the mudline is approximately the same as in water, a trend line is usually constructed with an approximate value of 5,000 ft/sec at the mudline as its initial point. The pore pressure is derived from the interval velocity by substituting the observed and normal velocity values into the Eaton equation.

The Eaton formula for calculating the pore pressure from the interval velocity is given by Eq. 3-29.

$$PP = OBG - (OBG - PP_n)(V/V_n)^3 \qquad (3\text{-}29)$$

Where,

PP is the pore-pressure gradient in ppg, kPa/m, etc.;

OBG is the vertical total stress, or overburden gradient, in ppg, kPa/m, etc.;

PP_n is the normal pressure gradient in ppg, kPa/m, etc.;

V is the seismic velocity in ft/sec, m/s, etc.; and

V_n is the velocity from the normal-compaction trend line in ft/sec, m/s, etc.

Eq. 3-29 is expressed in terms of gradients, but it can be expressed in terms of stresses and pressures by multiplying the gradient terms by the appropriate true vertical depth (TVD) and unit conversion factor (e.g., to convert from gradients expressed in ppg with TVD in ft to stress in psi, multiply the gradient by 0.052*TVD).

Pore Pressure from Sonic – Eaton

The data used in this analysis are obtained from the sonic tool measurements. The travel times measured in normally compacted sediments, especially in shales, decrease with depth, presumably because their porosity decreases. This decrease is considered to be a normal trend. Travel times that decrease less than the normal trend imply that compaction is inhibited because pore fluids cannot flow out of the sediment. Eaton's (1972) method uses the difference in the measured and estimated normal-trend travel times to infer the increased pore pressure.

The method uses a trend line typically developed from data collected up-hole. The Eaton formula for calculating pore pressure from sonic is shown in Eq. 3-30.

$$PP = OBG - (OBG - PP_n)(\Delta t_n / \Delta t)^3 \qquad (3\text{-}30)$$

Where,

PP represents the pore-pressure gradient in ppg, kPa, etc.;

OBG is the overburden gradient in ppg, kPa, etc.;

FORMATION PRESSURES

PP_n denotes the normal pore-pressure gradient (usually 8.7–9 ppg);

Δt_{tn} is the sonic transit time from the normal compaction trend in μ/ft, μ/m, etc.; and

Δt is the sonic interval transit time in ft/sec, μ/sec, etc.

Eq. 3-30 is expressed in terms of gradients, but it can be expressed in terms of stresses and pressures by multiplying the gradient terms by the appropriate TVD and unit conversion factor (e.g., to convert from gradients expressed in ppg with TVD in ft to stress in psi, multiply the gradient by 0.052*TVD).

Curved-Compaction Trend

It has been observed that abnormal pressures begin at or near the mudline in deep water, which leaves no observable normal-compaction trend from which to work. Therefore, a curved-compaction trend based on work originally performed by Bowers with subsequent refinements (1994–1999) was used in this analysis.

The curved normal-compaction trend line is based on a velocity/effective-stress function, which is derived using a relationship expressed in terms of seismic interval velocities, as shown in Eq. 31.

$$V_n = V_{mudline} + a[(s_v - p_n)]^b \qquad (3\text{-}31)$$

Where,

V_n is the resultant velocity normally pressured regime in ft/sec, m/s, etc.;

$V_{mudline}$ represents the seismic interval velocity at the mudline in ft/sec ($\approx 5{,}000$ ft/sec, 1,520 m/s);

s_v denotes the overburden or vertical total stress in psi, kPa, etc.;

p_n is the normal pore pressure in psi, kPa, etc.;

a is an empirically derived coefficient, which is unit dependent (usual

range is 10–25 when stress is in psi and velocity is in ft/sec); and b is an empirically derived exponent (usual range is 0.60–0.75).

Rearranging Eq. 3-31 in terms of sonic Δt gives:

$$\Delta t_n = 10^6/(10^6/\Delta t_{mudline} + a(s_v - p_n)^b) \tag{3-32}$$

Where,

Δt_n is the resultant Δt in a normally pressured regime in μsec/ft or μs/m, and

$\Delta t_{mudline}$ is the sonic Δt at the mudline in μsec/ft (200 μsec/ft, 660 μs/m).

Coefficients, a and b, can be varied as necessary to meet differing conditions. Note that because a multiplies the vertical effective stress to the power b with resulting units (ft/sec or m/s), a has non-standard units and care must be taken to transform it (e.g., a for σ in kPa = a/(6.895)^b in psi for velocities in ft/sec). Unless otherwise noted, typical values of a are given when stresses are measured in psi. When using Halliburton Drillworks® Predict software, this transformation is automatically accounted for.

Bowers' Method

Since Bowers' method can be characterized as a self-consistent pore-pressure prediction technique, the a and b parameters that are used to develop a normal-compaction trend can be used directly in a pore-pressure prediction. This can be done be as follows:

$$p = s_v - [(V - V_{mudline})/a]^{1/b} \tag{3-33}$$

Where,

p represents the predicted pore pressure in psi or kPa,

s_v denotes the overburden vertical total stress in psi or kPa,

V is the velocity at a given depth in ft/sec or m/s, and

$V_{mudline}$ = is the seismic interval velocity at the mudline in ft/sec ($\approx$ 5,000 ft/sec, 1,520 m/s).

Eq. 3-33 also can be written in terms of transit time by simply substituting $10^6/\Delta t$ for V and $10^6/\Delta t_{mudline}$ for $V_{mudline}$.

The a and b parameters, then, are essentially material properties that describe the velocity effective-stress relationship for any sediment undergoing compaction. We would normally expect these parameters and, hence, the compaction trend to be functions of the sediment type.

Note, again, that the above relationship only applies to sediments that are undercompacted (i.e., sediments whose current vertical effective stress is also the maximum value of the vertical effective stress experienced by that sediment). This type of condition is common in deepwater Gulf of Mexico and anywhere else subjected to rapid sedimentation. Bowers (1994) had also presented a method for modifying Eq. 3-31 for pressure prediction for cases in which the sediment's current effective stress is less than some maximum value it had experienced in the past. This reduction in effective stress is termed "unloading." Accounting for unloading can be complex. Refer to Bowers' 1994 paper for more details.

Miller's Method

Like Bowers' method, Miller's method can also be characterized as a self-consistent pore-pressure prediction technique, as there is a unique velocity effective-stress relationship for normal compaction. Miller's method differs from Bowers' method in that the velocity is asymptotic to the velocity of the sediment's matrix at high effective stresses. Miller's method also includes a provision to model the effects of "unloading," where the vertical effective stress decreases in response to some pressure-generating source. The governing equations are as follows when excess pore pressures result from compaction disequilibrium (undercompaction).

$$V = V_{mudline} + (V_{matrix} - V_{mudline})[1 - exp(-\lambda\sigma)] \quad (3\text{-}34)$$

Where,

V is the velocity at a given depth in ft/sec or m/s,

$V_{mudline}$ is the seismic interval velocity at the mudline in ft/sec ($\approx$ 5,000 ft/sec, 1,520 m/s),

V_{matrix} represents the velocity of a sediment's matrix material in ft/sec ($\approx$ 14,000 ft/sec to 17,000 ft/sec for most shales),

λ is an empirical parameter that provides the best fit for a normal compaction trend, and

σ denotes the vertical effective stress (psi).

Eq. 3-34 can also be written in terms of transit time by simply substituting $10^6/\Delta t$ for V and $10^6/\Delta t_{mudline}$ for $V_{mudline}$.

$V_{mudline}$, V_{matrix}, and λ are essentially material properties that describe the velocity effective-stress relationship for any sediment undergoing compaction. We would normally expect these parameters and, hence, the compaction trend to be functions of the sediment type. In theory, these parameters ($V_{mudline}$, V_{matrix}, and λ) can be varied as necessary to meet differing conditions. However, the values of $V_{mudline}$ and V_{matrix} are physically constrained (see typical values above).

To determine pore pressures, one simply solves for σ in Eq. 3-34 and subtracts that result from the overburden, as shown in Eq. 3-35.

$$pp = OBG \times depth \times ucf - \sigma \qquad (3\text{-}35)$$

Where,

pp represents the pore pressure,

OBG is the overburden gradient,

depth represents the depth, *ucf* denotes a unit correction factor that converts the product of the overburden gradient and depth to the appropriate units (done automatically in Drillworks® Predict software), and

FORMATION PRESSURES

$$\sigma = (1/\lambda) \ln \left[\frac{(V_{matrix} - V_{mudline})}{(V_{matrix} - V)} \right] \quad (3\text{-}36)$$

Note, again, that the above relationship only applies to sediments that are undercompacted (i.e., sediments whose current vertical effective stress is also the maximum value of the vertical effective stress experienced by that sediment). This type of condition is common in deepwater Gulf of Mexico and anywhere else subjected to rapid sedimentation.

Pore Pressure from Resistivity – Eaton

If shale-water salinity is assumed constant, then changes in resistivity imply a variation in shale porosity and, hence, its compaction state. Eaton's (1972) method uses the resistivity changes that differ from those expected for normally compacted sediments to infer pore pressure.

The method relies on data collected up-hole to infer the normal-compaction trend line for the resistivity data. The pore pressure is derived from the measured resistivity data by relating it to the normal-trend resistivity values extrapolated to the same depths.

The Eaton formula for calculating pore pressure from resistivity is given by Eq. 3-37.

$$PP = OBG - (OBG - PP_n)(R_o/R_n)^{1.2} \quad (3\text{-}37)$$

Where,

PP represents the pore-pressure gradient,

OBG is the overburden gradient,

PP_n denotes the normal pore-pressure gradient (typically 8.7 ppg, 10.1 kPa/m),

R_o is the observed resistivity, and

R_n is the resistivity from the normal-compaction trend line.

Eq. 3-37 is expressed in terms of gradients, but it can be expressed in terms of stresses and pressures by multiplying the gradient terms by

the appropriate TVD and unit conversion factor (e.g., to convert from gradients expressed in ppg with TVD in ft to stress in psi, multiply the gradient by 0.052*TVD).

Resistivity Temperature Normalization Using the Arps Equation

Resistivity is affected by the salinity of the connate water, as well as by temperature. Arps proposed a relationship between temperature and resistivity, which is useful in normalizing resistivity values for temperature effects. When formation temperatures are available, the Arps equation can be used to normalize resistivity values to a single reference temperature as follows:

$$R_{ref} = R \times (T+6.77)/(T_{ref}+6.77) \qquad (3.38)$$

Where,

R_{ref} is the resistivity at the reference temperature,

R is the observed resistivity,

T is the temperature at which observed resistivity was measured in °F, and

T_{ref} is the reference temperature in °F.

In theory, the chosen reference temperature is unimportant. However, in practice, the reference temperature is usually chosen to correspond to the formation temperature somewhere near the midpoint of the well being analyzed. Normalizing resistivities to a single reference temperature makes it easier to identify an appropriate normal-compaction trend.

References

Alixant, J.L. and Desbrandes, R. 1991. Explicit Pore-Pressure Evaluation: Concepts and Application. *SPEDE*, **6**(03).

Arps, J.J. 1964. Engineering Concepts Useful in Oil Finding. *AAPG Bull.*, **48**: 157–165.

Bowers, G.L. 1994. Pore Pressure Estimation From Velocity Data: Accounting for Overpressure Mechanisms Besides Undercompaction. Paper IADC/SPE 27488 presented at the IADC/SPE Drilling Conference, Dallas, Texas, 15–18 February.

Bowers, G.L. 1999. State of the Art in Pore Pressure Estimation. Paper DEA-119 presented at the Pore Pressure Advisory Board Meeting, Houston, Texas, 25 May.

Dix, C.H. 1955. Seismic Velocities from Surface Measurements. *Geophysics*, **20**: 68–66.

Eaton, B.A. 1968. Fracture Gradient Prediction Techniques and Their Application in Drilling, Stimulation and Secondary Recovery Operations. Paper SPE 2163 presented at the 43rd Annual Fall Meeting of the Society of Petroleum Engineers of AIME, Houston, Texas, 29 September–2 October.

Eaton, B.A. 1972. Graphical Method Predicts Geopressures Worldwide, *World Oil*, 51–56.

Eaton, B.A., and Eaton, T.L. 1997. Fracture Gradient Prediction for the New Generation, *World Oil*, 93–100.

Gardner, G.H.F., Gardner, L.W., and Gregory, A.R. 1974. Formation Velocity and Density – The Diagnostic Basis for Stratigraphic Traps. *Geophysics*, **39**(6): 2085–2095.

Issler, D.R. 1992. A New Approach to Shale Compaction and Stratigraphic Restoration, Beaufort-McKenzie Basin and McKenzie Corridor, Northern Canada. *AAPG Bulletin*, **76**(8): 1170–1189.

Mathews, W.R. and Kelly, J. 1967. How to Predict Formation Pressure and Fracture Gradient. *The Oil and Gas Journal*, 92–106.

Raiga-Clemenceau, J., Martin, J. P., and Nicoletis, S. 1986. The Concept of Acoustic Formation Factor for More Accurate Porosity Determination from Sonic Transit Time Data. SPWLA-1986-G presented at the 27th Annual Logging Symposium, Houston, Texas, 9–13 June.

Samuel, R. Class Notes, Drilling and Completions, University of Houston.

Terzaghi, K. 1943. **Theoretical Soil Mechanics**. New York: John Wiley & Sons, Inc.

Vidrine, D.J. and Benit, E.J. 1986. Field Verification of the Effect of Differential Pressure on Drilling Rate. *JPT*, **20**(7): 676–682.

CHAPTER **FOUR**

Well Design

Planning is the first and most important step in drilling a well. A complete understanding of customer requirements and expectations is crucial in developing a "fit-for-purpose" design. In extended-reach drilling (ERD), context well requirements may not be all that different from conventional wells in terms of reaching untapped reserves or providing a geological reservoir control point. The primary deviation, and where project teams usually get it wrong, is the part of expectations. An ERD well is far from being an ordinary well; past experience–if not a similar ERD profile–is irrelevant. Previous drilling performance, risks, and known issues are not valid benchmarks in measuring progress and building authority for expenditure (AFE) curves. For that reason, it is very important to have a risk management process implemented as early as possible in the project life cycle to accommodate for ERD challenges in the design.

Well Profiles and Terminology

A few simple terminologies involved in the ERD well design are shown in **Fig. 4.1** and are briefly explained below. These parameters include:

- Location (surface location)
- Inclination
- Azimuth
- Survey stations
- Kick-off point (KOP)
- Buildup rate (BUR)
- True vertical depth (TVD)
- Departure
- Tangent section

Location

Surface location (SL)

Inclination

The hole angle, or *inclination*, is always expressed in terms of the angle of the wellbore from the vertical.

Azimuth

The direction, or azimuth, of the well is expressed with respect to some reference plane, usually true north. The location of a point in the well is generally expressed in Cartesian coordinates with the wellhead or the rig's *rotary kelly bushing* (RKB) as the reference location.

Survey Stations

Survey stations are the measurement depths at which inclination and azimuth are measured.

WELL DESIGN

Kick-Off Point

The *kick-off point* is the beginning of the build section.

Buildup Rate

A build section is frequently designed at a constant *buildup rate* (BUR) until the desired hole angle or *end-of-build* (EOB) target location is achieved. BUR is normally expressed in terms of degrees per hundred feet (°/100 ft), which is simply the measured change in angle divided by the measured depth (MD) drilled.

True Vertical Depth

True vertical depth (TVD) is usually expressed as the vertical distance below the RKB.

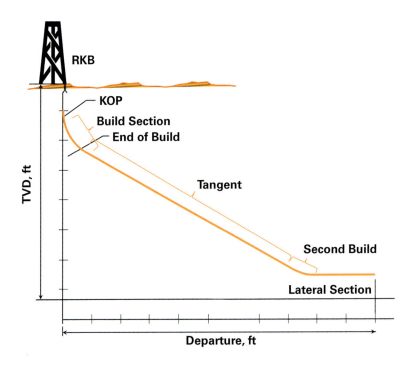

Fig. 4.1 – Well Profile Terminology.

Departure

Departure is the distance between two survey points as projected onto the horizontal plane. The EOB is defined in terms of its location in space as expressed by coordinates and TVD. The EOB specification also contains another important requirement, which is the angle and direction of the well at that point.

Tangent Section

A tangent section is shown after the build section. The purpose of the tangent is to maintain the angle and direction until the next target is reached.

Build Rates

Build or drop rates are expressed in degrees per 100 feet (°/100 ft) or degrees per 30 meters (°/30 m). It is the rate at which the wellpath is built or dropped.

Factors in Well Path Design

The following criteria are important in selecting the well path design:

- *Completion and reservoir drainage*

    Completion and reservoir-drainage considerations are key factors in the well path design. For fracturing, gravel packing, completion in weak formations, or depletion-induced compaction, it may be desirable to limit the inclination of the well through the reservoir or even to require a vertical or near-vertical trajectory.

- *Drainage of reservoir*

    Often, it may be desirable for the well path in the reservoir to be horizontal to provide as much reservoir drainage and production as possible. In horizontal wells, optimum TVD placement will minimize gas coning or water production. In vertically fractured formations in which the fractures may aid in the flow of hydrocarbons, the direction of the well path in the reservoir may be chosen to intersect multiple fractures.

WELL DESIGN

- *Faults and folding*

    Alternatively, it may be desirable to place the wellbore in a given direction to avoid faults that are expected to permit water migration. Optimal placement of the wellbore in the reservoir will result in maximum production and should actually be the starting point for well path design.

- *Other considerations*

    Additional considerations will influence the design of the trajectory from the surface location to the reservoir-target entry point. Some shallow formations in sedimentary geologies are weak, and, as a result, building inclination is difficult because of the lack of reactive forces against the BHA. If this condition is anticipated, the KOP should be designed deeper, where formations are more competent.

- *Casing program*

    The casing program influences the planned trajectory in several ways – although, in general, for a given casing design, the trajectory plan should be optimized for operational efficiency.

- *Troublesome zones*

    In troublesome zones, such as underpressured sands or reactive shales, which can increase the risk of stuck pipe, it may be desirable to avoid directional work that requires *sliding* (drilling without rotating the drillstring). Thus, the design of a build section may need to include a short tangent through the troublesome section so that it can be rotary-drilled as rapidly as possible.

Types of Wells

Typically, the different types of wells can be broadly classified as:

- Long-radius wells
- Medium-radius wells
- Intermediate wells
- Short-radius wells

The industry commonly refers to four main build types (**Fig. 4.2**).

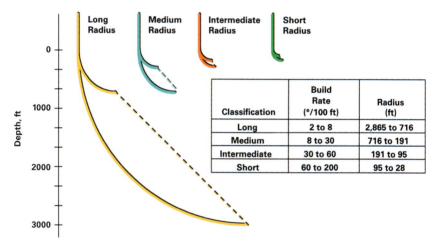

Fig. 4.2 – Build-Rate Classification

Long Radius

A long-radius horizontal well is characterized by build rates of 2–8°/30 m (100 ft), which results in a radius of 290–900 m (1,000–3,000 ft). This profile is drilled using conventional directional-drilling tools. Lateral sections of up to 2,500 m (8,000 ft) have been drilled. This profile is well suited for an application where a long horizontal displacement is required to reach the target entry.

Advantages/Disadvantages of Long Radius

Advantages

- Lower dogleg severity
- Long lateral section (compared to short radius)
- Higher departure possible from the surface location
- Adaptation of conventional directional-drilling techniques and equipment
- Greater amount of rotary drilling allows for improved drilling performance
- Uses standard tubulars and casing
- Fewer restrictions on hole/equipment sizes
- Wider range of completion options possible
- More readily logged and cored
- Can be drilled with steerable motor assemblies

Disadvantages

- Well path must be controlled over a greater length
- Greater length of openhole section exposed (potentially more problems)
- Greater overall measured depth
- Possible cost increase
- More casing required

Medium Radius

Medium-turning-radius horizontal wells have build rates of 8-30°/30 m (100 ft), radii of 50–300 m (160–1,000 ft), and lateral sections of up to 2,500 m (8,000 ft) in length. These wells are drilled with specialized

downhole mud motors and conventional drillstring components. Double-bend assemblies are designed to build angles at rates up to 35°/30 m (100 ft). The lateral section is drilled with conventional steerable-motor assemblies (SMAs). This profile is common for land-based applications and for reentry horizontal drilling.

In practical terms, a well has a medium radius if the BHA cannot be rotated through the build section at all times. At the upper end of the medium radius, drilling the maximum build rate is limited by the bending and torsional limits of API tubulars. Small holes with more flexible tubulars have a higher allowable maximum dogleg severity (DLS).

Advantages/Disadvantages of Medium Radius

Advantages

- Less openhole exposure compared to long radius
- Conventional drilling equipment can be used
- May result in less torque and drag
- Well path is controlled over a shorter interval; a combination of equipment design and fewer changes in formation makes it easier to achieve consistent buildup rates
- Long reach may be achieved compared to short radius
- Wider range of completion options compared to short radius
- Can be logged and cored
- Less restriction on hole sizes of 98 mm to 311 mm (3-7/8 in. to 12-1/4 in.) compared to short radius
- Multiple laterals possible from a single well

Disadvantages

- Some specialized tools may be required, such as double-bend BHAs.

- Some specialized drilling techniques are required (e.g., a lack of drillstring rotation while BHA is in the buildup section makes hole cleaning more difficult). If drillstring rotation is required (e.g., reaming tight hole), then large cyclic-bending stresses cause more rapid fatigue of BHA components.

- Non-API connections and more expensive casing and tubing may be needed.

- Large dogleg severity (compared to long radius) restricts logging and completion options.

Short Radius

Short-radius horizontal wells have build rates of 60-200°/30 m (100 ft), which equates to radii of 6.1–12.2 m (20–40 ft). The lengths of lateral sections vary between 60 m and 275 m (200 ft and 900 ft). Short-radius wells are drilled using specialized drilling tools and techniques. This profile is most commonly drilled as a reentry from an existing well.

In most applications, a vertical well is entered, and a short-radius curve is drilled immediately above, or in, the reservoir. The procedure is to set a packer/whipstock in the required orientation and then to kick off the building angle with a special-angle build assembly. Once 90° is reached, a special-angle hold assembly is run to drill the horizontal section. This special-angle hold assembly is driven by articulated tubulars to allow for rotation through the tight radius. Short-radius articulated motor systems have also been used on several wells to date.

Most wells drilled with this system have been less than 3,000 m (10,000 ft) TVD with lateral reaches of 90–120 m (300–400 ft), although lateral reaches up to 350 m (900 ft) have been obtained.

Advantages/Disadvantages of Short-Radius Wells

Advantages

- Shorter curved section
- Minimum departure allows for accurate structure definition

EXTENDED-REACH DRILLING

- KOP is closer to the reservoir
- Multiple laterals possible from a single well
- Minimum measured depth
- Easy reentry of existing wells

Disadvantages

- Specialized drilling equipment
- Unconventional drilling techniques are used
- Typically, limited reach – 90–120 m (300–400 ft) – with rotary systems, but potentially up to 450 m (1,500 ft) with motor systems
- Restricted hole sizes (107 mm to 158 mm or 4-1/2 in. to 6-1/4 in.)
- Poor azimuth control in horizontal section (rotary)
- Presently cannot be logged
- Completion options are limited (generally openhole)
- Time consuming (multiple BHA changes/low ROP)

Ultra-Short Radius

In addition to the above, there is also an ultra-short-radius system that can turn a well from vertical to horizontal in a radius of 0.3–0.6 m (1–2 ft). This is not a drilling system in the conventional sense, but a specialized application of a high-pressure water jet. The water jet drills a diameter hole of 3.8–6.4 cm (1.5–2.5 in.) to a length of 30–61 m (100–200 ft). It is our opinion that this technology has lacked commercial success.

Selecting the ERD Well Type

Drilling the Build Section

Typically, steerable motors are run in the build section because they can compensate for almost any deviation from the plan. General well-planning

guidelines are used to design the steerable motor with a dogleg capability of about 25–50 percent more than the planned build rate; the motor is then rotated as required to eliminate the excess build rate. In the build section, however, the greatest risk is falling "behind the curve." To prevent this from occurring, the tendency is to design the steerable motor for a greater build rate than what is needed. Such a selection can result in the creation of excessive doglegs in the build section, as the assembly repeatedly builds more than is needed; then, the motor must be rotated to reduce the overall build rate. When the motor is first rotated after each interval of oriented drilling, it will also encounter bit side loads that may reduce its life.

Drilling the Tangent Section

In a tangent section or lateral, typically, the goal is to drill straight in the direction established at the end of the build. Steerable motors, of course, are designed to drill straight ahead in the rotating mode. Therefore, the inherent advantage of steerable motors – that when the rotary-mode directional tendency deviates from the plan, it is possible to correct by sliding – can also be a trap. Since corrections are relatively easy to make, there may be less effort to optimize the rotary-mode directional characteristics during the planning phase, especially if the focus is on merely hitting targets or "staying on the line" geometrically.

However, compelling reasons exist for optimizing the rotary-mode tendency of steerable motors. One simple reason is economics. Experience has shown that, even in conventional directional wells without severe torque/drag problems, sliding ROP is typically only about 60 percent of rotary-mode ROP. In severe wells, effective ROP can be as low as 5–10 percent. Secondly, the doglegs created by excessive sliding can cause problems with drillpipe fatigue or with further attempts at sliding later in the well. Doglegs may also limit the drillable depth of the well.

Drilling the Short-Radius Lateral

Although articulated motors may be run in the lateral, non-articulated tools can be expected to provide more predictable control. Motors with flexible housings may be required for passing through the build section without yielding or getting stuck. At the beginning of the build sec-

tion, the lateral motor may need to be oriented so that it can be tripped through that section without bending. To minimize stress cycles, top drives or power swivels should be used to turn the drillstring as slowly as possible, preferably at 1–10 rpm. Drilling operators should particularly avoid picking up the drillstring or tripping out of the hole, since the combined stresses in the build section will be at their maximum in this condition. Drillpipe-fatigue cracks can usually be detected as washouts before the cracks part, so the drillstring should be tripped at the first sign of any loss in pump pressure.

Because most short-radius footage is drill-oriented or drilled at a low rate, the drillstring cannot be relied on to agitate the cuttings beds and lift cuttings into the annular flow stream. High annular velocities and drilling-fluid rheology must remove cuttings; sliding wiper trips may also be necessary.

Well Path Planning

The first step in the well design process is to determine with a preliminary well path from the defined surface location that is practical, efficient, and achieves downhole target intersections. The well path must meet any additional requirements, such as specific dogleg limitation in the overburden for torque management in long, deep ERD wells, and for completion-running specifics or inclination limitations related to formation stability in high-step-out wells. The well path must accommodate all design specifications of drilling tools to be used in different sections, rig specifications and capabilities, as well as anticipated casing design. Such preliminary well paths will be, in most cases, adjusted once a risk management process and other well design simulations are conducted.

Risk Management Process

The drilling project team must identify all potential risks that might exist related to the intended well path, using any of the risk analytical methods existing in the industry. Potential risks must be evaluated for severity and frequency of occurrence. Although ERD wells do not have any specific risk issues compared to ordinary wells, the severity and frequency of such

risks tend to be highly elevated in such profiles. A detailed description of each risk issue and its consequence must be clearly documented in the well-risk registry – such as a risk map or a risk – that will be updated during the execution and evaluation phases.

The second part of the risk management process is to develop contingency plans that will help manage the identified risks in terms of preventing the issues from materializing or mitigating the severity of such materialization. On the prevention front, the contingency plan must include all design specifics that reduce the likelihood of the event from occurring, such as BHA composition, mud design, or any other well design requirements. On the mitigation front, the plan must clearly state how the problem will be detected during execution, what actions should be taken, when they should be taken, and who is the responsible party to execute such actions.

Survey Management

The well survey program, in general, must satisfy all anti-collision requirements that may exist around the well path at all stages of the drilling process, as well as meet well-positioning objectives within the structure. Survey by part is the industry-chosen approach to reflect different phases of drilling progress through different well sections, which has not yet changed for ERD wells. The largest deviation from the norm in terms of ERD is the survey tool's error code of choice. As ERD wells tend to have much longer-than-usual sections due to the higher displacement requirement and the advancement of rotary steerable systems (RSSs), which allow for one-run sections, it is safe to say that using normal tool error codes, such as standard measurement while drilling (MWD), will result in a huge ellipse of uncertainty by the end of the section that will not satisfy well-positioning requirements. For that reason, most ERD projects tend to use gyro surveys or drilling-efficient advanced-survey calculation methods, such as in-field referencing (IFR) or something similar, that produce smaller error. The ERD survey management process must be documented in a specific surveying procedure that lists the steps of real-time survey corrections and details the responsibility of field crew and survey specialists.

BHA and Drillstring Design

The BHA design must fulfill the section directional objective – build, hold, or drop – along with formation evaluation requirements to reach anticipated targets in the most cost-effective, efficient way; the fewer instrumented components, the better. The BHA must also comply with survey requirements in terms of survey-point distance from the bit, as well as magnetic interference and azimuthal error. The selection of drill collars, heavy-weight drillpipe, and normal drillpipe is important for all simulations – hydraulics, vibration, and torque and drag – to come. Stabilization size and placement have a critical effect on BHA behavior under different drilling modes. Using the correct BHA tendency analysis and components-estimated deflection software is a key element in improving directional-drilling efficiency.

Hydraulics Management

Hole cleaning is often one of the major risks encountered in ERD wells due to the presence of long sections with critical inclination (between 30° and 60°). Add to that a long drillstring producing high hydraulic friction that affects the ability to circulate at the optimum flow due to maximum pressure limitation, a higher mud-weight requirement for borehole stability at high inclination across the soft-overburden formations, and/or a narrow equivalent circulating density (ECD) window, making ERD wells – especially shallow ones – very hydraulically challenging. The hydraulic design must account for the limitation of BHA components and rig specifications. The mud program must provide optimum cuttings-carrying capacity, formation stability, and other rheological properties needed for wellbore stability. In ERD wells, it is a wise investment to implement real-time hydraulics-management monitoring services, either on the rig or in a real-time operations support center, to ensure that hydraulics-related risks are properly managed.

Torque and Drag Management

ERD wells often incorporate high stresses exerted on the drillstring components in the form of axial loading for deep ERD wells, buckling, and

torsional forces on connections due to their extended profile. Torque-and-drag simulations must be done with great care and must cover all types of drilling activity based on BHA type, such as rotary drilling, slide drilling, reaming in/out, and tripping-load analyses. Effort must be spent on identifying the correct formation friction factors to be used in the simulation. Several drillstring failures have been attributed to the use of incorrect friction factors during simulations. Torque-and-drag simulations must be performed for different points along the well path based on directional changes and section length. For each case, a simulation must at least be conducted at every 500-m (1,500-ft) section interval. As most downhole drilling issues are first detected by a deviation in the torque-and-drag profile—pickup, slack-off, and free rotating weight—it is always recommended to include real-time drillstring-integrity services in ERD wells.

Vibration Management

A high-vibration level is a major contributor to service interruption in ERD wells; while axial and lateral vibration modes are common in top holes, torsional vibration is almost a common factor in all ERD wells due to their high-deviation profile. Managing such vibration levels might be extremely difficult, especially in torsional mode, where it is certain that most, if not all, vibration-management approaches will fail to eliminate stick slip from ERD wells. Vibration-management efforts should concentrate on reducing the consequences of torsional vibration rather than exceeding drillstring component limits. The first step in good vibration management is the inclusion of high-definition vibration sensors in the BHA, preferably at different locations to provide more depth to vibration detection and analysis. During the BHA and drillstring design phase, critical RPMs of the system must be determined by simulation software to be avoided during execution; side forces and bending stresses must be contained within reasonable levels to reduce the likelihood of equipment failure. Mud lubrication capacity should be designed and maintained at an optimum level during execution. Again, real-time vibration-management services are essential in ERD drilling during the execution phase.

Design Control

The well design must have all the verifications and assumption validations that conform to customer requirements, and all ambiguities must be communicated to all stakeholders. The design must contain the acceptance criteria of all services to be provided on the ERD well, along with a detailed benchmarking of anticipated drilling performance for measurement-efficiency purposes. Detailed reviews must be conducted among stakeholders at different stages of the design preparation to assess the adequacy of the plan and contingencies, and to confirm the compatibility of all measures included in the design. The process must include enough measures to detect major deviations from the design and to ensure that they are subject to the same level of engineering analysis and review.

Drilling Tangent Sections

Tangent sections are portions of the well-profile design that have constant hole inclination. Small adjustments in azimuth are occasionally planned (e.g., to account for expected right-hand walk if rotary assemblies are used).

Tangent sections may be used for a variety of reasons, including to:

- Increase horizontal displacement to reach the target entry point
- Correct for target-entry TVD uncertainties due to geological uncertainties
- Correct for imperfect directional performance
- Accommodate completion requirements (e.g., setting a submersible pump in a "straight" section, pulling a production packer without excessive torque and drag, and successfully running coiled tubing to bottom).

In cases where the tangent section is used to correct for uncertainties in geology or directional performance, it is best to locate the tangent section closer to the most critical section of the well. Another consideration for choosing the location of the tangent section includes the angle of hole inclination at which it occurs. For example, designing the tangent section

at the lowest-possible angle will result in the least amount of drillstring weight supported by the wellbore wall. This reduces drillstring torque and drag and casing wear. Another consideration is hole cleaning.

Since the worst-case conditions for hole cleaning occur between 35° and 55°, the tangent section in this range should be avoided if hole cleaning is problematic. Finally, practical considerations, such as the ability for under-reamer arms to stay fully open at high angles of hole inclination, may impact the design of the tangent section.

In some cases, more than one tangent section may be used to serve more than one purpose. For example, the first tangent section may be planned to increase the horizontal displacement, while the second tangent section may be planned to accommodate uncertainties in geological markers.

References

Azar, J.J. and Samuel, R. 2006. *Drilling Engineering*. PennWell Publishing.

An Engineering Approach to Horizontal Drilling – Halliburton Manual, 1992.

Banks, S.M., Hogg, T.W., and Thorogood, J.L. 1992. Increasing Extended-Reach Capabilities Through Wellbore Profile Optimization. Paper SPE 23850 presented at the SPE/IADC Drilling Conference, New Orleans, Louisiana, 18–21 February.

Dawson, R. and Paslay, P.R. 1984. Drillpipe Buckling in Inclined Holes. *JPT*, **36**(10): 1734–1738.

Hogg, W.T. and Thorogood, J.L. 1990. Performance Optimization of Steerable Systems. *ASME PD*, **27** 49–58.

Justad, T., Jacobsen, B., Blikra, H., Gaskin, G., Clarke, C., and Ritchie, A. 1994. Extending Barriers to Develop a Marginal Satellite Field from an Existing Platform. Paper SPE 28294 presented at the SPE Annual Technical Conference and Exhibition, New Orleans, Louisiana, 25–28 September.

Mueller, M.D., Quintana, J.M., and Bunyak, M.J. 1991. Extended-Reach Drilling from Platform Irene. *SPEDE*, **6**(02): 138.

Oag, A.W. and Williams, M. 2000. The Directional Difficulty Index – A New Approach to Performance Benchmarking. Paper IADC/SPE 59196 presented at the 2000 IADC/SPE Drilling Conference, New Orleans, Louisiana, 23–25 February.

Samuel, R. and Liu, X. 2007. *Advanced Drilling Engineering – Principles and Designs*. PennWell Publishing.

Sheppard, M.C., Wick, C., and Burgess, T. 1987. Designing Well Paths to Reduce Drag and Torque. *SPEDE*, **2**(04): 344–350.

Thorogood, J.L. 1990. Instrument Performance Models and Their Practical Application to Directional Surveying Operations. *SPEDE*, **5**(04): 294–298.

Thorogood, J.L. and Sawaryn, S.J. 1991. The Traveling Cylinder – A Practical Tool for Collision Avoidance. *SPEDE*, **6**(01).

Williams, C., Mason, J.S., and Spaar, J. 2001. Operational Efficiency on Eight-Well Sidetrack Program Saves $7.3 Million vs. Historical Offsets in MP 299/144 GOM. 2001. Paper SPE/IADC 67826 presented at the SPE/IADC Drilling Conference, Amsterdam, The Netherlands, 27 February–1 March.

CHAPTER **FIVE**

Well Paths

Drilling ERD and ultra-ERD (u-ERD) wells and extending the reach to greater depths requires improved models for well placement. Wellbore friction is an important issue for ultra-long wells, and optimizing the well path design is an effective means to reduce torque and drag. Selecting the ERD well path involves well service issues, hole issues, and possible drillstring design problems, as well as cementing and completion problems.

Factors Influencing ERD Well Path Design

Some of the factors that influence the well path design include (**Fig. 5.1**):

- Hole issues
    - Wellbore stability
    - Casing wear
    - Hole cleaning

- Running casing
- Cementing
- Differential sticking
- Drillstring issues
  - Torque and drag
  - Buckling
  - Combined loading
- Well service issues
  - Evaluation
  - Cleanout
  - Completion
  - Workover
  - Well abandonment
- Other issues
  - Surveying
  - Anti-collision
  - Sliding and rotating in the long tangent section
  - Sliding and rotating in the lateral section
  - BHA changes
  - Tortuosity

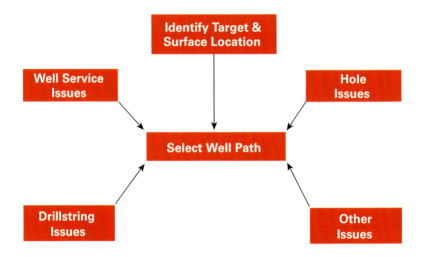

Fig. 5.1 – Factors Influencing ERD Well Path Design.

Basic Well Path Designs

ERD well path designs, along with accurate placement, not only provide solutions for restricted reservoir production, but also help to eliminate additional platforms. ERD techniques and technologies have rapidly evolved, and step-out wells have incrementally increased since 1993 when the ERD program began accessing offshore reserves under Poole Harbour in the U.K. from land-based wellsites (Robertson et al. 2005). Also in the U.K., the Wytch Farm oil field was at the forefront of extended-reach drilling. In 1997, Well M11 broke the 10-km (6-mi) departure milestone to set a new world record. In 2000, Well M16 established another world record at 10,727 m (35,194 ft) m and a measured depth of 11,278 m (37,001 ft) (Robertson et al. 2005; Meader et al. 2000). Mason and Judzis (1998) indicated that it will be possible to drill and complete u-ERD wells in the future.

There are several designs, based on the displacement needed; the following are general designs:

- Build and hold
- Build, hold, and drop

- Combination build
- Undersection build
- Combination of build and undersection

The build-and-hold design (**Fig. 5.2**):

- Is relatively easy to construct
- Is used to maximize rotary drilling
- Has a potential for high torque
- Has a potential for high casing and pipe wear

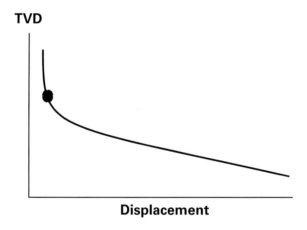

Fig. 5.2 – Build-and-Hold ERD Well Path Design.

The build, hold, and drop design (**Fig. 5.3**) is similar to the conventional S-type design.

- This design has a drop section, which improves wellbore stability.
- The drop section also reduces differential sticking.
- It results in a higher tangent angle.

- Followed by the long tangent section, the dropping section may be hard to initiate.
- It results in increased measured depth.

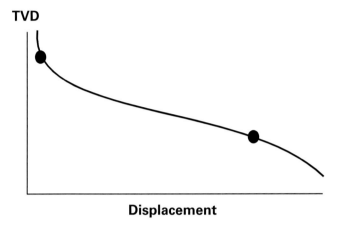

Fig. 5.3 – Build, Hold, and Drop ERD Well Path Design.

Similar to a continuous build design, a combination build design (**Fig. 5.4**) results in:

- Lower surface torque,
- Lower casing wear,
- Higher tangent angle, and
- Increased measured depth.

An undersection-build design is shown in **Fig. 5.5**. This design results in:

- Lower surface torque,
- Lower casing wear,
- Higher tangent angle, and
- Possible tubular buckling in the vertical section.

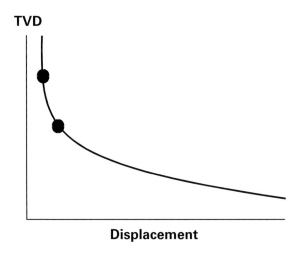

Fig. 5.4 – Combination-Build ERD Well Path Design.

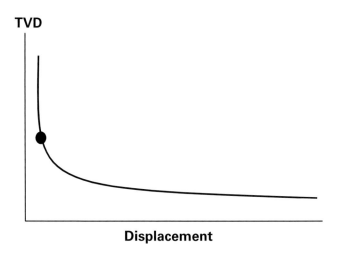

Fig. 5.5 – Undersection-Build ERD Well Path Design.

Combination builds and undersections (**Fig. 5.6**) result in a deep kickoff second build. This design is essentially a double-build design, with the second build very close to the lateral section.

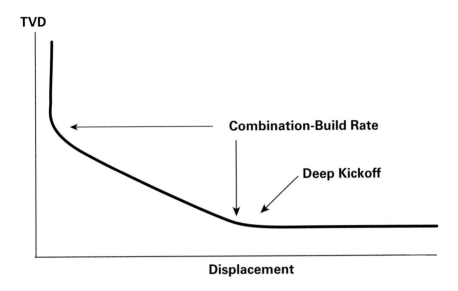

Fig. 5.6 – Combination-Undersection-Build ERD Well Path Design.

Catenary Design

The catenary profile was first introduced to the oil and gas industry by McClendon and Anders (1985). Early attempts have not had the expected effect because of the constraint of techniques and technologies. Du and Zhang (1987) illustrated two field cases, using catenary trajectories drilled in China. Han (1987, 1997) and Liu (2007) discussed the methods for planning a catenary profile. The catenary profile is assumed by a uniform line suspended between two points, as shown in **Fig. 5.7**. A rope, cable, chain, or any other line of uniform weight that is suspended between two points assumes a shape called a catenary. Common examples include the curves formed by an electrical wire hanging between two telegraph poles and a chain attached to a vessel, as well as an anchor to keep the vessel in place.

Based on the inherent nature of the curve, the catenary build results in lower torque and lower casing wear, but it may require more sliding than with a build-and-hold path, depending on the steering system used.

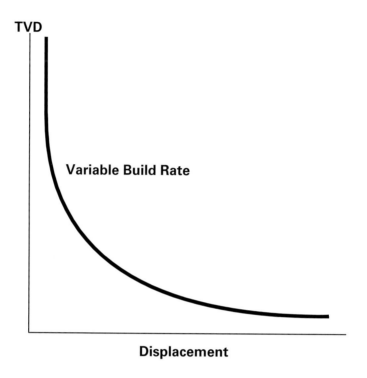

Fig. 5.7 – Catenary-Build ERD Well Path Design.

2-D Catenary Well Path

When string obtains a catenary shape, the classical catenary equation is as follows:

$$y = a\cosh\frac{x}{a} \qquad (5\text{-}1)$$

Where,

y is the y-coordinate, m,

x is the x-coordinate, m, and

a is the characteristic parameter of catenary, m.

The incremental increase in coordinates of the catenary segment can be given in the form of dimensionless abscissa and ordinates as:

$$\Delta H = a(Y_b - Y) \qquad (5\text{-}2)$$

$$\Delta S = a(X_b - X) \qquad (5\text{-}3)$$

Where,

X is the nondimensional x-coordinate, dimensionless, and

Y is the nondimensional y-coordinate, dimensionless.

$$X = -\ln\left(\tan\frac{\alpha}{2}\right) \qquad (5\text{-}4)$$

$$Y = \frac{1}{\sin\alpha} \qquad (5\text{-}5)$$

Where,

α is the inclination angle in degrees.

The calculation of the inclination at any point on the catenary section is given by Eq. 5-6.

$$\tan\alpha = \frac{1}{\dfrac{1}{\tan\alpha_b} - \dfrac{\Delta L}{a}} \qquad (5\text{-}6)$$

This calculation avoids using an inconvenient hyperbolic function to estimate the course-coordinate position parameters, while using the exact mathematical solution. This process also avoids the trial and error of iterative calculations.

Design of the 2-D Catenary Profile

A typical catenary profile is shown in **Fig. 5.8** and consists of the following four well sections:

- An inclined section,
- A straight section to the kickoff point,
- An initial buildup section to the start of the catenary section,

- The catenary section, and
- A straight-sail section to the target.

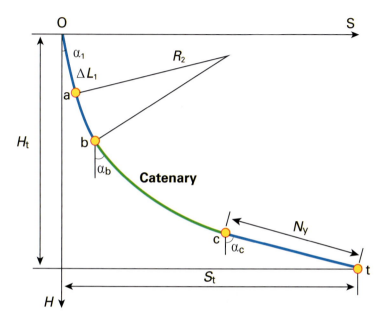

Fig. 5.8 – 2-D Catenary-Build ERD Well Path Design (Liu and Samuel 2009).

The first section is assumed to be an inclined straight section because a slant rig may be used for land drilling. Generally, it is a vertical section, i.e. when $\alpha_1 = 0$. The initial buildup section is required because the catenary section cannot begin vertically. If a slant rig is used, this section can be eliminated, and the rig mast should be positioned at the exact inclination to enter the catenary smoothly. In addition, the sail section is usually necessary for the design of u-ERD wells.

When planning a well profile, the total vertical depth and horizontal displacement at the target are known. The other geometric parameters of the profile include the following (Fig. 5.8):

- Inclination of the slanted section, α_1

- Length of the slanted section, ΔL_1
- Curvature radius of the initial buildup section, R_2
- Catenary characteristic parameter, a
- Starting inclination of the catenary section, α_b
- End inclination of the catenary section, α_c
- Length of the straight-sail section, ΔL_4

The first three parameters, α_1, ΔL_1, and R_2, are usually given when planning a catenary profile in which R_2 is calculated from the predetermined buildup rate based on the performance of the BHA design.

The end inclination of the catenary section, α_c, equals the sail inclination.

Critical Inclination Angle

Wellbore friction is an important issue for ultra-long wells, and optimizing the well path design is an effective means for reducing torque and drag. One of the characteristics of ERD wells is that the maximum angle of any section of the well can enable the drillstring and wireline tools to advance through that section by the force of gravity alone – that is, without being pushed or pumped down. This criterion would normally limit the maximum angle to about 65–80°, depending on friction factors.

The critical wellbore angle, θ_c, which is the angle above which the drillstring will no longer advance down the hole under the force of gravity alone, is given by Eq. 5-7.

$$\alpha_c = \tan^{-1}\left[\frac{1}{\mu}\right] \qquad (5\text{-}7)$$

Where,

μ is the coefficient of friction.

The following example will provide the effect of the friction factor and critical inclination angle.

Calculate the critical wellbore angle for a friction factor of 0.3 while drilling.

The wellbore angle is planned for casing flotation, and, when running the casing string, the expected friction factor is 0.7. Calculate the limit angle for this section.

Substituting the first friction factor into the equation, $\theta_c = \tan^{-1}\left[\dfrac{1}{\mu}\right]$, the critical inclination angle while drilling is $\theta_c = \tan^{-1}\left[\dfrac{1}{0.3}\right] = 73^0$.

Substituting the second friction factor into the same equation, the critical inclination angle during drilling is $\theta_c = \tan^{-1}\left[\dfrac{1}{0.7}\right] = 55^0$. Therefore, the limiting angle for this section is 55°.

The coefficient of friction between the string and the hole is an important factor for high-angle wells and can be altered by changing the drilling fluid or lubrication. The sail inclination is usually less than the critical inclination, i.e. $\alpha_c < \alpha_{cr}$, to ensure that the drillstring or casing slides downward.

One of the essential elements of planning a catenary profile is the determination of the shape and position of the catenary section. Only three parameters, α, α_b, and ΔL_4, must be determined. Because two constraint equations are required to determine the horizontal displacement and total vertical depth of the target, the catenary profile can be defined if one of them is given.

It is convenient and generally used to provide the value of α_b; thus, the solutions to a and ΔL_4 are as follows:

$$a = \frac{H_0 \sin \alpha_c - S_0 \cos \alpha_c}{b \sin \alpha_c - c \cos \alpha_c} \tag{5-8}$$

$$\Delta L_4 = \frac{bS_0 - cH_0}{b \sin \alpha_c - c \cos \alpha_c} \tag{5-9}$$

Where,

$$H_0 = H_t - \Delta L_1 \cos \alpha_1 - R_2(\sin \alpha_b - \sin \alpha_1)$$

$$S_0 = S_t - \Delta L_1 \sin \alpha_1 - R_2(\cos \alpha_1 - \cos \alpha_b)$$

$$b = \frac{1}{\sin \alpha_b} - \frac{1}{\sin \alpha_c} \qquad c = \ln\left(\frac{\tan \dfrac{\alpha_c}{2}}{\tan \dfrac{\alpha_b}{2}}\right)$$

Finally, the length of catenary section can be calculated using Eq. 5-10.

$$\Delta L_3 = a\left(\frac{1}{\tan \alpha_b} - \frac{1}{\tan \alpha_c}\right) \qquad (5\text{-}10)$$

3-D Catenary Well Path

During directional-drilling operations, bit-walk objectively exists along an actual drilled well trajectory. Drilling experience has shown that taking the physical bit-walk into account provides an effective measure to control a well's trajectory if the rate of the bit-walk can be accurately estimated. Because the planned results of the bit-walk path can evidently reduce the frequency of azimuth correction and drillstring trips, as well as lessen the difficulty and workload of trajectory control, it will undoubtedly improve the rate of penetration and the quality of well trajectory, and reduce the cost of drilling.

Bit-walk is the natural tendency of the drill bit to drift in a lateral direction during drilling, which occurs in every operation. Operators who plan and design wellbore trajectories must consider planning 3-D paths, especially in areas where the amount of bit-walk is considerable. The tendency and degree of bit-walk indicates the bit-walk rate; the industry describes bit-walk behavior as the rate of azimuth change. Assuming that the rates of azimuth change remain constant, the azimuth function vs. measured depth can be expressed by:

$$\phi = \phi_b + \frac{\kappa_\phi}{C} \Delta L \qquad (5\text{-}11)$$

Where,

ϕ is the azimuth angle in degrees,

κ_ϕ is the rate of azimuth change (decreasing azimuth is a negative value) in °/30 m, and

C is the constant related to the rate unit.

The incremental lengths are given by:

$$\begin{cases} \Delta N = \int_{L_b}^{L} \sin\alpha \cos\phi \, dL \\ \Delta E = \int_{L_b}^{L} \sin\alpha \sin\phi \, dL \\ \Delta H = \int_{L_b}^{L} \cos\alpha \, dL \\ \Delta S = \int_{L_b}^{L} \sin\alpha \, dL \end{cases} \quad (5\text{-}12)$$

Where,

N is the north coordinate (south is negative) in m,

E is the east coordinate (west is negative) in m.

H is the vertical depth in m, and

S is the horizontal curvilinear departure, in m.

Eqs. 5-11 and 5-12 can be used to calculate the incremental course coordinates in the catenary section; for more explicit points, numerical integration must be used. In addition, the borehole curvature and torsion for the catenary section can be estimated using the following equations:

$$\kappa = \sqrt{\kappa_\alpha^2 + \kappa_\phi^2 \sin^2\alpha} \quad (5\text{-}13)$$

$$\tau = \kappa_\phi \left(1 - \frac{\kappa_\alpha^2}{\kappa^2}\right) \cos\alpha \quad (5\text{-}14)$$

Where,

$$\kappa_\alpha = \frac{180 C}{\pi a} \sin^2\alpha$$

Design of the 3-D Catenary Profile

In the vertical profile, the inclination change rate of the hold section is zero, and the rate of the build/drop section is constant. The inclination of the catenary profile has been given by Eq. 5-8. Thus, the relationship of the inclination with depth changes by section; each well inclination

unit should have its own inclination equation, according to its different inclination characteristics.

The azimuth change of the well trajectory is related to many factors with certain rules, including the direction of the formation layer, formation anisotropy, bit type, bit anisotropy, BHA, BHA mechanics, weight on bit, bit rotational speed, well profile, and well geometry parameters.

A single well section represents a well inclination unit, and a formation layer represents an azimuth unit. The azimuth units can be divided by the azimuth drifting rates; thus, an azimuth unit is not exactly one formation layer. **Fig. 5.9** shows the combined relationship between the inclination unit and the azimuth unit. An azimuth unit may cover an entire well inclination unit, so it is not necessary to divide this inclination unit. An azimuth unit can also cover several inclination units, which can also be divided at the top and bottom edges of the azimuth unit. Therefore, the objectives of combining the inclination units and azimuth units are to divide the well profile into more detailed sections and to create smaller units with a constant inclination change rate and constant azimuth change rate. Obviously, the number of smaller units after combining is often more than the number of well sections.

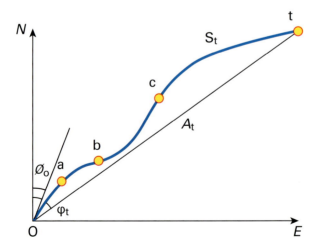

Fig. 5.9 – 3-D Catenary – Build ERD Well Path Design (Liu and Samuel 2009) – Horizontal Projection Plot.

Because the parameters of a bit-walk profile are interrelated and interdependent, it is too difficult to plan the 3-D bit-walk path with the aid of 2-D well path planning methods; however, operators must design the well path to reach the predetermined target. Different rock layers show varying natural deflecting behaviors and have varying bit-walk rates. Combining bit-walk units with inclination units divides the well profile into shorter intervals.

Thus, the sum of the coordinate increments over each interval must equal the given coordinate difference between the wellhead and target, which can be expressed as follows:

$$\left(\sum_{i=1}^{m} \Delta N_i\right)^2 + \left(\sum_{i=1}^{m} \Delta E_i\right)^2 = A_t^2 \qquad (5\text{-}15)$$

$$\sum_{i=1}^{m} \Delta E_i = \tan \varphi_t \sum_{i=1}^{m} \Delta N_i \qquad (5\text{-}16)$$

$$\sum_{i=1}^{m} \Delta H_i = H_t \qquad (5\text{-}17)$$

Fig. 5.9 shows the schematic drawing of a bit-walk path in the horizontal plot. To compensate a well trajectory for bit-walk effects, a lead angle is necessary. The value of the lead angle may be positive or negative because, although bit-walk generally occurs as right-hand drift, it occasionally occurs as left-hand drift. Well designers must plan a 3-D well path and provide the lead angle as one of the calculated parameters accounting for bit-walk effects.

Using these design-constraint equations, three unknowns can be solved in the design of the 3-D drift path of an ERD well. The solution must be found by using an iterative method, because the system of equations is nonlinear. In principle, a three-level iterative method should be used with three unknowns. However, it is possible to have fewer iterations and to improve the convergence by selecting the proper iterative method.

Transition Curves

Trajectories are typically designed with constant-curvature, well-defined arcs that act as the transition well paths between the tangent sections. The

transition curves that are used are defined as the curve segments connecting the tangent sections of the well path to the build or drop sections. Although the transition between the tangent section and build section or tangent section and drop section appears to be smooth, there will be discontinuity, which can result in multiple stresses in the tubulars. Discontinuity is obvious when two circular arcs or one tangent section and circular arc and tangent sections are joined together. To avoid this problem, continuous build or drop sections are planned, and, even with these designs, there exists a discontinuity in the transition zones. To avoid the discontinuity, curvature-bridge curves can be used.

Several mathematicians and physicists have previously studied the properties of several curves. Out of which, the Cornu's spiral (or clothoid) or Euler spiral (also known as linarc) are of great interest due to the very nature of the special properties of this curve. In fact, Euler described several properties of the curve, including the curve's quadrature. It is also widely known as the Fresnel spiral. The insertion of clothoid sections between the tangent and build or drop section of the well path will result in curvature continuity. This curvature bridge will alleviate the drag problems that will enable the design engineers to extend the reach of the well with the given mechanical limitations.

Clothoid Curve

Clothoid curves are spiral curves whose curvatures change linearly from zero to a desired curvature with respect to the arc length. In other words, the radius of curvature at any point on the curve varies as the inverse of the arc length from the starting point of the curve.

$$R \propto \frac{1}{L} \tag{5-18}$$

or $\quad L_1 \times R_1 = L_2 \times R_2 = ... = L_n \times R_n = \sigma \tag{5-19}$

$$\kappa(s) = \kappa(0) + \sigma s \tag{5-20}$$

Where,

    R is the radius of curvature,

    L is the length of the curve,

    κ is the curvature,

    σ is the sharpness of the curve, and

    s is the arch length of the curve.

The clothoid curves can be given parametrically as follows:

$$f(\ell) = (C_f(\ell), S_f(\ell))$$
$$C_f(\ell) = \xi \int_0^\ell \cos\left(\frac{\pi u^2}{2}\right) du$$
$$S_f(\ell) = \xi \int_0^\ell \sin\left(\frac{\pi u^2}{2}\right) du \quad (5\text{-}21)$$

Where,

    ξ is the characteristic parameter.

The Fresnel sine and cosine integrals are given in Eq. 5-22.

$$FresnelC_f(\ell) = \int_0^\ell \cos\left(\frac{\pi u^2}{2}\right) du$$
$$FresnelC_f(\ell) == \int_0^\ell \sin\left(\frac{\pi u^2}{2}\right) du \quad (5\text{-}22)$$

Since it is not possible to obtain a closed-form solution to the above equations, several approximate numerical computations have been presented in the literature using the Taylor, Power Series, and Maclaurin expansions. Brandse et al. (2007) obtained a simple expression using the Maclaurin expansion, and the coordinates can be expressed in terms of the length of the spiral arc, as shown by Eq. 5-23.

$$y = \frac{L^3}{6\xi^2} - \frac{L^7}{336\xi^6} + \frac{L^{11}}{42240\xi^{10}} + \ldots$$
$$x = L - \frac{L^5}{40\xi^4} + \frac{L^9}{3456\xi^{10}} + \ldots \quad (5\text{-}23)$$

Omitting higher-order terms, Eq. 5-23 can be written as Eq. 5-24, which is cubic parabolic in nature.

$$y = \left(6\xi^2 x\right)^{\frac{1}{3}} \tag{5-24}$$

Based on the properties of the clothoid curve, the relationship between the curvature and the scale parameter can be given as:

$$L_1 \times R_1 = L_2 \times R_2 = ... = L_n \times R_n = \xi^2 \tag{5-25}$$

It can also be noted that the tangents at the connection point between the clothoid spiral and the straight segment are the same. It has been found that the Cornu spiral's path reduces the lateral stresses on the tubulars that pass through the section. A necessary condition for the curvature bridge is that, at the start of the build section, the spiral should have the same curvature and end with the same curvature that fits to the tangent section. In the same way, the spiral section should end with the curvature of the tangent section.

Fig. 5.10 illustrates the well path with and without a clothoid spiral in a curved section. It can be seen that the well path consists of the following sections with curvature bridging:

- Fresnel spiral arc from the kickoff depth
- Circular arc with maximum curvature
- Fresnel spiral arc, including partial tangent section
- Partial tangent section
- Fresnel spiral arc, including partial hold section
- Hold horizontal section

Fig. 5.11 presents a simple diagram that illustrates the curvature of the wellbore with and without a clothoid spiral in the curved sections, as well as straight sections along the wellbore. It can be seen that the curvature changes between the sections are smooth.

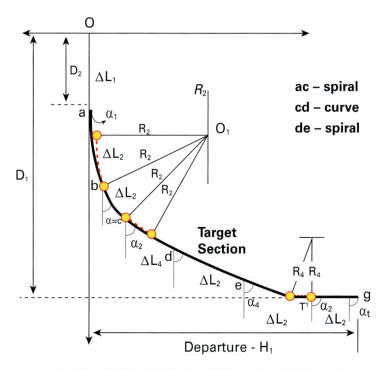

Fig. 5.10 – Well Paths With and Without Clothoid Spiral.

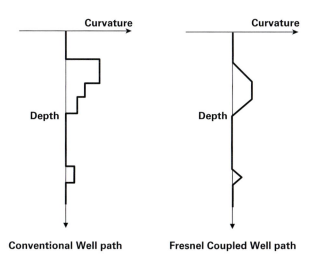

Fig. 5.11 – Curvature Comparison With and Without Bridging Curves.

Curvature Bridging

Curvature bridging is important for the torque-and-drag and fluid-mechanics analyses, such as cuttings transport and swab-and-surge wellbore pressure calculations. **Fig. 5.12** illustrates the curvature bridging of a standard S-type well. The figure is embedded with the commonly used method, along with clothoid spiral arcs. The well path consists of the following sections with clothoid arc lengths:

- Fresnel spiral arc from the kickoff depth – build section
- Fresnel spiral arc, including drop-and-hold sections

The well path with circular arc lengths consists of the following sections:

- Straight section up to the kickoff depth
- Circular arc from the kickoff depth – build section
- Second circular arc – build section

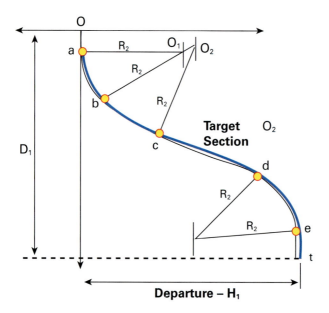

Fig. 5.12 – S-Type Well Paths with Circular Arc and Bridging Curves.

- Tangent section
- Circular arc – drop section
- Hold section

Fig. 5.13 illustrates the curvatures for both options. It can be seen that the curvature bridging is smooth with Fresnel spiral-arc wellbore paths.

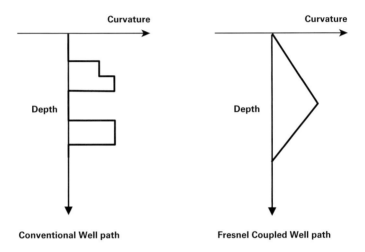

Fig. 5.13 – Curvature Comparison With and Without Bridging Curves.

Trajectory Calculations

Accurate estimation of well path parameters and coordinates is important for the precise placement of wellbores. The following discussion describes the method for estimating these parameters. Let s be the current position of a point in the hole with coordinates (N_s, E_s, H_s) and measured depth, m_s. Let the inclination and azimuth at point, s, be a_s and ϕ_s, respectively. The objective is to reach target, t, with coordinates (N_t, E_t, H_t).

The unit vector, $c_s = (c_N, c_E, c_H)$, represents the direction of the borehole at s. According to the theory of differential geometry, the direction cosines of the vector c in the O-*NEH* coordinate frame are:

$$\begin{cases} c_N = \sin\alpha_s \cos\phi_s \\ c_E = \sin\alpha_s \sin\phi_s \\ c_H = \cos\alpha_s \end{cases} \quad (5\text{-}26)$$

Eq. 5-24 can be used to calculate the course coordinates based on the differential mode of the wellbore trajectory as follows (Liu and Samuel 2008):

$$\begin{cases} \Delta N_i = \int_{L_{i-1}}^{L_i} \sin\alpha(L)\cos\phi(L)dL \\ \Delta E_i = \int_{L_{i-1}}^{L_i} \sin\alpha(L)\sin\phi(L)dL \\ \Delta H_i = \int_{L_{i-1}}^{L_i} \cos\alpha(L)dL \end{cases} \quad (5\text{-}27)$$

The coordinates for the i-th measured section for all the sections, including the clothoid section, are calculated using the coordinate increment, as shown by Eq. 5-28.

$$\begin{cases} N_i = N_{i-1} + \Delta N_i \\ E_i = E_{i-1} + \Delta E_i \\ H_i = H_{i-1} + \Delta H_i \end{cases} \quad (5\text{-}28)$$

Starting from the wellhead point, the calculation proceeds downward with the incremental calculation of all the coordinates, and the horizontal displacement and closure angle at any survey station are given by:

$$A_i = \sqrt{(N_i - N_o)^2 + (E_i - E_o)^2} \quad (5\text{-}29)$$

$$\tan\varphi_i = \frac{E_i - E_o}{N_i - N_o} \quad (5\text{-}30)$$

Finally, the measured depth and horizontal departure can be calculated by:

$$\begin{cases} \sum_{i=1}^{n} \Delta D_i = D_T \\ \sum_{i=1}^{n} \Delta H_i = H_T \end{cases} \quad (5\text{-}31)$$

Curvature and Torsion

Using the Fresnel equations (Eq. 5-22), the curvature and torsion for clothoid transition sections can be obtained as follows (Samuel and Liu 2009):

$$\kappa(s) = \frac{\pi a}{\sigma^2 + b^2} u \qquad (5\text{-}32)$$

$$\tau(s) = \frac{\pi b}{\sigma^2 + b^2} u \qquad (5\text{-}33)$$

As the parameter, u, varies from $u = 0$ and $u = 2\pi$, the point on the clothoid curve advances in the vertical direction a distance of $2\pi|b|$, and the x and y components return to their original values. It can also be noted that since κ = constant and τ = constant, and when both are greater than zero, then the curve is part of the clothoid or κ/τ = constant.

Quantification of Borehole Complexity

With the advent of new and complex downhole assemblies, there is a growing need to monitor the performance of these tools, along with the difficulty involved in drilling the predefined well paths. Alternating between sliding and rotary drilling modes results in hole spiraling. Further, wellbore oscillation becomes more pronounced with the length of time spent in sliding mode. Qualitative assessment and quantitative characterization of the well path are critically important in each phase of the well construction. They not only allow subsequent adjustments to the well plan when combined with pay-zone geo-steering tools, but also the successful completion of extended-reach and complex wells. The increasing use of complex well paths requires accurate estimation of torque and drag.

Another equally important objective is to characterize and provide a method for evaluating the complexities involved in constructing the well paths. The ability to provide a reasonable quantitative estimate of wellbore-trajectory complexity can provide reliable guidance for performing sensitivity studies on different well profiles. Published papers, such as Oag and Williams (2000), typically describe the complexities of drilling the hole in qualitative, rather than quantitative, terms. Furthermore, there are no clear criteria for defining wellbore quality unless they have a physical

basis or underlying theory to support their validity. In the present study, space-curve fundamental equations are used to quantify the difficulty of a wellbore design. Dodson and Dodson (2003) proposed a mechanical-risk index using drilling variables, such as measured depth, vertical depth, horizontal displacement, and other factors with associated arbitrary weighting factors. If the weighting factors based on the empirical development are not assigned properly, they will skew the results. Shirley (2003) used a difficulty index to simulate the difficulty of drilling an extended-reach well. This weighted method is similar to the mechanical-risk index.

The drilling-difficulty index presented by Dodson and Dodson (2003) is based on an empirical approach that estimates the difficulty of drilling a well by measuring the total accumulated dogleg over the total measured depth. In defining the directional-difficulty index, tortuosity is used purely as a measure of how difficult the well is to drill, not how smoothly it was drilled. Samuel et al. (2005) and Luo et al. (2003) summarize the methods used for quantifying and calibrating tortuosity. Absolute tortuosity is the tortuosity of the initial well path before artificial tortuosity was applied. Relative tortuosity is used to characterize the tortuosity of the well path relative to the absolute tortuosity. Using tortuosity to define the drilling-difficulty index provides a somewhat simpler approach that is used to define the threshold difficulty of drilling a smoother hole. While all these methods provide a simple method for estimating well difficulty or complexity that can be used for classifying and comparing wells, they lack a physical basis. An estimation of well difficulty is also useful for estimating the difficulty in using clothoid curves in well path designs or modifying existing configurations. Therefore, a simple and reliable quantitative methodology is needed for describing well paths.

The methods listed below represent several geometrically based options that use the properties of the well path but do not require predefined weights or weighting functions. The discussion of the various techniques used to quantify borehole quality is based on the following methods:

- Relative distance change
- Total curvature change

- Strain energy of the wellbore
- Inflection point – to quantify the sinusoidal nature
- Binormal vector – to quantify the helical nature
- The analysis is an attempt to describe the space curves between different survey stations in a relatively simple way.

Wellbore Indices

The complexity of drilling a well can be characterized using indices, such as the directional difficulty index (DDI), difficulty index (DI), mechanical-risk index (MRI), and modified mechanical-risk index (MMRI). These indices have been defined and used under various circumstances to evaluate and establish the complexity of drilling and completing the well. These limitations and assumptions must be considered in evaluating the complexity of the wells.

The DDI, described by Oag and Williams (2000), is defined by the following equation:

$$DDI = \log\left(\frac{D \times H \times T}{S}\right) \qquad (5\text{-}34)$$

Where,

D is the depth in ft,

H is the total vertical depth in ft,

T is the tortuosity, and

S is the horizontal curvilinear departure in ft.

The classification for the difficulty of drilling based on the DDI is calculated by using Eq. 5-34. The MRI (Williams et al. 2001) includes several variables, such as measured depth, kickoff depth and water depth, mud-line suspension, and subsea wellheads for offshore wells. The method is based on the commonly used well path design variables, including vertical depth, departure, casing-setting depths, number of drilling phases,

mud weight, water depth, and weighting factors. It also includes other well design variables.

The weighting factors, when not properly applied or tuned, will result in the overestimation or gross underestimation of the complexity of the well path design. Other modified risk indices are proposed, but they lack clear definitions, a basis for development, and magnitude of the severity of drilling variables.

The difficulty index (DI) for estimating the complexity (Shirley 2003) is similar to MRI, but uses a different method for applying weight to the input variables. The weights and biases used to control the influences of key drilling parameters will have a large influence on the result and may shift the origin of influence on the outcome. The weights need constant calibration as the well is drilled.

The wellbore score card (WSC) described by Mason et al. (2006) to gauge the quality of the hole is more subjective in nature than quantifying the hole quality. During the planning stage, the estimate is grossly subjective, as it is with uncertainty and variability for actual operations. It must be based on previously drilled offset wells and may be applicable only to the area in which the well is being planned.

Another well path design index, called the trajectory risk index (TRI) (Liang 2007), encompasses the risks and difficulties associated with the trajectory, collision, torque, drag, and buildup rate, and is given as:

$$TRI = \log\left(TDI + R_{cl} + R_{tq} + R_{d} + R_{bu}\right) \tag{5-35}$$

Where,

TDI is the trajectory difficulty index,

R_{cl} is the collision risk,

R_{tq} is the torque risk,

R_d is the drag risk, and

R_{bu} is the buildup risk.

Samuel's Wellbore Energy Index

An additional mathematical criterion for quantifying the complexity of the well path design can be based on physical reasoning, rather than on the geometric meaning, and is an excellent criterion for considering the simplicity of producing smooth curves. The strain energy (E_s) of the well profile is given as the arc-length integral of the curvature squared plus the wellbore torsion squared, and can be given by the Samuel's criterion as:

$$E_{(abs)_n} = \left(\frac{\sum_{i=1}^{n}\left(\kappa_i^2 + \tau_i^2\right)\Delta D_i}{D_n + \Delta D_n} \right) \quad (5\text{-}36)$$

Where,

τ is the torsion of wellbore trajectory in (°)/30 m or (°)/100 ft,

ΔD is the distance between the survey stations in m or ft,

κ is the curvature of the wellbore trajectory in (°)/30 m or (°)/100 ft,

i is the survey-station index, and

n is the index.

Total Strain Energy Change

Ideally, a mathematical technique for measuring borehole difficulty should be based on both physical and geometrical principles. In nonlinear curve modeling, the thin elastic line that bends the least while passing through a given set of points is known as the minimum-energy curve. It is considered an excellent criterion because of its simplicity for producing smooth curves (i.e., describing the minimum energy of the wellbore path). An additional advantage is that it more effectively emphasizes the undulation of well path curvature of tortuous well paths than can be obtained using the previous method.

The strain energy of the wellbore path is given as the square of the arc-length integral of the curvature.

WELL PATHS

$$E = \int_0^\ell \kappa(x)^2 dx \qquad (5\text{-}37)$$

It is important to also take into consideration the torsion of the well path profiles, which depicts the rotating rate of the bi-normal vector with respect to the curve length, or the measure of the rate at which the osculating plane changes its direction. It not only ensures a smooth well path, but also reduces the torque and drag in ERD and u-ERD wells. The importance has been described by Samuel (2007) and Liu and Samuel (2008).

With the inclusion of the torsion parameter as the arc-length integral of the torsion squared to make it more comprehensive, the energy of the well profile, which is referred to as Samuel's criterion, can be defined as:

$$E = \int_0^\ell \left(\kappa(x)^2 + \tau(x)^2\right) dx \qquad (5\text{-}38)$$

Where,

E is the strain energy based on curvature,

κ is the curvature of wellbore trajectory in °/ft, and

τ is the torsion of the wellbore trajectory in °/ft.

Relative Strain Energy

The well-profile energy can be further normalized to a standard wellbore course length between survey stations, as given by Eq. 5-39.

$$E_{(abs)_n} = \left(\frac{\sum_{i=1}^{n} \left(\kappa_i^2 + \tau_i^2\right) \Delta D_i}{D_n + \Delta D_n} \right) \qquad (5\text{-}39)$$

In order to quantify how the well trajectory has changed after applying the artificial tortuosity, relative energy is defined as the energy of the wellbore relative to the absolute energy, which is given by:

$$E_{s(rel)_n} = E_{s(abs)_n}^{tor} - E_{s(abs)_n}^{notor} \qquad (5\text{-}40)$$

Minimizing the total energy of the curve will result in less torque and drag during several operations. This method is defined for curves in space, R_3, and is simple, fast, and deterministic. The previous method based on the inflection point will fail when the well path changes both direction and azimuth and is helical in nature. In this case, the inflection point will be constant and will fail to capture and quantify the wellbore oscillation. In addition, the computation using the two-dimensional model with only curvature will be incapable of capturing the change azimuthally. However, a three-dimensional comprehensive estimate with both curvature and torsion provides better prediction.

Tortuosity

Tortuosity is a measure in which the sum of all the increments of curvature along the section of interest is subtracted from the planned curvature and then divided by the footage drilled. In the well-planning phase, specific tortuosity guidelines should be generated for each section of the well based on torque-and-drag modeling.

Tortuosity is given as:

$$T = \frac{\sum_{i=1}^{m} \alpha_{n-1} + \Delta D \times \delta_i}{D_i - D_{i-1}} \qquad (5\text{-}41)$$

Several methods render planned (smooth) well profiles in a form that can predict loads more realistically. These methods provide an indirect formulation to quantify the degree to which the wellbore will undulate from the planned path and is usually expressed in °/100 ft, which is similar to the expression of dogleg severity.

Rippling or undulation is applied based on the following four methods (Luo et al. 2003, Samuel et al. 2005, Azar and Samuel 2009):

- Sine-wave method
- Helical method
- Random inclination and azimuth method
- Random inclination-dependent azimuth method

Tortuosity limitations generally should be the most stringent in the upper portion of the well and in the build section, where high drillstring tension causes high-side loading, which results in torque and drag, key seating, and worn tool joints and casing. Reducing tortuosity requires an integrated engineering approach, as described below.

- The rotary-drilling directional tendency of BHAs should be tracked, quantified, and refined to yield rotary behaviors that are as close as possible to planned build rates. This process minimizes oriented drilling as a means of inclination control.

- When steering is required, it should be executed in a controlled manner. For example, doglegs can be minimized by sliding for only part of a joint, or a single joint or stand; then, rotary drilling can be used for the remaining footage. This process can then be repeated as required to offset the build, drop, or turn behavior of the rotary BHA that is causing the problem.

- Sliding repeatedly in short intervals is greatly preferred over executing one continuous, long, sliding section, which will cause a significant and sharp dogleg.

Sine-Wave Method. For this method, the sine-wave equation is used, and the angle change is modified by using the following relationship:

$$\Delta\alpha = \sin\left(\frac{D}{P} \times 2\pi\right) \times M \tag{5-42}$$

Where,

M is the magnitude,

P is the pitch, and

D is the depth.

The new angle and azimuth are given as follows:

$$\begin{cases} \alpha_n = \alpha + \Delta\alpha \\ \phi_n = \phi + \Delta\alpha + \psi_{xvc} \end{cases} \tag{5-43}$$

Where,

α is the inclination angle in degrees,

ϕ is the azimuth angle in degrees, and

Ψ_{xvc} is the cross-vertical azimuth-correction angle in degrees.

Helical Method. The helical method (Samuel et al. 2005, Azar and Samuel 2009) modifies the inclination and azimuth of the survey points by superimposing a helix along the wellbore path using the specified magnitude (radius of the cylinder in the parametric equation) and period (pitch). This method uses the circular helix, which is defined as:

$$f(u) = a\cos(u) + a\sin(u) + bu \qquad (5\text{-}44)$$

The generalized parametric set of equations for the helix used to superimpose the wellbore path is given by:

$$\begin{cases} x(u) = M\cos(u) \\ y(u) = M\sin(u) \\ z(u) = \dfrac{P}{2\pi}u \end{cases} \qquad (5\text{-}45)$$

Random Inclination and Azimuth Method. This method applies a random variation to the survey inclination and azimuth within the magnitudes specified using random numbers between –1.0 and +1.0. The incremental change in angle is given as follows:

$$\Delta\alpha = \zeta \times \frac{AD}{P} M \qquad (5\text{-}46)$$

The new angle and azimuth are given as follows:

$$\begin{cases} \alpha_n = \alpha + \Delta\alpha \\ \phi_n = \phi + \Delta\alpha + \psi_{cvc} \end{cases} \qquad (5\text{-}47)$$

Random Inclination-Dependent Azimuth Method. The random inclination-dependent azimuth method is similar to the random inclination and azimuth method previously described, except that the azimuth variation

is independent of inclination. The change in angle, new angle, and new azimuth are given by:

$$\begin{cases} \alpha_n = \alpha + \Delta\alpha \\ \phi_n = \phi + \dfrac{\Delta\alpha}{2\sin\alpha_n} + \psi_{cvc} \end{cases} \quad (5\text{-}48)$$

References

An Engineering Approach to Horizontal Drilling – Halliburton Manual, 1992.

Azar, J.J. and Samuel, R. 2006. *Drilling Engineering*. PennWell Publishing.

Bai, J.Z. 1982. Bottomhole Assembly Problems Solved by Beam Column Theory. Paper SPE 10561 presented at the International Petroleum Exhibition and Technical Symposium, Beijing, China, 17–24 March.

Bourdet, D., Ayoub, J.A., and Pirard, Y.M. 1989. Use of Pressure Derivative in Well Test Interpretation. *SPEFE*, **4**(2): 293–302. SPE 12777-PA.

Brandse, J., Mulder, M., van Paassen, M.M. 2007. Clothoid-Augmented Trajectories for Perspective Flight-Path Displays. *International Journal of Aviation Psychology*, **17**(1): 1–29.

Chen, S., Collins, G.J., and Thomas, M.B. 2008. Reexamination of PDC Bit Walk in Directional and Horizontal Wells. Paper SPE 112641 presented at the IADC/SPE Drilling Conference, Orlando, Florida, 4–6 March.

Dodson, J., and Dodson, T. 2003. Drilling Efficiency Numbers Static. *Offshore*, **63**(1): 26–28.

Du, C.W. and Zhang, Y.J. 1987. The New Technology in Directional Drilling – Catenary Profile. *Oil Drilling & Production Technology*, **9**(1): 17–22, 37.

Han, Z.Y. 1987. The Method of Practical Design of Catenary-Shape Profile. *Oil Drilling & Production Technology*, **9**(6): 11–17.

Han, Z.Y. 1997. Method of Non-Dimensional Design of Cautionary Shape Profile of Directional Well. *Oil Drilling & Production Technology*, **19**(4): 13–16.

Han, Z.Y. and Huang, G.L. 2005. Method of Trajectory Design for Single-Target Directional Wells With Bit Walk Considered. *China Offshore Oil and Gas*, **17**(1): 38–40.

Ho, H.-S. 1987. Prediction of Drilling Trajectory in Directional Wells via a New Rock-Bit Interaction Model. Paper SPE 16658 presented at the SPE Annual Technical Conference and Exhibition, Dallas, Texas, 27–30 September.

Horn, B.K.P., 1983. The Curve of Least Energy. *ACM Transactions on Mathematical Software (TOMS)*, **9**(4): 441–460.

Juliano, T., Domnich, V., Buchheit, T., and Gogotsi, Y. 2004. Numerical Derivative Analysis of Load-Displacement Curves in Depth-Sensing Indentation. *Materials Research Society Symposium Proceedings*, **791**.

Kaiser, M.J., 2007. A Survey of Drilling Cost and Complexity Estimation Models. *International Journal of Petroleum and Technology*, **1**(1): 22.

Liu, X.S. 2007. Study on the Methods for Planning a Catenary Profile. *Natural Gas Industry*, **27**(7): 73–75.

Liu, X.S. 2008. New Techniques Accurately Model and Plan 3D Well Paths Based on Formation's Deflecting Behaviors. Paper IADC/SPE 115024 presented at the IADC/SPE Asia Pacific Drilling Conference and Exhibition, Jakarta, Indonesia, 25–27 August.

Liu, X.S., Liu, R.S., and Sun, M.X. 2004. New Techniques Improve Well Planning and Survey Calculation for Rotary-Steerable Drilling. Paper SPE 87976 presented at the IADC/SPE Asia Pacific

Drilling Technology Conference and Exhibition, Kuala Lumpur, Malaysia, 13–15 September.

Liu, X. and Samuel, G.R. 2008. Actual 3D Shape of Wellbore Trajectory: An Objective Description for Complex Steered Wells. Paper SPE 115714 presented at the SPE Annual Technical Conference and Exhibition, Denver, Colorado, 21–24 September.

Liu, X. and Samuel, R. 2009. Catenary Well Profiles for Extended and Ultra-Extended-Reach Wells. Paper SPE 124313 presented at the SPE Annual Technical Conference and Exhibition, New Orleans, Louisiana, 4–7 October.

Liu, X.S. and Shi, Z.H. 2002. Technique Yields Exact Solution for Planning Bit-Walk Paths. *Oil & Gas Journal*, **100**(5): 45–50.

Liu, X.S., Shi, Z.H., and Fan, S. 1997. Natural Parameter Method Accurately Calculates Wellbore Trajectory. *Oil & Gas Journal*, **95**(4): 90–92.

Lubinski, A. and Woods, H.B. 1953. Factors Affecting the Angle of Inclination and Dog-Legging in Rotary Boreholes. *API Drill and Prod. Pract.*, 222–250.

Luo, Y., Bharucha, K., Samuel, R., and Bajwa, F. 2003. Simple Practical Approach Provides a Technique for Calibrating Tortuosity Factors. *Oil & Gas Journal*, **15**.

Ma, D. and Azar, J.J. 1986. A Study of Rock-Bit Interaction and Wellbore Deviation. *Journal of Energy Resources Technology*, **108**(3): 228–233.

Maidla, E.E. and Sampaio Jr., J.H.B. 1989. Field Verification of Lead Angle and Azimuth Rate of Change Predictions in Directional Wells Using a New Mathematical Model. Paper SPE 19337 presented at the SPE Eastern Regional Meeting, Morgantown, West Virginia, 24–27 October.

Maidla, E.E., Cordovil, A.G., Pereira, J.J., and Falcao, J.L. 1991. Computerized Directional Well Planning for a Dual-Target Objective. Paper SPE 22315 presented at the Petroleum Computer Conference, Dallas, Texas, 17–20 June.

Mason, C.J. and Judzis, A. 1998. Extended-Reach Drilling – What is the Limit? Paper SPE 48943 presented at the SPE Annual Technical Conference and Exhibition, New Orleans, Louisiana, 27–30 September.

Mason, C.J. and Chen, C-K. 2005. The Perfect Wellbore. Paper SPE 95279 presented at the SPE Annual Technical Conference and Exhibition, Dallas, Texas, 9–12 October.

McClendon, R.T. and Anders, E.O. 1985. Directional Drilling Using the Catenary Method. Paper SPE 13478 presented at the SPE/IADC Drilling Conference, New Orleans, Louisiana, 5–8 March.

McMillian, W.H. 1981. Planning the Directional Well – A Calculation Method. *JPT,* **33**(6): 952–962. SPE-8337-PA.

Meader, T., Allen, F., and Riley, G. 2000. To the Limit and Beyond –The Secret of World-Class Extended Reach Drilling Performance at Wytch Farm. Paper SPE 59204 presented at the IADC/SPE Drilling Conference, New Orleans, Louisiana, 23–25 February.

Millheim, K., Jordan, S., and Ritter, C.J. 1978. Bottomhole Assembly Analysis Using the Finite-Element Method. *JPT,* **30**(2): 265–274. SPE-6057-PA.

Millheim, K.K. and Warren, T.M. 1978. Side-Cutting Characteristics of Rock Bits and Stabilizers While Drilling. Paper SPE 7518 presented at the SPE Annual Fall Technical Conference and Exhibition, Houston, Texas, 1–3 October.

Oag, A.W. and Williams, M. 2000. The Directional Difficulty Index – A New Approach to Performance Benchmarking. Paper IADC/SPE 59196 presented at the 2000 IADC/SPE Drilling Conference, New Orleans, Louisiana, 23–25 February.

Payne, M.L., Cocking, D.A., and Hatch, A.J. 1994. Critical Technologies for Success in Extended-Reach Drilling. Paper SPE 28293 presented at the SPE Annual Technical Conference and Exhibition, New Orleans, Louisiana, 25–28 September.

Planeix, M.Y. and Fox, R.C. 1979. Use of an Exact Mathematical Formulation to Plan Three-Dimensional Directional Wells. Paper SPE 8338 presented at the SPE Annual Technical Conference and Exhibition, Las Vegas, Nevada, USA, 23–26 September.

Robertson, N., Hancock, S., and Mota, L. 2005. Effective Torque Management of Wytch Farm Extended-Reach Sidetrack Wells. Paper SPE 95430 presented at the SPE Annual Technical Conference and Exhibition, Dallas, Texas, 9–12 October.

Samuel, G.R., Bharucha, K., Luo, Y. 2005. Tortuosity Factors for Highly Tortuous Wells: A Practical Approach. Paper SPE 92565 presented at the SPE/IADC Drilling Conference, Amsterdam, The Netherlands, 23–25 February.

Samuel, G.R., 2007. *Downhole Drilling Tools – Theory and Practice for Students and Engineers.* Gulf Publishing.

Samuel, G.R. and Liu, X. 2010. *Advanced Drilling Engineering – Methods and Applications.* Gulf Publishing.

Samuel, R. 2010. Ultra-Extended-Reach Drilling (u-ERD: Tunnel in the Earth) - A New Well-Path Design. Paper SPE 119459 presented at the SPE/IADC Drilling Conference and Exhibition, Amsterdam, The Netherlands, 17–19 March.

Samuel, R. 2015. *Solutions and Applications.* Halliburton.

Shirley, K. 2003. Extended-Reach Drilling: The Viable Alternative for Field Development. *American and Gas Reporter*, **46**(4): 97–104.

Walker, B.H. and Freedman, M.B. 1977. Three-Dimensional Force and Deflection Analysis of a Variable Cross-Section Drillstring. *Journal of Pressure Vessel Technology*, **56**(4): 367–373.

CHAPTER **SIX**

Drilling Hydraulics

Extended-reach wells, particularly those with ultra-long horizontal displacements, represent some of the greatest challenges for drilling fluids. Stuck pipe, barite sag, excessive torque and drag, shale instability, poor hydraulics, and inadequate hole cleaning are among the potential limitations. Formation damage may also be critical, especially if the productive interval is drilled horizontally and completed open hole. Problems with torque and drag and hydraulics are linked most often with extended-reach wells.

Oil- and synthetic-based muds are the drilling fluids of choice for most extended-reach wells, primarily because of their high levels of lubricity and inhibition. Well design and optimization require extensive modeling for torque and drag. Payne and Abbassian (1996) derived representative friction factors by analyzing historical data (**Table 6.1**). These friction factors vary with mud type and wellbore material (open hole or casing). Friction factors can also be measured in the laboratory, but correlations with field results have been difficult.

Table 6.1 – Representative Friction Factors for Different Muds (Payne and Abbassian 1996)

Mud Type	Cased Hole Friction Factor	Open Hole Friction Factor
WBM	0.24	0.29
OBM	0.17	0.21
Brine	0.30	0.30

Many extended-reach wells are drilled with downhole motors. Some have horizontal departures approaching 25,000 ft (7,620 meters), and sail angles on most vary from 65° to 75°. For these conditions, optimizing well hydraulics for penetration rates, hole cleaning, and barite sag can be difficult. Minimum high-shear-rate viscosity (plastic viscosity) is necessary, both for reasonable flow rates without exceeding pump horsepower limits and for maximizing bit hydraulic horsepower. Plastic viscosity increases with mud weight and solids content. Elevated low-shear-rate viscosities improve hole cleaning and minimize barite sag.

Hydraulics and Wellbore-Pressure Management

Hydraulic modeling of wellbore-service fluids to optimize their performance is one of the most important parts of the well-planning process. If the fluid system(s) and operational parameters are not carefully considered in the planning process, there is a greater likelihood of nonproductive time (NPT) and remedial treatments. Good wellbore-pressure-management practice is essential to maintain efficient operations and safety. Some key parameters for wellbore hydraulics and wellbore pressure management, as well as the basic process for modeling wellbore hydraulics, are outlined below.

Wellbore Hydraulics Modeling Outline

- Input the configuration parameters
  - Wellbore
    - Trajectory, azimuth, hole angle

DRILLING HYDRAULICS

- Casing and hole sizes
- Drillstring and BHA configuration
– Thermal gradient
- Formation
- Water
– Operational parameters
- Pump rate
- Revolutions per minute (RPM)
- Hours pumping (used to model the effects of heat transfer)
- Average diameter and specific gravity of cuttings
- Rate of penetration (ROP)
- Hole cleaning ("pump and rotate," time, and speed)
- Connection times
- Choke pressure (if used)
- Running speeds
– Fluid systems
- Base fluids – Algorithms will model density (T, P)
- Fluid formulation – Algorithms will model MW (T, P, ASG, OWR, base fluid, WPS, TVD)
- Rheology – Algorithms will model rheology (T, P)
- Calculate
    – Equivalent static density (ESD) – Fluid temperature and pressure gradient, fluid formulation
    – Equivalent circulating density (ECD) modeling and optimization to determine the most efficient operational conditions for the wellbore with all (T, P)-dependent properties included
    – ECD surge and swab

Modeling wellbore hydraulics requires a detailed description of the wellbore geometry, hardware, and operational methods, as well as a good understanding of the wellbore fluid(s) from various standpoints, including:

- Fluid compressibility and thermal expansion
- Fluid rheological properties at wellbore temperatures and pressures
- Cuttings transport
- Heat transfer and drilling-time effects on wellbore-fluid temperatures

A detailed discussion on some of these topics related to drilling fluid rheology and hydraulics modeling is provided in the following text.

Mud Consideration

Some of the parameters to be considered for ERD wells include:

- Economic issues
- Rig issues
- Hole issues
- Other issues
  - Environmental
  - Safety

Economic Issues

Economic issues are related to various factors, such as:

- Maintenance
- Buy back
- Disposal
- Lost circulation

DRILLING HYDRAULICS

Rig Issues

Rig issues mainly cover the logistics related to remote locations, mud systems, and solids-disposal systems. Depending on the complexity, some well designs may require special rigs and associated rig and handling systems.

Hole Issues

Fluid compressibility and thermal expansion can have a profound impact on wellbore pressure management, as shown in **Fig. 6.1**. Since all wellbore-servicing fluids are compressible and thermally expansive, these properties must be considered for accurate wellbore-pressure modeling. For example, ESD is commonly calculated. ESD is the equivalent fluid density that would be required to exert the same pressure at bottomhole as the compressible and thermally expansive wellbore fluid. In terms of both ESD and ECD, compressibility and thermal expansion of the fluids may cause these modeled wellbore pressures to vary at bottomhole by several tenths of a lb/gal, as shown in **Fig. 6.2**. Each base fluid will have a unique pressure-volume-temperature (PVT) signature that must be modeled for accurate ESD and ECD calculations. **Table 6.2** illustrates the typical variation for two common base oils, with the only difference between the two fluids being the bottomhole temperature.

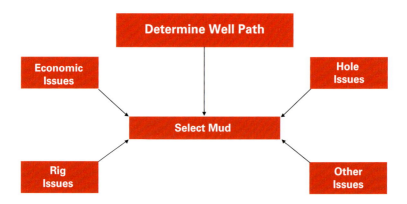

Fig. 6.1 – ERD Mud Consideration.

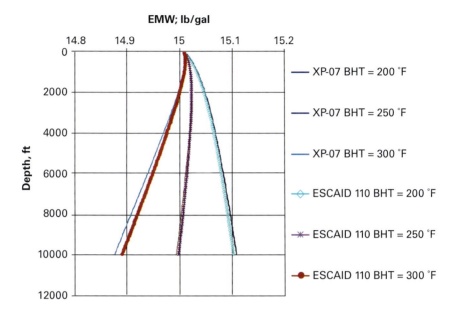

Fig. 6.2 – Depth vs. Equivalent Mud Weight.

Table 6.2 – Density vs. Pressure and Temperature

°F psi	40	80	120	160	200	240	280	320	360	400
0	0.770	0.753	0.737	0.721	0.704	0.688	0.672	0.655	0.639	0.623
2,000	0.781	0.766	0.751	0.736	0.722	0.707	0.692	0.677	0.662	0.647
4,000	0.789	0.775	0.761	0.747	0.733	0.719	0.705	0.691	0.677	0.664
6,000	0.795	0.782	0.769	0.756	0.743	0.730	0.717	0.704	0.691	0.678
8,000	0.801	0.789	0.777	0.765	0.752	0.740	0.728	0.716	0.703	0.691
10,000	0.807	0.796	0.784	0.773	0.761	0.749	0.738	0.726	0.715	0.703
12,000	0.813	0.802	0.791	0.780	0.769	0.758	0.748	0.737	0.726	0.715
14,000	0.818	0.808	0.797	0.787	0.777	0.767	0.757	0.746	0.736	0.726
16,000	0.823	0.813	0.804	0.794	0.785	0.775	0.765	0.756	0.746	0.737
18,000	0.828	0.819	0.810	0.801	0.792	0.783	0.774	0.765	0.756	0.747
20,000	0.832	0.824	0.816	0.807	0.799	0.791	0.782	0.774	0.766	0.757

Other Issues

Selection of the base fluids and chemicals added should be environmentally safe. Disposal of the cuttings and mud should always comply with the regulatory safety standards.

Impact of Hole Cleaning and Cuttings Transport on ECD Management

For accurate ECD modeling, the impact of the cuttings on the fluid density must be included in hydraulics modeling. Cuttings loading will increase both the ESD and ECD in the wellbore. Typically, the higher the ROP, the higher the cuttings loads in the wellbore and the higher the ESD. Cuttings typically have a specific gravity of about 2.6. This is considerably higher than most drilling fluids, and, thus, a minimal cuttings load can have a significant impact on the ESD and, ultimately, the ECD.

The general recommendation for total cuttings load is roughly 3% for deviated and ERD wells and 5% for vertical holes. Well trajectory and drilling practices may permit a more aggressive ROP, which will result in a higher cuttings load. In some cases, it is common to have portions of the wellbore with higher cuttings loads than the general recommendations for wellbore averages. In such cases, higher torque and drag will likely be experienced. Elements of good hole cleaning for ERD are given in **Fig. 6.3**.

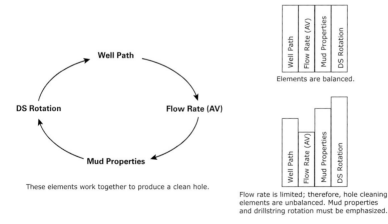

Fig. 6.3 – Elements of Good Hole Cleaning.

Effect of RPM on Cuttings Transport Efficiency

Pipe rotational speed (RPM) will have a major impact on the efficiency of cuttings transport (**Figs. 6.4 and 6.5**). Some of the major variables impacting cuttings transport are pipe RPM, mud weight, rheology (T, P), hole angle, wellbore/pipe geometry, the specific gravity (Sg) of the cuttings, cuttings diameter, and pump rate. In the chart below, a fluid with the following properties is shown to demonstrate the large impact that pipe rotation and cuttings diameter can have on cuttings transport: 12-in. hole, 5.5-in. pipe, $n = 0.789$, k = 0.263, $\tau_0 = 5.68$, average annular velocity = 107.7 ft/min, and the cuttings diameter = 0.25 in. In the following, V_f represents the average annular velocity, while V_c represents the velocity of the cuttings.

This transport efficiency (TE) data demonstrates the large impact that pipe rotation can have on deviated holes. In the deviated region, the transport efficiency is zero for pipe rotational speeds less than 25 RPM. In this example, to maintain the TE at a more efficient value of 0.3, the pipe speed should be approximately 125 RPM. It is important to note that this data is for one unique case; any of the fluid properties mentioned can impact these results.

Impact of Cuttings Size on Transport Efficiency

Cutting size can dramatically impact the ability to efficiently transport cuttings from the wellbore. In the following example, using the same fluid properties as before, the impact of cutting size alone is demonstrated. In this example, the transport efficiency of the cuttings significantly lowers as the cuttings diameter increases from 0.125 in. to 0.375 in. In cases where larger cuttings are expected, fluid properties may be changed to accommodate the larger cuttings. However, hydraulics modeling will help to determine the best compromise of properties for drilling in specific formations and operational limits.

Optimization and Operational Limits

Hydraulics modeling and optimization can touch many disciplines at the rigsite. Each discipline has its own unique goals and constraints; yet,

DRILLING HYDRAULICS

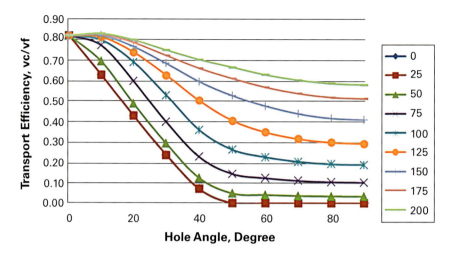

Fig. 6.4 – Transport Efficiency vs. RPM and Hole Angle.

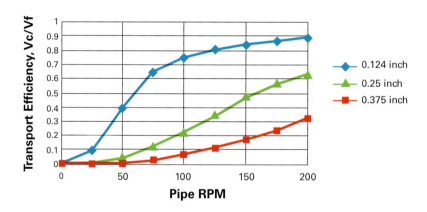

Fig. 6.5 – Transport Efficiency vs. RPM.

wellbore-pressure management is a key component to successful operations from any point of view. For example, the bit providers may want to maximize bit life and ROP. The measurement-while-drilling (MWD) team may have operational constraints related to pipe RPM to maximize tool life. The geomechanics team will provide maximum wellbore-pressure limits that must be regarded; however, the goal is to drill as fast as possible

without exceeding the fracture gradient (FG). All of these disciplines must work in concert with hydraulic simulations to provide the best-possible outcome in any drilling scenario.

Problems Related to Drilling Fluid

The following mud-related problems can delay, suspend, or even cancel a drilling project,

- Stuck pipe
- Lost circulation
- Wellbore instability

Stuck Pipe

Traditionally, causes of stuck pipe are categorized as either differential or mechanical. Differential sticking results when the drillstring is held tightly by differential pressure against a permeable formation. Mechanical sticking can be caused by key seating, inadequate hole cleaning, wellbore instability, and/or an undergauge hole. The percentage of incidents in either category depends on well type and drilling conditions.

The mechanics of differential sticking are well understood (Outmans 1958). When a nonmoving drillstring becomes embedded in a thick filter cake within a permeable formation, the cake can act as a pressure seal. Differential pressure plus any side forces (pipe weight) can hold the pipe with such great force that it cannot be pulled free. Inadequate fluid-loss control, poor filter-cake characteristics, excessive solids content, and high overbalance pressures exacerbate cake thickness and the severity of the problem. In water-based muds, lubricants may help free stuck pipe. Time is critical – sometimes, the pipe can be worked or jarred free if action is taken quickly. Reduction in mud hydrostatic pressure is an alternative, but this must be done carefully so that it does not compromise well control. Finally, spotting a fluid designed to penetrate the filter-cake seal is recommended (full circulation is usually possible). A soak time of at least

12 hours should be allowed. After approximately 24 hours, the probability of success diminishes rapidly.

Mechanical sticking usually requires working or jarring to free the pipe. Thereafter, the cause of the sticking must be corrected, and the stuck zone will need to be reamed or otherwise reconditioned. Additional mud weight may be required to handle wellbore instabilities caused by formation stresses, while reactive shales may require a more inhibitive mud or a fresh-water pill may need to be spotted to free the pipe grabbed by plastic salts.

Lost Circulation

Lost circulation is a perennial drilling problem characterized by the loss of whole mud into downhole formations. Other hole problems, including stuck pipe, hole collapse, and loss of well control, can also affect the likelihood or extent of lost circulation. Drilling costs can be excessive, especially when using synthetic-based drilling fluids.

Lost circulation can occur in formations that are:

- Fractured (natural or induced),
- Highly permeable and/or porous (massive sands, gravel beds, reef deposits, shell beds), and
- Cavernous/vugular (limestone, dolomite, chalk).

Induced fractures are caused by excessive annular pressures.

Lost circulation in naturally occurring voids and unconsolidated formations typically cannot be avoided; however, the following preventive measures apply in other cases:

- Casing should be set so that it protects weak formations and provides a formation fracture gradient sufficient to support drilling-fluid-imposed pressures in the annulus.
- Minimal mud weight should be maintained for the drilling conditions.
- Excessive downhole pressures should be avoided, including those caused by improper rheology/hydraulics, high flow rates, thick

filter cakes, surge pressures during tripping in the hole, bridges, high shut-in underpressures, or sloughing shales.

Proper control of lost circulation involves keeping the hole full to prevent a kick, avoiding stuck pipe, sealing off lost-circulation zones, and cautiously regaining circulation. Leakoff can often be corrected by the addition of lost-circulation materials (LCMs) to the mud. These LCMs include sized calcium-carbonate or cellulosic fibers. For partial losses, the bit should be pulled safely above the lost-circulation zone; the hole should be kept full with low-weight mud or base fluid and allowed to stand full for 4 to 8 hours. The bit should then be returned to bottom carefully. If returns are still not achieved, an LCM pill or a high-fluid-loss slurry squeeze should be mixed and circulated. For oil-based muds, gunk squeeze (organophilic clay in water) is recommended. Complete losses usually require a high-fluid-loss slurry squeeze (such as cement-bentonite, cement-Gilsonite™, or bentonite-cement-diesel oil slurries) or a hard plug, such as cement.

LCM bridging agents that are larger than normal mud solids are used to seal off lost-circulation zones.

LCMs are classified as:

- Fibrous (paper, cottonseed hulls),
- Granular (nut shells), and
- Flakes (cellophane, mica).

Wellbore Instability

Wellbore instability can be caused by mechanical factors and/or physio-chemical interactions between the mud and formation. Chapter 3 describes several problems related to wellbore stability and rock mechanics. Most, but not all, wellbore-instability problems occur in shales. Mechanical factors include formation stresses (low mud weight), erosion, surge/swab pressures, and pipe whip, as well as unconsolidated sands and plastic salt flows. **Fig. 6.6** shows the mud-weight window for different inclinations. As the inclination increases, the pore and frac window reduces, which results in a low-wellbore-stability region.

DRILLING HYDRAULICS

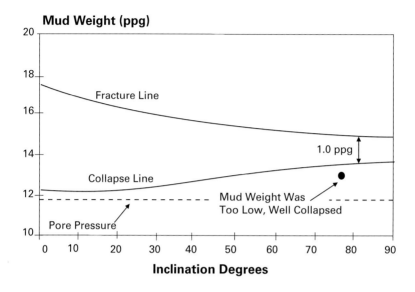

Fig. 6.6 – Mud Weight, Inclination, and Stability.

Unconsolidated sands lack natural cohesion among individual grains. Control of drilling-fluid properties is essential when drilling through these formations (Stephens and Bruton 1992). Some degree of overbalance should always be maintained without the use of excessive mud weights. Properly controlled filtration, spurt loss, and filter-cake properties are critical for the prevention of hole erosion and stuck-pipe problems; bridging solids are especially important. Non-damaging fluids should be used if the unconsolidated formation is a potential producer. Finally, mud rheology should be set so that proper hole cleaning can be provided at relatively low flow rates to minimize hydraulic erosion.

Hole Cleaning

Practically speaking, hole cleaning in most vertical wells can be improved by increasing the mud viscosity (yield point) and flow rate (annular velocity). However, hole cleaning in directional wells (extended-reach, horizontal, and multilateral) can be an order of magnitude more difficult. In inclined intervals, the combination of skewed annular velocity profiles, unusual settling patterns, and force imbalances over the annular cross-

section can promote the formation of troublesome cuttings beds on the low side of the hole. Angles between 30° and 60° are the most difficult to clean, as beds formed over this range of angles can slide downward toward the bottom of the well. Poor drilling practices, low flow rates, and inadequate mud viscosity and suspension properties exacerbate the problem.

The goal of good hole cleaning for ERD wells is to maximize the average penetration rate by eliminating:

- Back-reaming trips
- Wiper trips
- Stuck pipe

Elements of Good Hole Cleaning

It is generally agreed that annular velocity is the key parameter affecting hole cleaning; however, mud viscosity, pipe rotation, and pipe eccentricity can be critical, and they even rival velocity in importance. Hole cleaning is also affected by specific hole conditions, formation properties, and, to some extent, personal preference. The conventional yield point is not a good measure of hole-cleaning capability. Better indicators include:

- A field viscometer reading at 3 or 6 RPM,
- A low-shear-rate yield point determined from 3- and 6-RPM readings, or
- An ultra-low-shear-rate viscosity measured with nonstandard viscometers.

With the ever-increasing measured depths and horizontal displacements in ERD wells, good hole cleaning remains a major challenge. Recently, a hole-cleaning model for fluids in laminar flow was presented to the industry. Since its introduction, the model has been used on many occasions to characterize hole-cleaning efficiency in post-well analysis, evaluate fluid performance during the drilling of ERD wells, and predict fluid rheological properties and pump output levels for optimum cleaning in pre-well planning.

DRILLING HYDRAULICS

The basic elements of hole cleaning that work together include:

- Well path,
- Drillstring rotation,
- Flow rate, and
- Mud properties.

These elements must be balanced, so that an optimal drilling rate can be achieved.

Well Path

Well path design is critical to hole cleaning in extended-reach wells. The cuttings slip velocity changes in the vertical section, build section, long tangent section, and horizontal section, if present.

Some considerations for hole cleaning with reference to different well path designs are (**Fig. 6.7**):

- Cuttings slip velocity – maximize annular velocity (AV)
- Cuttings backsliding – maximize AV, increase low-end rheology in laminar flow.

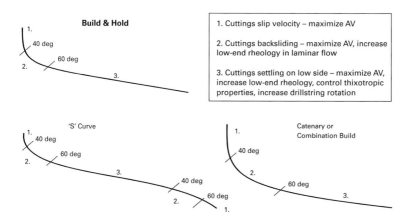

Fig. 6.7 – **Well Paths and Hole Cleaning.**

- Cuttings settling on low side – maximize AV, increase low-end rheology, control thixotropic properties, increase drillstring rotation

These hole-cleaning considerations are shown in **Fig. 6.7** against each portion of the well – build and hold, S-type or catenary, or combination build when drilled.

Drillpipe Eccentricity

The position of the drillpipe while rotating in the eccentric annulus is the greatest unknown. While drillpipe eccentricity (E) is considered to be near zero in vertical wellbores, it is assumed to increase with wellbore deviation due to the increasing effect of gravity. In flow-loop testing at high angles of deviation, the drillpipe lies against the lower side of the annulus (e.g., E = 1) when there is no drillpipe rotation, and rises up or levitates when drillpipe rotation rates greater than 30 rev/min are applied. Further complicating things, in a skewed annulus, there is an infinite number of eccentricities at a given angle of deviation. Hence, it is appropriate to use a particular level of drillpipe eccentricity as an average to cover those situations when the rotating drillstring is lifted off bottom. The effect of drillpipe eccentricity on cleaning potential was documented in an earlier work, which showed that, at very low levels of drillpipe eccentricity (E = 0 – 0.3) and at very high levels of drillpipe eccentricity (E = 0.7 – 1.0), fluids with very different rheological properties behaved similarly in cleaning efficiency when pump rates were held constant. Differences in fluid-cleaning efficiency stand out in the midrange of drillpipe eccentricity (E = 0.3 – 0.7). To determine the average values of drillpipe eccentricity that are valid to use in the modeling process, a wide range of eccentricities in this midrange are considered, and the results are then compared to field information. For high-angle situations, where the drillstring is being rotated, a drillpipe eccentricity level of 0.5 is often used because it most closely correlates with field information.

Lift Factors

Lift factors represent ratios between the net upward velocity of the drilling fluid moving under the eccentric drillpipe (v up) and the net down-

DRILLING HYDRAULICS

ward velocity of the particle as it is settling under the drillpipe (v down). They are calculated very similarly to the general transport ratio in vertical wellbores, where the fluid velocity moving upward is nearly always greater than the drilled cuttings settling velocity.

However, sometimes, fluid velocity can be very small or even zero (0) when the drillpipe is highly eccentric. While it is best to have highly positive lift factors for efficient cleaning, in highly deviated wellbores (70° to 90° from vertical), a lift factor of 0 is often acceptable. In these high-angled situations, there can be very little net upward velocity, and, at times, the best option is to at least have the net upward velocity approximate the particle-settling velocity. Lift factors of –1 denote little to no mud velocity moving upward under the eccentric drillpipe and represent a "free fall" of drilled cuttings that leads to cuttings-bed accumulation. Drilling ahead can proceed carefully when lift factors are temporarily –1. However, when lift factors remain at –1 for an extended period of time, hole-cleaning problems are predicted and action in the form of increased pump output, major changes in fluid rheological properties, and/or increased drillpipe rotation should be taken in order to avoid problems with excessive torque, packing off, or stuck pipe.

Hole-Cleaning Management

One of the main challenges in deep water, which can generate increased nonproductive time (NPT) in the drilling process, is the narrow mud-weight window, which is caused by a lack of formation compaction. Multiple unplanned events can be related to the narrow mud-weight window and the ability to manage hole cleaning efficiently. The following paragraphs present an example of hole-cleaning management, including potential problems encountered.

Due to potential problems, a drilling road map was developed that included the lower and upper limit of the mud-weight window. A sensitivity analysis was performed to determine the maximum ROP allowed to keep the ECD within limits. An upper ROP limit of 50 m/hr was used in the planning stage. During execution, a further limit was required based on real-time data and live road maps.

In this scenario, mud losses were experienced below the 13⅜-in. casing shoe due to an excess of cuttings from cleaning out the rat hole. The mud weight was adjusted and drilling resumed. The well was drilled to TD with no additional loss events. The ROP was controlled to 30 m/hr while drilling practices were implemented to maximize hole cleaning.

A torque-and-drag road map helped to monitor downhole drilling conditions and identify deviations from the normal trend. **Fig. 6.8** shows actual pick-up, rotating, and slack-off loads while drilling the 12¼-in. hole. Real-time monitoring allowed the team to make decisions regarding ROP, drilling parameters, and drilling practices to ensure proper hole cleaning.

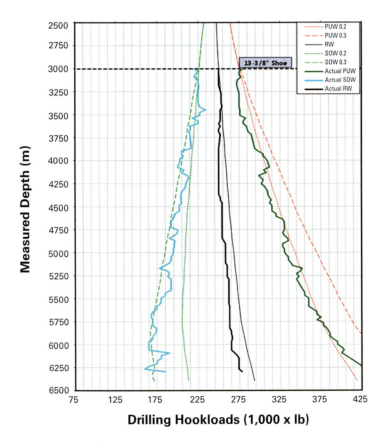

Fig. 6.8 – Real-Time Torque-and-Drag Road Map.

The drilling drag profile also provides an estimation of the cuttings accumulation. **Fig. 6.9** illustrates the drag vs. the measure depth. The convergence and divergence of the pick-up and slack-off weight provide insight into the accumulation of cuttings, as shown in **Fig. 6.9**. Both deteriorating and improving hole conditions can clearly be seen.

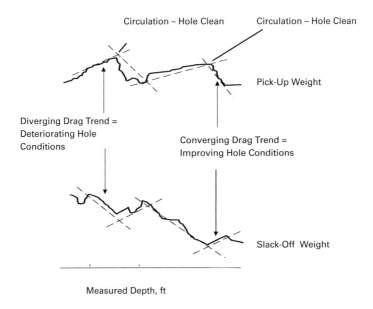

Fig. 6.9 – Real-Time Torque-and-Drag Road Map – Drag.

Fig. 6.10 illustrates ECD monitoring using the pressure-while-drilling (PWD) tool.

While drilling ERD wells, this tool is intended to help:

- Control the ECD while drilling,
- Monitor cuttings load in the annulus,
- Control surge/swab pressures on connections when reciprocating pipe and during trips,
- Detect early kick, and
- Detect wellbore breathing.

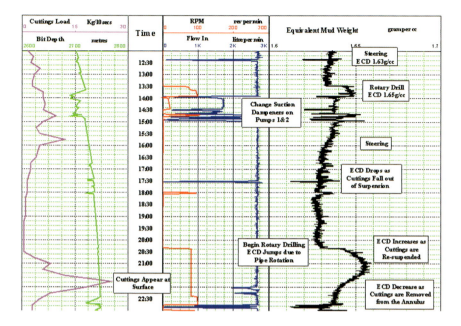

Fig. 6.10 – Cuttings Load Monitoring with the PWD Tool.

Barite Sag

Barite sag can lead to serious problems in high-angle wells drilled with weighted muds. Barite sag is a significant variation in mud density caused by the settling of barite or other weight material. The greatest density variation occurs during the first bottoms-up circulation after a trip or other operation where the mud has been static for a period. Therefore, sag was originally believed to be primarily a static problem. However, Hanson et al. (1990) proved that three key mechanisms were involved: dynamic settling, static settling, and slumping.

Most of the barite bed forms on the low side of the inclined hole under dynamic conditions. Low annular velocities, stationary pipe (no rotation), and poor, low-shear rheology exacerbate the settling. Additional settling occurs when circulation stops, although gels formed in the mud can significantly slow down this process. Studies by Bern et al. (1996) showed that the most difficult angle range is 60–75°. The biggest problem occurs when the barite bed slumps downward toward the bottom of the hole.

Slumping, which rarely occurs at angles greater than 75°, causes the characteristic density variation and can lead to problems with lost circulation, stuck pipe, induced wellbore instability, and loss of well control.

References

Alfsen, T.E., Heggen, S., Blikra, H., and Tjotta, H. 1995. Pushing the Limits for Extended-Reach Drilling: New World Record from Platform Statfjord C, Well C2. *SPEDC*, **10**(02): 71. *Trans.*, AIME, **299**.

Barker, J.W. and Gomez, R.K. 1989. Formation of Hydrates During Deepwater Drilling Operations. *JPT*, **41**(03). SPE 16130.

Bassal, A. 1996. The Effect of Drillpipe Rotation on Cuttings Transport in Inclined Wellbores. M.S. thesis, University of Tulsa, Tulsa, Oklahoma.

Bern, P.A., Zamora, M., and Slater, K.S. 1996. The Influence of Drilling Variables on Barite Sag. Paper SPE 36670 presented at the SPE Annual Technical Conference and Exhibition, Denver, Colorado, 6–9 October.

Bleier, R.D., Leuterman, A.J.J., and Stark, C.L. 1993. Drilling Fluids: Making Peace with the Environment. *JPT*, **45**(01): 6–10.

Bradley, W.B., Jarman, D., Plott, R.S., et al. 1991. A Task Force Approach to Reducing Stuck Pipe Costs. Paper SPE 21999 presented at the SPE/IADC Drilling Conference, Amsterdam, The Netherlands, 11–14 March.

Carter, T.S. and Faul, G.L. 1992. Successful Application of the AOBM System in a Deep West Texas Well. Paper SPE 24590 presented at the SPE Annual Technical Conference and Exhibition, Washington, D.C., 4–7 October.

Chien, S.F. 1994. Settling Velocity of Irregularly Shaped Particles. *SPEDC*, **9**(04): 281.

Haciislamoglu, M. and Cartalos, U. 1996. Fluid Flow in a Skewed Annulus. *Journal of Energy Resources Technology*, **118**, 89.

Hanson, P.M., Trigg, T.K., Rachal, G., and Zamora, M. 1990. Investigation of Barite 'Sag' in Weighted Drilling Fluids in Highly Deviated Wells. Paper SPE 20423 presented at the SPE Annual Technical Conference and Exhibition, New Orleans, Louisiana, 23–26 September.

Hemphill, T. 1996. Prediction of Rheological Behavior of Ester-Based Drilling Fluids Under Downhole Conditions. Paper SPE 35330 presented at the SPE International Petroleum Conference and Exhibition of Mexico in Villahermosa, Mexico, 5–7 March.

Hemphill, A.T. and Pogue, T. 1999. Field Applications of ERD Hole Cleaning Modeling. *SPEDC*, **14**(4). SPE 59731.

Hemphill, T., Pilehvari, A., and Campos, W. 1993. Yield-Power Law Model More Accurately Predicts Mud Rheology. *Oil & Gas Journal*, **45**.

Hough, R. 1995. Slimhole Wells Present Tremendous Economic Opportunity. *Pet. Eng. Intl.*, 22–27.

Jerez, H., Dias, R., and Tilley, T. 2013. Offshore West Africa Deepwater ERD: Drilling Optimization Case History. Paper SPE/IADC-163485-MS presented at the SPE/IADC Drilling Conference and Exhibition held in Amsterdam, The Netherlands, 5–7 March.

Jones, F.V., Moffitt, C.M., and Leuterman, A.J.J. 1987. Drilling Fluids Disposal Regulations: A Critical Review. *Drilling*, 21–24.

Jones, R.D. and Sherman, J. 1986. Controlling Hydrates in Deep Water. *Offshore*, 27–29.

Kenny, P. 1996. Hole Cleaning Capabilities of an Ester-Based Drilling Fluid System. *SPEDC*, **11**(01): 3.

Kenny, P., Sunde, E., and Hemphill, T. 1996. Hole-Cleaning Model:

What Does the Fluid-Flow Index Have To Do With It? *JPT*, 1055.

Lai, D.T. and Dzialowski, A.K. 1989. Investigation of Natural Gas Hydrates in Various Drilling Fluids. Paper SPE 18637 presented at the SPE/IADC Drilling Conference, New Orleans, Louisiana, 28 February–3 March.

RP 13D, *Recommended Practice on the Rheology and Hydraulics of Oil-Well Drilling Fluids*, third edition. 1995. API.

Scott, P. 1994. Drilling Fluids with Scavengers Help Control H2S. *Oil & Gas Journal*, 72–75.

Sorelle, R.R., Jardiolin, R.A., Buckley, P., and Barios, J.R. 1982. Mathematical Field Model Predicts Downhole Density Changes in Static Drilling Fluids. Paper SPE 11118 presented at the SPE Annual Technical Conference and Exhibition, New Orleans, Louisiana, 26–29 September.

Stephens, M.P. 1991a. Drilling Fluid Design Based on Reservoir Characterization. In *Reservoir Characterization II*. ed. Lake et al. Academic Press.

Stephens, M.P. 1991b. Drilling Fluid Key Factor in Preventing Damage. *Am. O&G Rep.*, 47–51.

White, W.W., Zamora, M., and Svoboda, C.F. 1996. Downhole Measurements of Synthetic-Based Drilling Fluid in Offshore Well Quantify Dynamic Pressure and Temperature Distributions. Paper SPE 35057 presented at the SPE/IADC Drilling Conference, New Orleans, Louisiana, 12–15 March.

Zamora, M. 1996. On the HPHT Rheology and Hydraulics of Synthetic-Based Drilling Fluids. Trans., *Nordic Rheological Soc.*, **4**, 16–19.

Zamora, M. and Hanson, P. 1991. Rules of Thumb to Improve High-Angle Hole Cleaning. *Pet. Eng. Intl.*, Part 1: 44–51 and Part 2: 22–27.

EXTENDED-REACH DRILLING

CHAPTER **SEVEN**

Drillstring Mechanics

Understanding drillstring mechanics is critical in determining whether a desired well path can actually be drilled and cased, especially in ERD wells. Issues related to tubular mechanics include torque-and-drag estimates, BHA selection for different types of wells, string vibration, and tubular stresses and buckling conditions. The drillstring design for ERD wells is complex and involves a coupled analysis of engineering and rig limits. BHA components should be appropriately selected and placed so that operation parameters can be optimized effectively. In ERD and u-ERD wells, torque demands may exceed the capacity of the rotary table, top-drive system, or drillstring members, so it is imperative that these issues be evaluated through an accurate estimation of the torque and drag, and, thus, the hook-load calculation.

Drillstring Design

Drillstring design involves the expected load calculations, which are further related to the following issues:

- Profile design and optimization
- Well type
    - Onshore
    - Offshore
    - High pressure/high temperature
    - Deepwater
    - Multilateral
- Operating limits
- Casing design
- Economic issues
- Rig issues
- Torsion/tension/torque and drag
- Buckling
- Hole issues
- BHA components
    - Jar placement
    - Other component placements
- Operating parameters
    - Rotary
    - Sliding
    - Backreaming
    - Tripping
    - Jarring
    - Fishing

Modified from ERD guidelines and Hill et al. 1996, **Fig. 7.1** shows the components involved in the drillstring design for ERD wells.

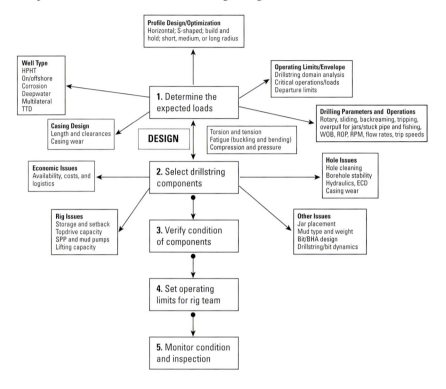

Fig. 7.1 – Drillstring Guidelines.

In addition, simulator models, real-time measurements, and optimization, as shown in **Fig. 7.2**, are important components in the drillstring design.

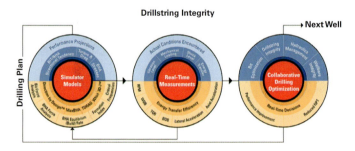

Fig. 7.2 – Drillstring Integrity Requirements.

Torque and Drag

Torque and drag are factors that can determine whether or not a given well path can be drilled and cased. Typically, models consider well trajectory, drillstring configuration, doglegs, friction factors, and casing depth to predict torque and drag in the well. Torque-and-drag modeling is used for various purposes, including:

- Evaluating and optimizing well paths to minimize torque and drag,
- Fine-tuning well paths to minimize local effects, such as excessive normal loads,
- Providing normal force loads for inputs into other programs, such as casing-wear models,
- Identifying depth or reach capabilities or limitations, both for drilling and running casing/tubing,
- Matching the strength of drillstring components to the loads (axial, torsional, or lateral) in the wellbore, and
- Identifying the hoisting and torque requirements of the drilling rig.

The most commonly used torque/drag models are based on:

- Soft string,
- Stiff string,
- Finite-element analysis (FEA),
- Multi-body system,
- Dynamic soft string, and
- Dynamic stiff string.

The details of the models are explained in the *Drilling Engineering* and *Horizontal Drilling Solutions and Applications* books by the same author.

Dynamic soft- and stiff-string calculations are also important for dynamic

pressures. Due to pipe movement, friction forces must be accounted for in the proper direction to estimate the axial tension (Eq. 7-1).

$$F(\xi) = F_0 e^{\pm \mu \xi} + \int_0^{\varsigma} \lambda(s) e^{\pm \mu(\xi - s)} ds \qquad (7\text{-}1)$$

Where,

$$\lambda = -Rwb(-t \pm \mu n)b, \quad \xi = \frac{AD}{R} \text{ and } b = t \times n.$$

The influence of coefficient of friction (CoF) is evident in the overall results in estimating the position of the pipe, as well as in solving the dynamic pressure-flow equations. Pipe elasticity is important in the calculation of dynamic wellbore pressures, because the surface-tripping velocity may not be the same as the velocity at the bottom of the workstring. Consequently, the pipe and annulus pressures must be combined through pipe velocity. The effects will be more pronounced in highly deviated and extended-reach wells. Frictional forces will play an important role in the estimation of the composite elasticity of the system while planning u-ERD wells or in wells where the fracture and pore margins are very narrow.

Trip Speed and Pipe Rotation

Field experience has shown that axial-drillstring drag is reduced when the drillstring is rotated. Torque-and-drag models account for this mathematically by the use of velocity vectors (Dellinger et al. 1980) (**Fig. 7.3**).

Where,

V_R is the resultant velocity,

V_A is the axial velocity,

V_C is the circumferential velocity, and

f is the coefficient of friction.

The resultant velocity, V_R, of a contact point on the drillstring is the vector sum of two components: circumferential velocity, V_C (caused by rotation), and axial velocity, V_A (affected by the drilling rate or tripping speed).

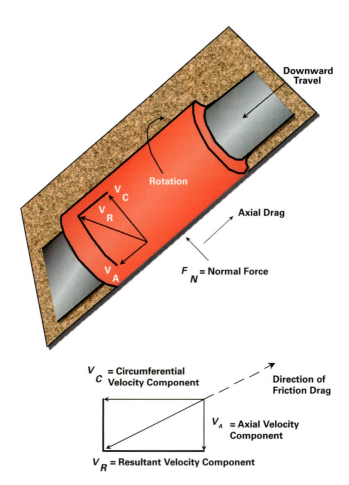

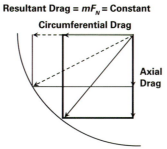

Axial drag is reduced when rotational speed is increased.

Fig. 7.3 – Effect of Drillstring Rotation on Axial Friction.

The *direction* of the resultant frictional force is assumed to act in the direction opposite to that of resultant velocity, V_R; therefore, its vector components will be in proportion to those of the resultant velocity.

The *magnitude* of resultant frictional force is simply the product of normal force, F, and friction coefficient, f, and does not vary with velocity. Since the magnitude of the vector sum of these components is a fixed quantity, as the circumferential component increases, the axial component must decrease. Logically, as drillstring rotation speed increases, it increases the circumferential component, which decreases the axial friction.

Well planning should include torque/drag modeling with worst-case friction factors to ensure that the drillstring can be advanced, rotated, or slid if oriented drilling is necessary, and pulled out of the hole. Similar modeling should be used to ensure that friction will not prevent the casing from being run and that the casing can be pulled if necessary. The torque and tension/compression at any point in the drillstring must be compared to the torsional, tension, and buckling capabilities of the drillstring and tool joints.

Preventive or remedial actions after damage occurs could include:

- Enhancing hole cleaning through higher flow rates, rotation, or modified drilling fluid rheology;
- Making short trips to condition the hole;
- Reaming out ledges, key seats, or doglegs;
- Changing mud type; or even
- Altering the well profile or changing the casing or hole program.

BHA Modeling

A good well plan provides rigsite personnel with the predicted capabilities and tendencies of each planned BHA. As a key component of well engineering, BHA modeling should identify the response of each BHA to variations in operating parameters, such as weight on bit (WOB), hole an-

gle, over-gauge or undergauge hole, stabilizer wear, and formation tendencies. Modeling should also identify the directional response to BHA design parameters, such as stabilizer diameter, drill-collar length, or motor bend angle.

BHA modeling can also be used for calculating bending moments and stresses. In some applications, bending stress caused by hole curvature may be high enough to cause additional problems of fatigue or overload. Side forces on bits and stabilizers can also be calculated. These values are useful for motor-component design work and as inputs into torque/drag and casing-wear programs.

Various types of directional prediction models exist, but all are based on the principle that directional control is accomplished when forces are applied to the bit that will cause it to drill in the desired direction.

Two kinds of BHA models are commonly used:

- Equilibrium (constant hole curvature) models
- Drill-ahead models.

Equilibrium Models

Equilibrium models are typically static-beam models that solve for the hole curvature in which all bending moments and forces on the beams and BHA components are in equilibrium. A typical 2-D model (Williamson and Lubinski 1986) applies known loads (including weight on bit, buoyancy, and the weight of the BHA itself) and derived loads (bit side-loads resulting from formation anisotropy) to the BHA elements. The effects of rotation or dynamics are not considered. A single, empirically derived, bit-formation interaction factor is normally used. The premise of the model is that, while both the bit and formation may have anisotropic properties, only the net effect can be measured. These models have proved to be reasonably accurate for a wide range of BHAs and formations.

Drill-Ahead Models

Drill-ahead models (Larson and Azar 1992) create a constantly chang-

ing wellbore path, the instantaneous direction of which is based on the combination of force vectors on the bit and anisotropy factors. Anisotropic cutting properties may be assigned to the bit, meaning that its ability to drill sideways in response to a given force is not the same as its ability to drill forward in response to the same force. Formation-anisotropy properties also may be assigned, meaning that the formation is more easily drilled in one direction than in another. Formation-anisotropy properties are oriented with respect to the dip angle and direction of bedding planes. Three-dimensional forces resulting from rotation or reactive torque can also be applied in drill-ahead models.

Formation Anisotropy

Formation anisotropy is a variable that can significantly affect the directional characteristics of a BHA. The exact mechanism of formation anisotropy is not known. Lubinski (1953) theorized that formations have a higher drillability perpendicular to the bedding plane than parallel to it. This theory would seem to be supported by the science of rock mechanics, since it is known that the compressive strength of many rocks is anisotropic. Rollins (1959) proposed that thinly laminated formations fracture perpendicular to the bedding plane, creating miniature whipstocks that force the bit updip. Murphy and Cheatham (1965) proposed the drill-collar moment theory, suggesting that, when a bit drills from a soft formation into a hard formation, the hard formation supports most of the bit load, causing a bending moment to be applied to the drill collar. The collar would then bow to the opposite side of the hole and point the bit updip.

Although the formation-anisotropy mechanism may not be fully understood, the manner in which BHAs respond to formation anisotropy and dip can be observed. For well-planning purposes, detailed information from offset wells should be compiled. This information should consist of data from intervals in which consistent operating parameters have been used. Formation dip and direction may be obtained either from seismic information or through the correlation of logs from several offset wells. BHA design, operating parameters, and hole curvature can be found in daily reports and well surveys. With these as input parameters, the BHA modeling program can solve for the remaining variable, which is the

formation-anisotropy factor. As field development progresses, factors should continually be evaluated, updated, and then applied to the planning of future wells.

BHA Response

When BHAs do not exhibit the predicted directional characteristics, parametric studies must be performed to isolate whether variation from the plan resulted from formation anisotropy or some other effect, such as hole erosion or stabilizer wear. In nearly all cases, predictive BHA modeling requires disciplined integration of mechanical models with empirical field experience. For example:

- BHA modeling should be used to make rig personnel aware of BHA responses to design and operating parameters.

- Knowing the response of BHAs to these parameters will enable the directional driller to vary BHA configuration or operating parameters to control directional tendencies, as well as to have BHAs available to respond to contingencies.

- Finally, modeling should be used to establish operating guidelines. In particular, the maximum dogleg in which each BHA can be rotated should be identified.

Rig Capabilities

In addition to geological, geometric, hydraulic, and mechanical considerations, directional planning must also consider the capabilities of the rig and associated drilling equipment. The "severity" of the directional well being planned can be limited by a number of rig aspects. (In this chapter, the term *severity* refers to a qualitative measure of the extent of doglegs, turns, angle, reach, depth, and other factors that influence hoisting, torsional, and hydraulic capabilities of the drilling rig.) Hoisting capability may impose directional limitations on the well, depending on the TVD of the target; the amount of frictional drag associated with lifting the drillstring or deep casing strings; and the amount of mechanical drag induced by doglegs, keyseats, etc. Directional wells induce greater rotary torque

than vertical wells. Top drives are becoming standard equipment on rigs for drilling directional wells. The ability to circulate and rotate while tripping is an absolute necessity in some directional wells, and is always a welcomed capability in others.

The drillstring hook load and surface torque change depending on the tangent angle, and, eventually, the rig torque capacity becomes a limiting factor. For example, **Fig. 7.4** shows the tension and torque values for a 5-in., 19.5-ppf drillpipe at 20,000 ft (6,096 m) measured depth (MD) in a well path with a kickoff point (KOP) at a depth of 1,000 ft and a build of 2°/100 ft (2°/30 m).

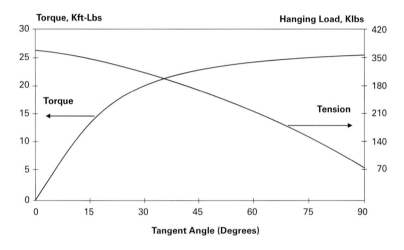

Fig. 7.4 – Drillstring Load vs. Inclination.

Rigs for drilling directional wells may need upgrades in depth-tracking, torque-sensing, and pressure-sensing equipment. Because measured depth is one of the main inputs for calculating well trajectory, knowing the exact measured depth is critical in directional wells. Accurate torque sensing is necessary because of the higher torque demands of directional wells; in fact, torque-limiting or even active torsional control systems with feedback loops may be necessary (Sananikone et al. 1992). High-resolution standpipe-pressure instrumentation that can detect motor-operating pressure fluctuations as low as 50 psi may be needed even when standpipe pressure is 3,000 psi to 5,000 psi.

Crossover subs, whether supplied by the drilling contractor or directional company, should be subjected to a higher level of design, quality, and inspection scrutiny than those used in vertical wells. Crossovers are subjected to high stresses in directional wells and are frequently weak points in the drillstring or BHA. Crossovers should have stress-relief features, and should be made from high-quality material, and be properly inspected at regular and frequent intervals.

Because inclined wells require higher flow rates to clean the cuttings from the well, the pressure and/or flow-rate capacity of the pumps and surface plumbing should be evaluated. The rig must generate enough power to simultaneously run the pumps, the rotary or top drive, and the draw-works at elevated operating parameters. Similarly, the rig's solids control system must have a volumetric capacity that matches the flow-rate requirements, or elevated flow rates will not be sustainable. Because of the various inter-relationships between drilling mechanics and the directional trajectory, an integrated and comprehensive approach to rig selection must be taken during the planning and evaluation of directional wells.

Drillstring Considerations

Drillstring considerations vary depending on the type of wells, and can be broadly classified as:

- Long radius
- Medium radius
- Short radius

In conventional directional wells, because the angle of the well is low enough to allow gravity to be used, drill collars are commonly used in the BHA to apply weight on bit. Unlike drillpipe, the collar's weakest part is the connection; therefore, rotating collars through high doglegs should be avoided.

Particularly in deep wells, unplanned doglegs in the build section should be minimized to reduce both drillstring fatigue and drag. In extremely deep directional wells with a high KOP, the planned build rate, itself,

DRILLSTRING MECHANICS

may have to be minimized. Conversely, if, for a given well depth, the KOP can be designed as deep as possible, higher build rates can be safely used. Higher build rates are possible with a deep KOP because less pipe is present below the KOP and because a higher percentage of its weight is supported by the borehole. The result of these factors is less tension in the drillpipe than in the build section of the hole.

Different drillstring configurations can be considered, as shown in **Fig. 7.5**, including consideration of the annular velocity (AV), drill pipe (DP), and heavy-weight drill pipe (HWDP).

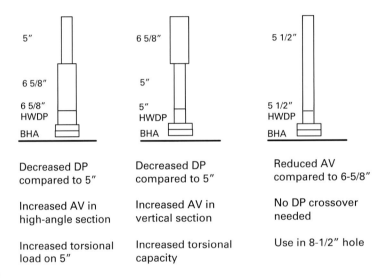

Fig. 7.5 – Drillstring Configurations.

Drillstring Dynamics

Drillstring dynamics are not unique to designer and ERD wells; drillstring dynamics occur in all well types and, in fact, are sometimes severe in vertical wells. Nevertheless, the extreme torque-and-drag levels of designer and ERD wells do result in more stored energy in the drillstring than in other wells. High torque-and-drag levels also cause drillstring components to be stressed near their limits so that additional loading from dynamic forces can result in failure.

Since static-force models usually predict BHA tendencies adequately, dynamic steady-state and transient behaviors are typically not an issue in terms of directional tendency prediction. This condition implies that the average behavior of a dynamically active BHA can be characterized by its static displacement and force state. However, dynamic behaviors still significantly impact other aspects, such as the structural integrity of the bit and BHA and equipment fatigue (Fear et al. 1997, Dufeyte and Henneuse 1991). Experience has shown that most fatigue failures, connection back-offs, and MWD/LWD electronics failures are associated with drillstring dynamics. Moreover, in some drilling situations, the dynamic behaviors can be quite dominant and can severely impact the directional-drilling operation (Birades 1986; Brakel 1986, Brett et al. 1989).

Managing excessive shocks and vibration is important, and the following should be considered:

- BHA design and integrity,
- Drillstring design and integrity,
- Equipment reliability,
- Protection from fatigue,
- Protection from excessive shocks and vibration, and
- Bit life.

This is achieved by fully understanding the expected conditions and by using all available tools to model, measure, and optimize:

- BHA forces and natural frequencies,
- BHA design, string design, and the selection of drilling parameters to prevent premature failure of drillstring components,
- Downhole forces and vibration in real time, as well as
- Performance of drilling assemblies to determine the most efficient design and bit selection.

Various modes of dynamic behaviors can be active in the "structure" composed of the drillstring, BHA, and bit. These modes include the following:

- **Axial vibrations or "bit bounce."** These vibrations are most commonly associated with three-cone bits drilling through hard rock, and are usually more prone to occur at shallow depths and in vertical wells.

- **Torsional vibrations of the drillstring.** Torsional vibration occurs when the drillstring "twists" according to the frequency of the primary torsional vibration mode. Torsional vibration can be induced purely from the frictional loads along the drillstring. It can also be exacerbated by the cutting behavior of PDC bits, which exhibit nonlinear-force rate behaviors. In extreme cases, torsional vibrations can become severe enough to cause "stick-slip" problems. Under stick-slip conditions, the bit exhibits an erratic speed profile, whereby it rapidly decelerates and accelerates as the torsional vibration arrives at, and reflects from, the bit. This erratic motion can rapidly damage the bit and cause very poor ROP performance.

- **Lateral vibrations of the BHA.** Harmonic instability or contact-induced motions, such as stick-slip, can cause BHAs and drillstrings to undergo severe lateral vibrations. These vibrations are most likely to occur when motor or drillstring stabilizers hang and then break free when rotating through formation stringers. The resulting lateral shocks and vibrations can cause fatigue failures or backoffs of BHA connections, along with rapid wear of tool joints and stabilizers.

- **Bit whirl.** PDC bits can exhibit a chaotic behavior, whereby they gyrate off-center and induce severe dynamic motion into the BHA. PDC bit whirl can cause cutter damage or failure, which rapidly results in failure of the bit itself. ROP is usually poor when bit whirl becomes active.

- **Other vibration modes.** A number of other vibration modes are associated with drillstring motion or with the interaction of some of the vibration modes discussed here. For more information about drilling dynamics, additional technical literature is available (Brett et al. 1989, Payne and Spanos 1992).

Types and Causes of Vibration

- Lateral vibration – Bit/BHA/Drillpipe whirl
  - Cannot be seen at the surface
  - Resonance/harmonics – at critical RPMs
- There are multiple critical RPM levels
  - BHA buckling
  - Hole washout
  - Tool kit: Whirl analysis, DDSr™ drillstring dynamics sensor, buckling analysis, ACAL™ acoustic caliper sensor on the CTN™ compensated thermal neutron sensor
- Torsional vibration – Stick-slip (higher downhole torque than surface torque)
  - Can be seen on the rig floor
  - Aggressive bits
  - Hard formations
  - Usually associated with rotary steerable BHAs
  - Tool kit: TEM™ torsional efficiency monitor sensor, DrilSaver™ III vibration monitoring system, DDSr™ drillstring dynamics sensor
- Axial vibration – Bit bounce

Fig. 7.6 illustrates an example of high vibration with displacement and bit-developed whirl. In this example, the well was displaced from drilling fluid to brine fluid starting at 19:30 hr, and the increase in both the surface torque and lateral shocks at the drillstring dynamics sensors were observed with little change in the RPM variation. The normal scale for peaks X and Y has been increased from 0 200 g (where, the unit, g, represents the gravitational acceleration).

DRILLSTRING MECHANICS

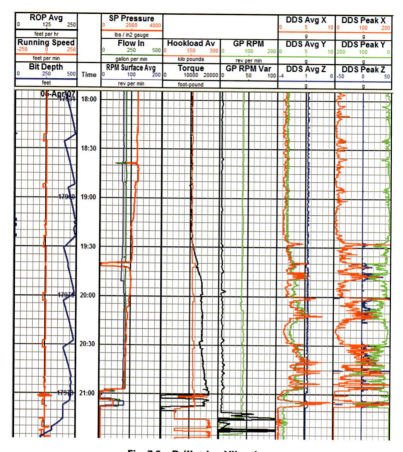

Fig. 7.6 – Drillstring Vibration.

Vibration Stability Plots

A large portion of the drilling cost is related to nonproductive time associated with drilling problems. With the identification of stick/slip and bit whirl as the two major causes of premature PDC bit failures, bit dynamics have become the subject of concern. These studies have involved a detailed analysis of surface and downhole vibration data, and have assisted with the theoretical investigation of various events, notably string-torsional (stick-slip) and bit-lateral (whirl) vibrations.

Bit-tooth wear also has significant effects on the ROP and is also a major cause of premature bit failures. There is no acceptable universal, math-

ematical model that describes bit wear accurately because of the complex nature of downhole conditions. Previous independent studies by Gouda et al. (2011) and Rashidi et al. (2010) used analytical models and real-time data analytics, respectively, to estimate and predict bit wear and, thus, ROP. Motaharri et al. (2008) proposed a model for PDC bits to estimate drilling rates, which also integrates the effect of bit wear. Owing to the unavailability of a standard correlation relating the ROP to the drilling parameters (such as weight on bit, bit rotary speed, flow rate, and torque), it is desirable to integrate hydro-mechanical specific energy (HMSE) with the stability plots.

The optimum ROP values are estimated at each depth of the drilling interval, considering the effect of bit wear and bit vibrations at that depth. Because the bit wears continuously while penetrating the rocks, discretization of depth is necessary for the ease of simulation. In addition, the vibration-stability analysis needs to be performed continuously, because, with changes in the formation and depth, the friction factor, rock strength, length of drillpipe, and other parameters change. Hence, discretization becomes all the more important for the approach being presented in this chapter. The drilling interval can be defined as the interval in which the drilling simulation is to be performed. Discretization is done by dividing the drilling interval into sub-intervals of 1 ft (0.3 m). The sub-interval selected is small enough such that the bit wear and the parameters used in the vibration analysis can be assumed to be constant over that range.

The vibration-stability analysis and bit-wear performance analysis can be combined to create a new buckling-stability plot. The different regions marked in **Fig. 7.7** can be explained as follows:

- Region A signifies all WOBs and RPMs for which the system is stable from torsional and lateral vibrations, and also shows that the bit wear is below the maximum-allowable wear.

- Region B signifies all WOBs and RPMs for which the system is stable from torsional and lateral vibrations, but the bit wear is greater than maximum-allowable wear.

- Region C signifies all WOBs and RPMs for which the system is unstable for torsional vibrations and stick-slip vibrations, as well as the existence of non-uniform bit motion.

- Region D signifies all WOBs and RPMs for which the system is unstable for lateral vibrations, as well as the existence of backward whirl.

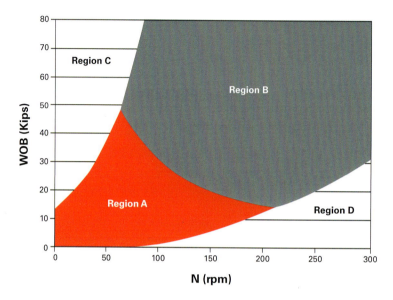

Fig. 7.7 – Drillstring Vibration – Stability Plot with Bit Wear

Deconvolution of Vibrational Data

As the drilling industry enters the era of big data, it has become necessary to find ways to organize and understand the vast amounts of real-time, high-frequency data recorded.

Shor et al. (2014) show that real-time accelerations recorded down hole actually differ from those predicted by various models, either in the high-frequency range or at peak values. These differences in vibration levels can be attributed to noise from various sources (such as the motor or surface equipment), design of measurement devices, uneven shape of the borehole, and/or dynamic effects (such as the dampening/cushioning of fluids, bit-rock interactions, and drillstring-borehole wall interactions). These differences can cause real-time drill-log analysts to miss instances of actual failure or to predict false failures.

The industry currently focuses on the peak and average values of the accelerations recorded down hole, and there is no established method to examine the trend of these accelerations. The methodology proposed in this book first focuses on obtaining the actual unmodulated acceleration values from the recorded downhole gauge data and then processes these values to understand the trend of acceleration as the drilling proceeds. This demodulation (or deconvolution) of the recorded data can reduce the likelihood of false predictions and, at the same time, increase the credibility of the mode of acceleration predicted (and, hence, more accurately predict failure), which currently relies only on the experience of the engineer. Thus, this technique can make real-time data monitoring more reliable and simple. Further, if combined with a gamma-ray log to understand the lithology of the formation being drilled, this data-monitoring technique can reveal a significant amount of information.

Any additional noise in the recorded data can broaden its base within a frequency spectrum, and the data can exhibit nonlinear offsets with an unclear cause. To differentiate the expected acceleration values from anomalies and purely focus the efforts on unwanted dysfunctions that should be mitigated, this problem is approached by blind-source deconvolution. The goal is to recover the unknown actual signal from the observed vibrational signal, given no information about the noise source. For this, it is proposed to use two deconvolution techniques: the minimum entropy deconvolution (MED) technique (linear) and the Teager-Kaiser energy operator (TKEO) (nonlinear).

Once the actual vibrational signal is derived from the observed signal, jerk values and jerk intensities are calculated to predict the failure of a downhole assembly. As discussed in later sections, the jerk intensity is observed to be a straight line plot, and, if any defect occurs, the intensity of jerk suffered at the drillstring begins to increase. This close monitoring of jerk intensity makes failure prediction obvious so that necessary remedial actions can be taken in time.

Using the premise that vibration patterns hold the key to vibration identification and, ultimately, mitigation, the recorded vibrational signal is decomposed into its intrinsic mode functions (IMFs), and trends have

been established for failure prediction. This technique is referred to as EMD. These calculations are performed on two different datasets: one in which failure occurred, and another in which failure did not occur. Final IMFs generated for these two cases are compared, and it is observed that the monotonic IMF, generated from the jerk intensity of the signal, follows a certain trend if failure occurs or is predicted to occur. However, to make this approach more robust and acceptable as an industry standard, additional data processing would be required.

The jerk intensities calculated for two datasets are decomposed into their IMFs, and the final monotonic function obtained in the case of failure and non-failure is observed.

Three different trends are noticed. After careful observation, the following can be summarized:

- A downward parabolic function is the normal (or general) case for lateral jerk.

- A downward parabolic function with skewness toward the right is the general case for longitudinal jerk.

- An upward parabolic function is the general case for longitudinal jerk in case of failure.

These observations are summarized in **Fig. 7.8**.

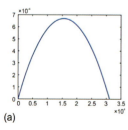
(a)
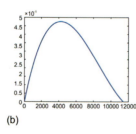
(b)
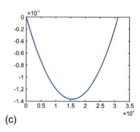
(c)

Fig. 7.8 – a) Downward parabolic function. This is observed as the normal case for lateral jerk. This trend is the same for failure and non-failure cases. (b) Downward parabolic function with skewness toward the right or left modality. This is observed as the normal case for longitudinal jerk. (c) Upward parabolic function. This is the case of longitudinal jerk when failure occurs.

Tool-Failure Prediction

The lateral and torsional components of jerk provide significant contribution to tool failure in comparison with the axial-jerk counterpart. The axial component of jerk corresponds to the accelerometer readings obtained along the "x" coordinates of the downhole measurement. The torsional and lateral components of jerk correspond to the "y" coordinates and "z" coordinates, respectively, based on accelerometer readings. For the sake of accuracy, evaluation must be done independently for the axial, torsional, and lateral components of jerk, as well as for the cumulative jerk. Field values obtained from the accelerometer and calculated jerk values can also be used to forecast potential future events.

Data-driven predictive analytics can also be effectively used for failure prediction combined with scientific/engineering approaches. Data-driven models have been officially implemented across various industries and have gained a reputation for being excellent problem-solving tools. Information obtained from similar historically recorded events can be productively used to forecast potential occurrences of future events. Based on the complexities associated with a given scenario, certain contextual data-driven models or strategic combinations can be used. Drawing elements from computational intelligence and machine learning, some data-driven modeling techniques include neural networks, fuzzy rule-based systems, and support-vector machines.

As shown in **Fig.7.9**, when these two powerful approaches (data-driven analysis + engineering) are combined, a well-devised tool-failure model can be created. Such a model can be used during both real-time drilling operations and for planning purposes before drilling begins. While planning before drilling, to facilitate qualitative decisions beforehand without the accelerometer tool, the model can highlight potential occurrences of failure in advance. During real-time operations, live values of downhole-tool recordings and other meaningful parameters can be fed to the prediction system, which will then process the information to match field conditions. The information can then be recorded and compiled to create a comprehensive log of useful datasets for subsequent accuracy improvements during future predictions.

DRILLSTRING MECHANICS

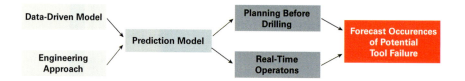

Fig. 7.9 – Combined Model for Tool-Failure Prediction.

Drillstring Buckling

The term *buckling* is used to refer to drillstring/tubular equilibrium configurations. In contrast, conventional mechanical engineering design considers buckling in terms of stability, that is, the prediction of the critical load at which the original configuration becomes unstable (Crandall et al. 1959).

Accurate analysis of buckling is important for several reasons:

- First, buckling generates bending stresses not present in the original configuration; if the stresses in the original configuration were near yield, this additional stress could produce failure, including a permanent, plastic deformation called *corkscrewing*.
- Second, buckling causes tubing movement.
- Third, buckling relieves compressive axial loads.

The accuracy and comprehensiveness of the buckling model is important for designing the drillstring. For example, the most commonly used buckling model, developed by Lubinski and Woods (Lubinski et al. 1962; Hammerlindl 1977, 1980), is accurate for vertical wells but must be modified for deviated wells (Kellingstad 1989, Mitchell 1988, Miska and Cunha 1995).

The hole size, as well as the well inclination, is important for the estimation of the critical buckling load. It can be seen that the critical buckling load is high for small hole sizes compared to the higher borehole diameters for the same drillpipe and mud density.

References

API 5C2, *Bulletin on Performance Properties of Casing, Tubing, and Drill Pipe*, 18th edition. 1982. API: Dallas.

API 5C3, *Bulletin on Formulas and Calculations for Casing, Tubing, Drill Pipe, and Line Pipe Properties*, fourth edition. 1985. API: Dallas.

API D7, *Casing Landing Recommendations*. 1955. API Specification 5B. API: Dallas.

Chen, Y.C., Lin, Y.H., and Cheatham, J.B. 1990. Tubing and Casing Buckling in Horizontal Wells. *JPT*, **42**(02).

Crandall, S.H. and Dahl, N.C. 1959. **An Introduction to the Mechanics of Solids**, 199. New York: McGraw-Hill Book Company.

Dawson, R. and Paslay, P.R. 1984. Drillpipe Buckling in Inclined Holes. *JPT*, **36**(10).

Hammerlindl, D.J. 1980. Packer-to-Tubing Forces for Intermediate Packers. *JPT*, **32**(03): 195–208.

Hammerlindl, D.J. 1977. Movement, Forces, and Stresses Associated with Combination Tubing Strings Sealed in Packers. *JPT*, **29**(02): 195–208.

Hill, T.H., Guild, G.J., and Summers, M.A. 1996. Designing and Qualifying Drill Strings for Extended-Reach Drilling. *SPEDC*, **11**(02). SPE-29349-PA.

Lakhanpal, V. and Samuel, R. 2016. Deconvolution of Vibrational Data to Reduce the Ambiguity in Downhole Tool Failure. Paper SPE 181491 presented at the SPE Annual Technical Conference and Exhibition, Dubai, UAE, 26–28 September.

Liu, Z., Marland, C., Li, D., and Samuel, R. 2014. An Analytical Model Coupled with Data Analytics to Estimate PDC Bit Wear. Paper SPE 169451-MS presented at the SPE Latin American and Caribbean Petroleum Engineering Conference, Maracaibo, Venezuela, 21–23 May.

Lubinski, A., Althouse, W.S., and Logan, J.L. 1962. Helical Buckling of Tubing Sealed in Packers. *JPT*, **14**(06): 655–670.

Mirani, A. and Samuel, R. 2015. Discrete Vibration Stability Analysis with Hydro-Mechanical Specific Energy. Proceedings of the ASME 2015 34th International Conference on Ocean, Offshore and Arctic Engineering, OMAE2015, St. John's, Newfoundland, Canada, 31 May–5 June.

Miska, S. and Cunha, J.C. 1995. An Analysis of Helical Buckling of Tubulars Subjected to Axial and Torsional Loading in Inclined Wellbores. Paper SPE 29460 presented at the SPE Production Operations Symposium, Oklahoma City, Oklahoma, 2–4 April.

Mitchell, R.F. 1996. Buckling Analysis in Deviated Wells: A Practical Method. Paper SPE 36761 presented at the SPE Annual Technical Conference and Exhibition, Denver, Colorado, 6–9 October.

Samuel, R., 2007. **Downhole Drilling Tools**, 1–550. Gulf Publishing Company.

Samuel, R. 2010. Friction Factors: What Are They for Torque, Drag, Vibration, Bottomhole Assembly Drill Ahead, and Transient Surge/Swab Analyses? Paper SPE 128059 presented at the IADC/SPE Drilling Conference and Exhibition, New Orleans, Louisiana, 2–4 February.

Samuel, R. and Gao, D. 2014. **Horizontal Drilling Engineering: Theory, Methods and Applications**. Houston, Texas: Sigma Quadrant Publishers.

Shor, R.J, Pryor, M., and van Oort, E. 2014. Drillstring Vibration Observation, Modeling and Prevention in the Oil and Gas Industry. Presented at the ASME Dynamic Systems and Control Conference, San Antonio, Texas, 22–24 October. DSCC2014-6147. http://dx.doi.org/10.1115/DSCC2014-6147.

EXTENDED-REACH DRILLING

CHAPTER **EIGHT**

Well Control

As the number of horizontal and ERD wells continues to increase, the importance of understanding well control in high-angle wells also increases. Within the industry today, there is very little information available on well control in extended-reach and ultra-extended-reach wells, and few well-control incidents have been recorded. The main objective of this section is to highlight the aspects of well control that are unique for ERD wells.

Well control is divided into three categories–primary, secondary, and tertiary.

Primary control is the proper use of the fluid's hydrostatic head (mud weight) to overbalance the formation pressure, thereby preventing entry of formation fluids into the wellbore.

Secondary control is the proper use of blowout prevention equipment to control the well in case primary control is lost.

Tertiary control refers to methods used when secondary control is in imminent danger of being lost or when it cannot be applied.

Fundamentals of Primary Well Control

The fundamentals of primary well control can be divided as follows:

- Maintaining primary control through well planning and operating procedures
- Detecting when primary control has been lost
- Taking appropriate action to regain primary control

A brief overview of these fundamental procedures for any well is given below. The following sections will concentrate on the different aspects of these fundamentals.

To maintain primary well control, the hydrostatic mud pressure must exceed the formation pressure. When the formation pressure exceeds the hydrostatic mud pressure, the well is said to be "*underbalanced*," and an influx of formation fluid (or "*kick*") may be taken into the annulus.

The methods for kick detection include:

- Drilling break
- Flow increase
- Pit gain
- Decreasing the circulating pressure
- Fluid or gas-cut mud or an increase in mud chlorides

These methods are described below.

A drilling break, or a large, sudden increase in the rate of penetration, sometimes occurs when drilling into formations of higher pore pressure. This results in underbalance if the formation pore pressure is greater than the bottomhole pressure provided by the mud weight. If the formation is permeable, then this underbalance will result in a kick. Although a drilling break does not always signify a kick, it is very useful, since it occurs as soon as the bit penetrates the higher-pressure zone and, therefore, helps alert the rig crew to the potential for a kick.

- A flow increase occurs when the flow coming out of the well exceeds the flow going into the well. This occurs whenever an influx is taken and usually indicates the first sign of a kick. Flow sensors with alarms are useful for drilling or tripping.

- A pit gain will also result from a kick, since the rig's fluid system is a closed system. This is usually monitored by some type of pit-level marker.

- A decrease in circulating pressure occurs after a kick, since the resistance to pumping the lighter-weight fluid is reduced. This kick indicator is usually the least sensitive.

Fluid- or gas-cut mud or an increase in mud chlorides is only observed when bottoms-up is obtained at the surface. Thus, it may be the last indication that a kick has occurred. Nevertheless, it may be very useful as a confirmation for other indicators that a kick has occurred.

After a kick has been detected, then primary well control is lost. Secondary well control is provided by blowout preventers (BOPs), which consist of annular or pipe rams. The BOPs seal the drillpipe annulus, thereby "*shutting-in*" the well and preventing additional influx.

After casing (annulus) and drillpipe (bore) pressures have stabilized, the shut-in casing pressure (SICP) and the shut-in drillpipe pressure (SIDPP) are read and recorded. The annulus is contaminated with drill cuttings and formation fluid of unknown density and volume, while the drillpipe is usually filled with mud of known density, denoted here as the original mud weight (OMW). Therefore, the SIDPP is normally used to calculate the degree of underbalance and the mud weight increase required to regain primary well control.

The well is then "*killed*," meaning that the kick and original-weight mud are circulated out and replaced by kill mud weight (KMW). An industry-accepted practice is to monitor drillpipe pressure while circulating out the kick through adjustable chokes. Excessive surface pressure can break down the casing shoe or other weak formations, which could result in lost circulation. Inadequate surface pressure allows additional kicks that, at a

minimum, lengthen and complicate the kill. Thus, maintaining the proper surface pressure while circulating out a kick is important.

The fundamentals described above apply to any well, including horizontal wells. However, there are aspects of well planning and operating procedures that differ for horizontal wells. These are discussed below.

Maintaining Primary Well Control

Fracture Gradient and Pore Pressure

The fracture gradient represents the maximum pressure that can be exerted in the wellbore without fracturing the formation. For wells that are not drilled horizontally, the fracture gradient typically increases with depth due to increasing overburden. For horizontal wells, the fracture gradient does not usually increase over the length of the lateral section because the True verical depth (TVD) (and, hence, overburden) is essentially constant.

Similarly, the pore-pressure gradient often increases with depth for non-horizontal wells, whereas the lateral section of horizontal wells usually remains in formations of approximately equal pressure (unless the well crosses through sealing faults). However, the circulating pressure losses in the annulus that result from friction continue to increase with the length of the lateral section. In a horizontal well, these annular pressure losses translate to an increasing equivalent circulating density (ECD) along the length of the lateral section.

Fig. 8.1 illustrates the relationship among pore pressure, static fluid pressure (*"mud weight"*), circulating fluid pressure (ECD), and fracture gradient. In this example, if the lateral section were long enough, then the ECD would approach the fracture gradient. Consequently, the maximum length of the lateral section that can be drilled could be limited by the fracture gradient and should be carefully considered during well planning.

NOTE: Friction losses can be reduced by decreasing the flow rate, increasing annular clearance between the drillstring and the borehole wall, or adjusting mud rheology.

WELL CONTROL

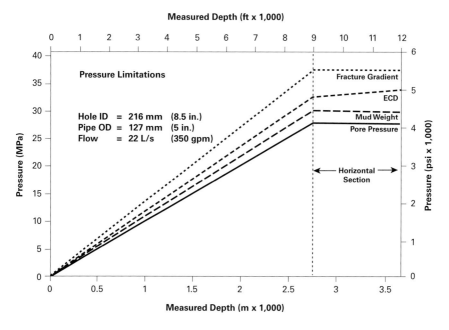

Fig. 8.1 – Pressure Limitations.

Swabbing

As pipe is pulled out of the hole, the drilling fluid tries to follow behind it. This upward movement of the fluid decreases bottomhole pressure, which can lead to momentary entry of formation fluids into the wellbore. This action is known as swabbing, and it is caused by highly viscous drilling fluid, small annular clearances (including balled-up bits, reamers, or stabilizers), or improper pipe-pulling speeds. As discussed earlier, the pore pressure generally does not increase in the lateral section of horizontal wells. However, the pressure drop caused by pulling the drillstring out of the hole (*"swabbing"*) does increase with the length of the lateral section. Therefore, horizontal wells are prone to swabbing.

Detection and correction of swabbing tendencies for horizontal wells are identical to those for conventional wells. Swabbing is detected by accurately measuring the amount of drilling fluid pumped into the hole to replace the drillpipe being removed from the hole. The use of small, calibrated (*"trip"*) tanks is an effective method to monitor the pump strokes

required to fill the hole. An adjustment of fluid properties and pipe-pulling speed may be necessary to correct swabbing action.

Another possibility is to turn on the pumps while pulling out of the hole in order to use the ECD as a way to increase overbalance. However, if these procedures fail to prevent swabbing, then the last resort is an increase in mud weight with its attendant disadvantages regarding lost circulation.

Surging

Surging is the opposite effect of swabbing and can result in lost circulation. It usually occurs when pipe is run into the hole too quickly. As previously noted, the fracture gradient does not increase in the lateral section of horizontal wells. Because the pressure drop caused by running the drillstring in the hole does increase with the length of the lateral section, horizontal wells are more likely to experience surging problems.

Kick Detection

As discussed earlier, the methods of kick detection used for conventional wells include drilling breaks, flow increase, pit gain, decrease in circulating pressure, and fluid- or gas-cut mud or an increase in mud chlorides. All of these kick indicators should be used in the usual manner for horizontal wells, with only one exception. For a gas kick, pit gain may be delayed due to a lack of gas expansion in the lateral section. If the gas kick goes undetected, then a very large kick may be taken in the lateral section.

In vertical wells, kicks may migrate up the annulus, even when a well remains shut in. This increases the pressure on the casing shoe (and other weak formations), as well as the surface pressure. For horizontal wells, the migration rate of a kick in the lateral section is extremely slow. This allows the rig personnel more time to plan and implement correct well-control procedures.

Kick Classification:

Dynamic bottomhole pressure (BHP) calculations are required to broadly classify the types of kicks taken under different operating conditions.

These kicks include:

- Kicks while drilling,
- Kicks after pump shutdown, and
- Swab kicks.

The different wellbore pressures under the different operations are given below.

Kicks While Drilling:

  Pore Pressure > Dynamic BHP > Static BHP

Kicks After Pump Shutdown:

  Dynamic BHP > Pore Pressure > Static BHP

Swab Kicks:

  Dynamic BHP > Static BHP > Pore Pressure

Expected Influx Volume

Kicks While Drilling

The sequence of events during the inflow period is divided into three time periods.

Time Period A:

- The time it takes to detect that a kick has occurred
- ROP = the drilling rate of penetration
- Mud flow rate = the drilling flow rate
- When the height of the penetration into the formation, h, goes from 0 to the maximum depth penetrated into the high-pressure zone

$$h = t \times ROP \tag{8-1}$$

Where,

t is Time Period A.

The pressure difference (ΔP) between the formation and the drilling-fluid column is between the pore pressure and the dynamic BHP, and results from both the hydrostatic pressure of the mud column and the frictional pressure loss in the annulus.

Because the height of penetration into the reservoir is increasing with time, the h parameter is expressed as "$t \times ROP$" in the model described above. Thus, for each 5-second time step, the height of penetration into formation increases by "$5 \times ROP$."

The values for influx volume, V, and flow rate, Q, are calculated for each 5-second time step.

Time Period A is determined by:

- For "Kick Detection Method" = "Flowrate Variation"
- When $Q >$ = "Flow Rate Variation"
- For "Kick Detection Method" = "Volume Variation"
- When $V - Q*$Detection Time Delay $>$ = "Volume Variation"

Time Period B:

- The time it takes to confirm that a kick has occurred
- $ROP = 0$, rotation is stopped
- Mud flow rate = the drilling flow rate
- h is now constant at "Time Period A * ROP"

The pressure difference (ΔP) between the formation and the drilling-fluid column is a result of both the hydrostatic pressure of the mud and influx columns and the frictional pressure loss in the annulus from the drilling mud and the influx.

The height of penetration into the reservoir is now a constant value at "h = Time Period A * ROP." The influx parameters are determined for Time Period B. The values of V and Q are calculated for each 5-second time step over Time Period B.

Time Period B = Time to Stop Rotation + Time to Pick Up Off Bottom + Time to Stop Pumps

Time Period C:

- The time it takes to secure the well
- *ROP = 0*, rotation is stopped
- Mud flow rate = 0, pumps are stopped
- h is constant at "Time Period A * ROP"

The pressure difference (ΔP) between the formation and the drilling-fluid column is now only due to the hydrostatic pressure of the mud and influx columns; no frictional pressure loss is generated because the mud pumps are off.

The height of penetration into the reservoir is still a constant value at "h = Time Period A * ROP." The influx parameters are determined for Time Period C. The values of V and Q are calculated for each 5-second time step over Time Period C.

Time Period C = Time to Perform Flow Check + Time to Open HCR + Time to Close BOP + Time to Close Choke

So,

Total Influx Volume = Time Period A Influx Volume

+ Time Period B Influx Volume

+ Time Period C Influx Volume

Influx Volume at Detection = Time Period A Influx Volume

Detection Time = Time Period A

Kick After Pump Shutdown

The sequence of events during the inflow period is divided into two time periods.

Time Period A:

- The time it takes to detect a kick has occurred
- $ROP = 0$, no rotation
- Mud flow rate = 0, the pumps are stopped
- h is constant at "Exposed Height"

The pressure difference (ΔP) between the formation and the drilling-fluid column results from the hydrostatic pressure of the mud and influx columns only; no frictional pressure loss is generated because the mud pumps are off.

The values of V and Q are calculated for each 5-second time step.

Time Period A is determined by:

- For "Kick Detection Method" = "Flowrate Variation"
- When $Q >$ = "Flowrate Variation"
- For "Kick Detection Method" = "Volume Variation"
- When $V - Q*$Detection Time Delay $>$ = "Volume Variation"

Time Period C:

- The time it takes to secure the well

- $ROP = 0$, rotation is stopped
- Mud flow rate = 0, pumps are stopped
- h is constant at "Exposed Height"

The pressure difference (ΔP) between the formation and the drilling-fluid column is now only due to the hydrostatic pressure of the mud and influx columns; no frictional pressure loss is generated because the mud pumps are off.

The height of penetration into the reservoir is still a constant value at "$h = Exposed\ Height$." The influx parameters are determined for Time Period C. The values of V and Q are calculated for each 5-second time step over Time Period C.

Time Period C = Time to Perform Flow Check + Time to Open HCR + Time to Close BOP + Time to Close Choke

So,

Total Influx Volume = Time Period A Influx Volume + Time Period C Influx Volume

Influx Volume at Detection = Time Period A Influx Volume

Detection Time = Time Period A

Regaining Primary Well Control

Lost Circulation

In the event that the fracture gradient is exceeded and lost circulation does occur, then there are several aspects of spotting lost-circulation material (LCM) that differ for horizontal wells. Full-scale tests have shown that conventional spotting procedures tend to preferentially plug the lower half-circumference of the wellbore. To ensure that the upper half-

circumference of the wellbore is plugged by LCM, the following steps are recommended:

1. Increase the concentration of the LCM.

2. Modify the mud rheology to increase the low-shear-rate viscosity of the drilling fluid to enhance its carrying capacity for the LCM.

3. Pump LCM through the open hole at lower flow rates.

Killing the Well

The circulating pressures during a horizontal-well kill differ significantly from those that occur in a vertical well. The industry-accepted practice for vertical wells requiring an increase in mud weight is to allow the drillpipe circulating pressure to decrease linearly with the cumulative volume of mud pumped. During this period, the original-weight mud in the drillpipe is displaced with kill-weight mud (**Fig. 8.2**). If this procedure is followed for a non-vertical well, then this implicitly assumes that the entire wellbore is slanted at a constant angle, regardless of the actual well path

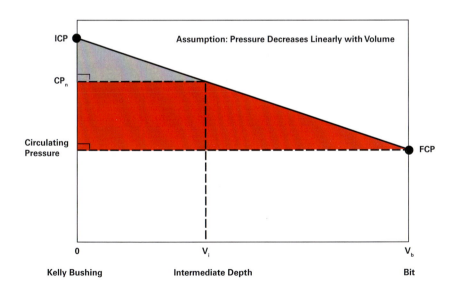

Fig. 8.2 – Pressure-Volume Schedules for Constant-Angle Wells.

(**Fig. 8.3**). The resulting error that occurs in circulating pressure is maximized in horizontal wells and should, therefore, usually be corrected.

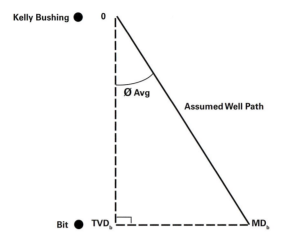

Fig. 8.3 – Assumed Well Path for Constant-Angle Wells.

The error in circulating pressure incurred by neglecting the directional profile results in overbalance (in addition to any margin) above the formation pressure until kill-weight mud reaches the bit. If the error is sufficiently large, then the additional overbalance could cause lost circulation and/or stuck pipe (Cheatham 1989). This method provides a means to estimate and, if desired, reduce this error in circulating pressure. The correction depends linearly on the degree of underbalance and nonlinearly on hole inclination and depths of kick-off points relative to the bit depth. Two examples are shown to illustrate the effect of a corrected circulating-pressure schedule.

Example 1: Deep Kick-Off Point

The first example shows the effect of a deep kick-off point with the following geometrical parameters:

Kick-Off Point	3,048 m (10,000 ft)
Measured Depth at TD of TYO	4,572 m (15,000 ft)
TD	3,353 m (11,000 ft)

These parameters result in the following calculated values:

Kill Mud Weight	1.31 sg (10.9 ppg)
Initial Circulating Pressure Final	8.3 MPa (1,200 psi)
Circulating Pressure	5.2 MPa (761 psi)

The drillpipe circulating-pressure schedule is shown in **Fig. 8.4**. The maximum error that would result from neglecting the horizontal nature of the well would be 1.2 MPa (167 psi), or 33% of the kick size.

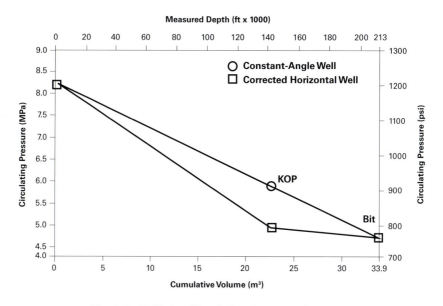

Fig. 8.4 – Drillpipe Circulating-Pressure Schedule

Example 2: Shallow Kick-Off Point

The second example shows the effect of a shallow kick-off point with the following geometrical parameters:

Kick-Off Point	305 m (1,000 ft)
Measured Depth at TD of TVD	3,048 m (10,000 ft)
TD	610 m (2,000 ft)

WELL CONTROL

The pressure parameters are identical to the first example, as follows:

Pump Pressure at Kill Speed	4.8 MPa (700 psi)
Original Mud Weight	1.2 sg (10.0 ppg)
Shut-In Drillpipe Pressure	3.4 MPa (500 psi)

These parameters result in the following calculated values:

Kill Mud Weight	1.77 sg (14.8 ppg)
Initial Circulating Pressure	8.3 MPa (1,200 psi)
Final Circulating Pressure	7.1 MPa (1,037 psi)

The drillpipe circulating-pressure schedule is shown in **Fig. 8.5**. The error that would result from neglecting the horizontal nature of the well would be 8.2 MPa (1,184 psi), or more than twice the size of the kick.

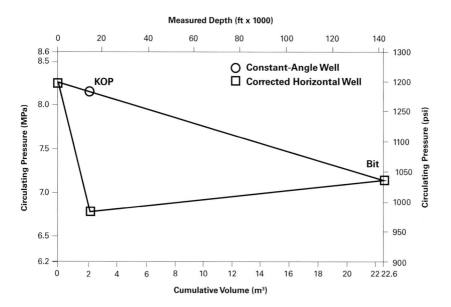

Fig. 8.5 – Drillpipe Circulating-Pressure Schedule.

In conclusion, it is very important to correct the pressure schedule for circulating out a kick in a horizontal well. Neglecting the horizontal nature can cause very large errors, thereby resulting in unnecessary overbalance in the open hole and at the surface.

Influence of Killing Variables

Computer simulations have shown that multiple variables can affect choke and casing-shoe pressures to different degrees. The following conclusions were reached for horizontal wells:

- The larger the pressure differential between the formation and wellbore pressures, the higher the choke pressure during the kill.

- The kick size had a major effect on the choke pressure magnitude. The bigger the kick, the higher the choke pressure.

- Differing wellbore geometries had a moderate effect on the annulus pressure. Smaller annular clearance resulted in the highest choke pressure and the shortest displacement time.

- Variations in the displacement rate had a moderate effect on choke and casing-shoe pressures. Higher pump rates resulted in higher pressures and a shorter displacement time.

- Changes in the lateral section length and buildup rate had a minor effect on the casing-shoe pressure.

Trapped Gas

If a well is killed off bottom, it is possible that some gas will remain trapped in the end of the lateral section. Since no pressure indications will be observed at the surface, bottoms-up should be circulated after the bit returns to bottom as a precaution before drilling commences again.

Even if the well is not killed off bottom, it is possible that gas will accumulate in undulating or overgauge hole sections after kicks (**Fig. 8.6**). Tests have shown that, at 90–92° inclination, an annular velocity of 30 m/min (100 ft/min) is sufficient to remove trapped gas, regardless of fluid rheology. Tests also showed that, while at 90° inclination, gas bubbles

Fig. 8.6 – Displacing Gas from Undulating Wellbore.

move at the same speed as the drilling fluid (i.e., without slip), but that, at 100°, the gas moves 10 times slower than the drilling fluid.

Kick Tolerance

The kick tolerance is usually determined by assuming that the gas is a single, continuous bubble, and wellbore pressures are calculated for the gas-bubble positions across the full range between the last casing setting depth and the influx depth. Further, the minimum gas volume required to fracture the formation at the assumed casing setting depth is calculated and compared against the allowable gas-kick volume. Gas-bubble volume is depth dependent and should be calculated as a function of local pressures, temperatures, volumes, and compressibility.

The stepwise calculations in CasingSeat™ casing design software (part of a Landmark software suite) for the Bottom-Up Design are as follows.

1. An iterative calculation starts with an initial guess for the casing setting depth, which is the midpoint between the first casing setting depth (Well/Design Parameters/General/First Casing Setting Depth) and well TD.

2. CasingSeat software will then calculate a gas-bubble height, starting with the bubble at well TD and circulating it out to the assumed casing setting depth using the Driller's Method. The bubble height is limited by the fracture gradient at the depth of the initial guess. Assumption: Since no other operating constraints are considered for this case, the mud-density gradient is considered to be equal to the maximum pore-pressure gradient in the open hole. If the pore pressure is increased by selecting other operating constraints, then

the new pore-pressure gradient will be used instead. The following calculations are done in order to calculate the gas height.

Pressure at the bit depth (initially well TD):

$$P_{bit} = 0.052(\rho_{ppBit} + \rho_{kickintensity})(D_{bit}) \tag{8-2}$$

Pressure of the mud column in the open hole:

$$P_{diff} = 0.052(\rho_{mud})(D_{bit} - D_{CS}) \tag{8-3}$$

Wellbore pressure at the assumed casing setting depth:

$$P_{CS} = P_{bit} - P_{diff} + H_{kick}(\rho_{mud} - \rho_{kick}) \tag{8-4}$$

Formation fracture pressure at the same depth:

$$P_{FracCS} = 0.052(\rho_{fracCS})(D_{CS}) \tag{8-5}$$

By equating the wellbore pressure with the formation fracture pressure at the same depth, the height of the gas bubble is obtained.

$$H_{kick} = \frac{\Delta P}{(\rho_{kick} - \rho_{mud})} \tag{8-6}$$

Where,

$$\Delta P = P_{bit} - P_{FracCS} - P_{diff},$$

ρ_{ppBit} is the pore pressure gradient at the bit depth,

$\rho_{kick\ intensity}$: In CasingSeat software, this is considered to be a safety margin for shifting (reducing) the fracture gradient to the left (well/design parameters, kick tolerance, kick intensity),

D_{bit} is the bit depth,

D_{CS} is the assumed casing setting depth,

ρ_{mud} is the mud density, and

ρ_{kick} is the gas kick density calculated at specific temperature and pressure conditions, assuming methane gas.

3. Assuming a gas kick-density at the bottom of the bubble, while the bubble is at bit depth, the height of the bubble is calculated (Step 2 above). This height is then used to calculate the average gas density (at the midpoint of the bubble) as a function of PVT-z. The new density is used to recalculate the bubble height, and this iterative process continues until a convergence for the average gas density is attained.

4. The above calculations (Steps 2 and 3) are performed repetitively for various gas-bubble locations, as the bubble is considered to migrate up the open hole. For each location, the gas volume required to fracture the formation is calculated knowing the wellbore geometry.

5. Steps 2 through 4 are repeated for all additional depths of interest (defined in the lithology, pore-pressure, and fracture-gradient spreadsheets) in order to find the minimum gas volume required to fracture the formation at each one of these depths.

6. A minimum of the all gas kick volumes obtained in Steps 4 and 5 is obtained and then compared with the allowable gas-kick volume. If this calculated minimum volume is less than the allowable gas-kick volume, a new casing setting depth will be assumed at half the distance between the initial assumption and the bit depth. All of the above calculations are then repeated for the newly assumed casing setting depth (Steps 1 through 5).

7. If this calculated minimum volume is greater than the allowable gas-kick volume, the newly assumed casing setting depth will go the opposite direction at half the distance between the first casing setting depth (user defined in Design Parameters dialog) and the initial assumption. This calculation is performed until a convergence is obtained with an allowable tolerance of 5 ft, and the last valid result will, thus, be saved.

8. Once the shoe depth is fixed, the same calculations are repeated to obtain the next casing shoe depth, assuming this depth to be bit depth, etc., until the first casing setting depth is reached.

9. This completes the one-casing-scheme solution, assuming that kick tolerance is the only operating constraint. The entire process is repeated by starting with a different hole size and obtaining various solutions of casing schemes until the maximum casing OD (well/design parameters, general/first casing OD) is reached.

Similar calculations are performed for the **top-down design**, except that, here, the variable is the bit depth and not the casing setting depth.

References

An Engineering Approach to Horizontal Drilling – Halliburton Manual, 1992.

Cheatham, C.A. 1989. Improved Pressure-Volume Schedules for Circulating Out Kicks in Directional Wells. Paper SPE 18715 presented at the SPE/IADC Drilling Conference, New Orleans, Louisiana, 28 February–3 March.

Hage, J.I., Surewaard, J.H.G., and Vullinghs, P.J.J. 1992. Application of Research in Kick Detection and Well Control. *SIPM* Paper presented at the IADC European Well Control Conference, Noordwijkerhout, The Netherlands, 2–4 June.

Rabia, H. 1987. *Fundamentals of Casing Design*. Graham and Trotman.

Swift, S.C. and Holmes, C.S. 1970. Calculation of Circulating Mud Temperatures. *JPT*, **22**(06).

Van Everdingen, A.F. and Hurst, W. 1949. The Application of the Laplace Transformation to Flow Problems in Reservoirs. *Trans. AIDE*, **186**, 305–324.

CHAPTER **NINE**

Casing Design

The casing program for an ERD well represents a significant portion of the total well cost. An approach is required to reduce the tubular cost without sacrificing the safety and integrity of the well. Casings for different drilling phases are selected in such a way that a minimal cost for casing design is achieved.

Properties of Casing

The American Petroleum Institute (API) has established standards for oil/gas tubing and casing. Within these standards, tubing is defined as pipe with nominal diameters from 1.0 in. to 4.5 in., while casing sizes range from 4.5 in. to 20 in.

Casing is classified according to the following five properties:

- Type of manufacturing
- Steel grade

- Type of joints
- Length range
- Wall thickness (unit weight).

Steel Grades

API has adopted a casing-grade designation to define the strength of casing steels. This designation consists of a grade letter followed by a number that indicates the minimum yield strength of the steel in kpsi (1,000 psi).

Proprietary steel grades are also widely used in the industry, but these grades do not conform to API specifications.

Pipe Strength

To design a reliable casing string, it is necessary to know the actual strength of pipe under different load conditions. Burst strength, collapse-pressure resistance, and tensile strength are the most important mechanical properties of casing and tubing.

Burst Strength

If the casing is subjected to internal pressure that is higher than the external pressure, it is said that the casing is experiencing burst pressure. Burst-pressure conditions may occur during such scenarios such as during well-control operations, integrity tests, and squeeze cementing.

The burst strength of the pipe body is determined by the internal yield-pressure formula (API Bulletin 5C3 1985).

$$p = 0.875 \left[\frac{2 Y_p t}{D} \right] \qquad (9\text{-}1)$$

Where,

p is the minimum internal yield pressure (psi),

Y_p is the minimum yield strength (psi),

t is the nominal wall thickness (in.), and

D is the nominal outside diameter (OD) of the pipe (in.).

Eq. 9-1, commonly known as the *Barlow equation*, calculates the internal pressure at which the tangential (or hoop) stress at the inner wall of the pipe reaches the yield strength of the material. The expression can be derived from the Lamé equation for tangential stress by making the thin-wall assumption that $D/t \gg 1$. Most oilfield casing has a D/t between 15 and 25. The factor of 0.875 appearing in the equation represents the allowable manufacturing tolerance of -12.5% for wall thickness, as specified in API Specification 5C2 (1982).

Collapse Strength

If the external pressure on the pipe exceeds the internal pressure on the pipe, the casing is subjected to *collapse*. Such conditions may exist during cementing operations and well evacuations.

The API collapse criteria (API Bulletin 5C3 1985) consists of four collapse regimes determined by yield strength and D/t.

- *Yield-strength collapse* – based on yield at the inner wall, using the Lamé thick-wall elastic solution

- *Plastic collapse* – based on empirical data from 2,488 tests

- *Transition collapse* – a numerical curve fit between the plastic and elastic regimes

- *Elastic collapse* – based on theoretical elastic collapse; this criterion is independent of yield strength and applicable to very thin wall pipe.

Most oilfield tubulars experience collapse in the *plastic* and *transition* regimes.

Nominal dimensions are used in collapse equations. Collapse strength is primarily a function of the material's yield strength and slenderness ratio, D/t. Collapse strength as a function of D/t is shown in **Fig. 9.1**.

Yield-strength collapse (Eq. 9-2) is based on yield at the inner wall, using the Lamé thick-wall elastic solution. This criterion does not represent a "collapse" pressure at all. For thick-wall pipes ($D/t < 15\pm$), the tangential stress will exceed the yield strength of the material before a collapse-instability failure occurs.

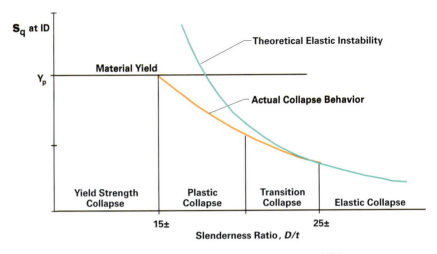

Fig. 9.1 – Collapse Strength as a Function of D/t.

$$p_{Y_p} = 2Y_p \left[\frac{(D/t)-1}{(D/t)^2} \right] \qquad (9\text{-}2)$$

Nominal dimensions are used in the collapse equations.

Plastic collapse is based on empirical data from 2,488 tests of K-55, N-80, and P-110 seamless casing. No analytical expression has been derived that accurately models collapse behavior in this regime.

The minimum collapse pressure for the plastic range of collapse is calculated using Eq. 9-3.

$$p_P = Y_p \left[\frac{A}{D/t} - B \right] - C \qquad (9\text{-}3)$$

Factors A, B, and C, and the applicable D/t range for the plastic collapse formula (Eq. 9-3) are shown in **Table 9-1**.

Transition collapse is obtained by a numerical curve fit between the plastic and elastic regimes. The minimum collapse pressure for the plastic-to-elastic transition zone, p_T, is calculated using Eq. 9-4.

$$p_T = Y_p \left[\frac{F}{D/t} - G \right] \qquad (9\text{-}4)$$

CASING DESIGN

Table 9.1 – Formula Factors and D/t Ranges for Plastic Collapse

1	2	3	4	5
		Formula Factor		
Grade•	A	B	C	D/t Range
H-40	2.950	0.0465	754	16.40 to 27.01
-50	2.976	0.0515	1056	15.24 to 25.63
J-K-55	2.991	0.0541	1206	14.81 to 25.01
-60	3.005	0.0566	1356	14.44 to 24.42
-70	3.037	0.0617	1656	13.85 to 23.38
C-75 & E	3.054	0.0642	1806	13.60 to 22.91
L-N-80	3.071	0.0667	1955	13.38 to 22.47
C-90	3.106	0.0718	2254	13.01 to 21.69
C-T-95 & X	3.124	0.0743	2404	12.85 to 21.33
-100	3.143	0.0768	2553	12.70 to 21.00
P-105 & G	3.162	0.0794	2702	12.57 to 20.70
P-110	3.181	0.0819	2852	12.44 to 20.41
-120	3.219	0.0870	3151	12.21 to 19.88
Q-125	3.239	0.0895	3301	12.11 to 19.63
-130	3.258	0.0920	3451	12.02 to 19.40
S-135	3.278	0.0946	3601	11.92 to 19.18
-140	3.297	0.0971	3751	11.84 to 18.97
-150	3.336	0.1021	4053	11.67 to 18.57
-155	3.356	0.1047	4204	11.59 to 18.37
-160	3.375	0.1072	4356	11.52 to 18.19
-170	3.412	0.1123	4660	11.37 to 17.82
-180	3.449	0.1173	4966	11.23 to 17.47

- Grades indicated without letter designation are not API grades, but are grades in use or grades being considered for use and are shown for informational purposes.

Factors, F and G, and the applicable D/t range for the transition-collapse pressure formula, are shown in **Table 9-2**.

Table 9.2 – Formula Factors and D/t Ranges for Transition Collapse

1	2	3	4
Grade•	Formula Factor F	Formula Factor G	D/t Range
H-40	2.063	0.0325	27.01 to 42.64
-50	2.003	0.0347	25.63 to 38.83
J-K-55	1.989	0.0360	25.01 to 37.21
-60	1.983	0.0373	24.42 to 35.73
-70	1.984	0.0403	23.38 to 33.17
C-75 & E	1.990	0.0418	22.91 to 32.05
L-N-80	1.998	0.0434	22.47 to 31.02
C-90	2.017	0.0466	21.69 to 29.18
C-T-95 & X	2.029	0.0482	21.33 to 28.36
-100	2.040	0.0499	21.00 to 27.60
P-105 & G	2.053	0.0515	20.70 to 26.89
P-100	2.066	0.0532	20.41 to 26.22
-120	2.092	0.0565	19.88 to 25.01
Q-125	2.106	0.0582	19.63 to 24.46
-130	2.119	0.0599	19.40 to 23.94
S-135	2.133	0.0615	19.18 to 23.44
-140	2.146	0.0632	18.97 to 22.98
-150	2.174	0.0666	18.57 to 22.11
-155	2.188	0.0683	18.37 to 21.70
-160	2.202	0.0700	18.19 to 21.32
-170	2.231	0.0734	17.82 to 20.60
-180	2.261	0.0769	17.47 to 19.93

• Grades indicated without letter designation are not API grades, but are grades in use or grades being considered for use, and are shown for informational purposes.

CASING DESIGN

Elastic collapse is based on theoretical elastic instability failure. This criterion is independent of yield strength and applicable to thin-wall pipe ($D/t > 25\pm$).

The minimum collapse pressure for the elastic range of collapse is calculated by Eq. 9-5.

$$p_E = \frac{46.95 \times 10^6}{(D/t)\left[(D/t) - 1\right]^2} \qquad (9\text{-}5)$$

The applicable D/t range for elastic collapse is shown in **Table 9-3**.

Table 9.3 – D/t Range for Eslastic Collapse

1	2
Grade•	Grade
H-40	42.64 and greater
-50	38.83 " "
J-K-55	37.21 " "
-60	35.73 " "
-70	33.17 " "
C-75 & E	32.05 " "
L-N-80	31.02 " "
C-90	29.18 " "
C-T-95 & X	28.36 " "
-100	27.60 " "
P-105 & G	26.89 " "
P-110	26.22 " "
-120	25.01 " "
Q-125	24.46 " "
-130	23.94 " "
S-135	23.44 " "
-140	22.98 " "
-150	22.11 " "
-155	21.70 " "
-160	21.32 " "
-170	20.60 " "
-180	19.93 " "

• Grades indicated without letter designation are not API grades, but are grades in use or grades being considered for use, and are shown for informational purposes.

Many manufacturers market "high-collapse" casing, which they claim has collapse performance properties that exceed the ratings calculated using the formulae in API Bulletin 5C3 (1985). This improved performance is the result of better manufacturing practices and stricter quality-assurance programs to reduce ovality, residual stress, and eccentricity.

If the pipe is subjected to both external and internal pressures, the equivalent external pressure, p_e, is calculated as follows:

$$p_e = p_o - \left(1 - \frac{2}{D/t}\right) p_i = \Delta p + \left(\frac{2}{D/t}\right) p_i \tag{9-6}$$

Where,

p_o is the external pressure,

p_i is the internal pressure, and

Δ_p is equal to $p_o - p_i$.

To provide a more intuitive understanding of this relationship, Eq. 9-6 can be rewritten as:

$$p_e D = p_o D - p_i d \tag{9-7}$$

Where,

d is the nominal inside diameter (ID).

Axial Strength

The axial strength of the pipe body is determined by the pipe-body yield-strength formula (API Bulletin 5C3 1985).

$$F_y = \frac{\pi}{4}\left(D^2 - d^2\right) Y_p \tag{9-8}$$

Where,

F_y is the pipe-body axial strength (in units of force).

Axial strength is the product of the cross-sectional area (based on nominal dimensions) and the yield strength.

Combined Stress Effects

All previous pipe-strength equations are based on a uniaxial stress state, a state in which only one of the three principal stresses is nonzero. Pipe in the wellbore, however, is always subjected to combined loading conditions.

To evaluate the pipe strength under combined loading conditions, the uniaxial yield strength is compared with the yielding condition. Perhaps the most widely accepted yielding criterion is based on the maximum distortion energy theory, which is known as the *Huber-Hencky-Mises yield condition*, or simply the *von Mises, triaxial*, or *equivalent stress* (Crandall and Dahl 1959).

Triaxial stress (equivalent stress) is not a true stress. It is a theoretical value that allows a generalized three-dimensional (3-D) stress state to be compared with a uniaxial failure criterion (the yield strength). In other words, if the triaxial stress exceeds the yield strength, a yield failure is indicated. The triaxial safety factor is the ratio of the material's yield strength to the triaxial stress.

For triaxial burst, the pipe stresses (axial stress, σ_a; bending stress, σ_b; circumferential stress, σ_θ; radial stress, σ_r; and torsional shear stress, τ) are calculated from the loads, using the Lamé equations (see API 5C3).

$$\sigma_a = \frac{F_a}{A_s} \tag{9-9a}$$

$$\sigma_b = \pm \frac{M_b}{I} r \tag{9-9b}$$

$$\sigma_\theta = \frac{p_i {}^*\!A_i - p_o A_o}{A_o - {}^*\!A_i} + (p_i - p_o)\frac{A_o}{A_o - {}^*\!A_i}\left(\frac{d_{min}}{2r}\right)^2 \tag{9-9c}$$

$$\sigma_r = \frac{p_i {}^*\!A_i - p_o A_o}{A_o - {}^*\!A_i} - (p_i - p_o)\frac{A_o}{A_o - {}^*\!A_i}\left(\frac{d_{min}}{2r}\right)^2 \tag{9-9d}$$

$$\tau = \frac{M_t}{J_p} r \tag{9-9e}$$

Where,

$d_{min} = OD - 2\,k_w\,WT$,

$A_o = \pi/4\,OD^2$,

*$A_i = \pi/4\,d_{min}^2$,

$A_s = \pi\,WT\,(OD-WT)$,

$d = OD - 2\,WT$, and

$I = \tfrac{1}{2} J_p = \pi/64\,(OD^4\,d^4)$.

Factor, k_w, accounts for the manufacturing tolerance of the pipe wall, and r represents the radial coordinate. Note that the stresses are linear, homogeneous functions of the load variables.

The von Mises equivalent stress is:

$$\sigma_{eq} = \sqrt{(\sigma_a + \sigma_b - \sigma_r)^2 - (\sigma_a + \sigma_b - \sigma_r)(\sigma_\theta - \sigma_r) + (\sigma_\theta - \sigma_r)^2 + 3\tau^2} \qquad (9\text{-}10)$$

And the yield envelope is given by $\sigma_{eq} = YS$.

For an arbitrary load point, Eq. 9-6 states that the safety factor, SF, is the multiplier to all load variables in order to reach the yield envelope. For the case of triaxial burst, it follows from Eqs. 9-9 and 9-10 that scaling the load variables by SF leads to stresses scaled by SF, and, thus, the equivalent stress is scaled by SF. The yield envelope is then reached when $SF\,\sigma_{eq} = YS$; hence, for this case, the safety factor is obtained as YS/σ_{eq}. Note that this familiar result is only found if all the load variables are scaled, exactly as Eq. 9-6 proposes.

Fig. 9.2 illustrates the axial, tangential, and radial stress components.

The calculated axial stress, σ_z, at any point along the cross-sectional area should include the effects of self-weight, buoyancy, pressure loads, bending, shock loads, frictional drag, point loads, temperature loads, and buckling loads. Except for bending/buckling loads, axial loads are normally considered to be constant over the entire cross-sectional area.

CASING DESIGN

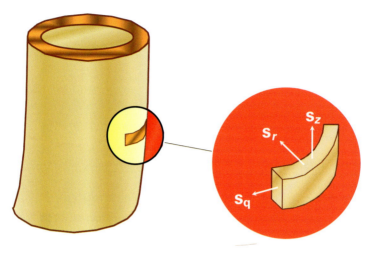

Fig. 9.2 – Axial, Tangential, and Radial Stress Components.

The tangential and radial stresses are calculated using the Lamé equations (Timoshenko 1961) for thick-wall cylinders as follows:

$$\sigma_\theta = \frac{r_i^2 + r_i^2 r_o^2/r^2}{r_o^2 - r_i^2} p_i - \frac{r_o^2 + r_i^2 r_o^2/r^2}{r_o^2 - r_i^2} p_o \qquad (9\text{-}11)$$

$$\sigma_r = \frac{r_i^2 - r_i^2 r_o^2/r^2}{r_o^2 - r_i^2} p_i - \frac{r_o^2 - r_i^2 r_o^2/r^2}{r_o^2 - r_i^2} p_o \qquad (9\text{-}12)$$

Where,

r_i is the inner-wall radius,

r_o is the outer-wall radius, and

r is the radius at which the stress occurs.

Combined Collapse and Tension

Assuming that σ_z and $\sigma_\theta \gg \sigma_r$, and setting the triaxial stress equal to the yield strength, the following equation of an ellipse results:

$$Y_p = \left[\sigma_z^2 - \sigma_z \sigma_\theta + \sigma_\theta^2\right]^{1/2} \qquad (9\text{-}13)$$

This well-known *biaxial* criterion used in API Bulletin 5C3 accounts for the effect of tension on collapse.

$$Y_{pa} = \left[\sqrt{1 - 0.75\left(\frac{S_a}{Y_p}\right)^2} - 0.5\frac{S_a}{Y_p}\right] Y_p \qquad (9\text{-}14)$$

Where,

S_a is the axial stress based on the buoyant weight of pipe (psi).

As S_a (in this case, tension) increases, the pipe's resistance to collapse pressure decreases. Plotting this ellipse allows a direct comparison of the triaxial criterion with the API ratings. Loads within the design envelope meet the design criteria.

Combined Burst and Compression Loading

Combined burst and compression loading corresponds to the upper-left quadrant of the design envelope. Triaxial analysis is most critical in this region because reliance on uniaxial criteria alone will not predict several possible failures.

For high burst loads (high tangential stress) and moderate compression, a burst failure can occur at a differential pressure that is less than the API burst pressure. For high compression and moderate burst loads, the failure mode is permanent corkscrewing, which is plastic deformation caused by helical buckling. This combined loading typically occurs when a high internal pressure is experienced (caused by a tubing leak or a buildup of annular pressure) after the casing temperature has been increased because of production. The temperature increase in the uncemented portion of the casing causes thermal growth, which can significantly increase compression and buckling. The increased internal pressure also results in increased buckling.

Combined Burst and Tension Loading

Combined burst and tension loading corresponds to the upper-right quadrant of the design envelope. In this region, reliance on the uniaxial criteria alone can result in a design that is more conservative than necessary.

For high burst loads and moderate tension, a burst yield failure will not occur until after the API burst pressure has been exceeded. As the tension approaches the axial limit, a burst failure can occur at a differential pressure that is less than the API value. For high tension and moderate burst loads, pipe-body yield will not occur until a tension greater than the uniaxial rating is reached.

By taking advantage of increased burst resistance in the presence of tension, design engineers can reduce casing costs without jeopardizing wellbore integrity. Similarly, engineers may wish to allow loads that fall between the uniaxial and triaxial tension ratings. However, great care should be taken in the latter case because of the uncertainty of what burst pressure may occur in conjunction with a high tensile load. In addition, connection ratings could limit an engineer's ability to design in this region.

Use of Triaxial Criterion for Collapse Loading

For most oilfield pipe, collapse is either an inelastic stability failure or an elastic stability failure independent of yield strength. Since the triaxial criterion is based on elastic behavior and the yield strength of the material, it should not be used with collapse loads. The one exception is for thick-wall pipes with a low D/t ratio that have an API rating in the yield-strength collapse region. This collapse criterion, along with the effects of tension and internal pressure (which are triaxial effects), result in the API criterion being essentially identical to the triaxial method in the lower-right quadrant of the triaxial ellipse for thick-wall pipes.

For high-compression and moderate-collapse loads experienced in the lower-left quadrant of the design envelope, the failure mode may be permanent corkscrewing as a result of helical buckling. Triaxial criterion should be used in this case. Typically, this load combination occurs only in wells that experience a large temperature increase as a result of production. The combination of a collapse load that causes reverse ballooning and a temperature increase, together, increases compression in the uncemented portion of the string.

Fig. 9.3 summarizes the triaxial, uniaxial, and biaxial limits that should be used in the casing design and provides a set of consistent design factors.

EXTENDED-REACH DRILLING

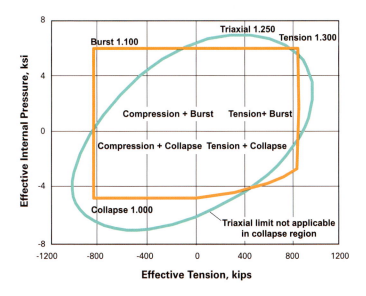

Fig. 9.3 – Triaxial, Uniaxial, and Biaxial Limits for Casing Design.

Although the von Mises criterion is the most accurate method for representing elastic yield behavior, its use in tubular design should be undertaken with the following precautions in mind:

- For most pipe used in oilfield applications, collapse is frequently an instability failure that occurs before the computed maximum triaxial stress reaches the yield strength. As a result, triaxial stress should *not* be used as a collapse criterion. Only in thick-wall pipe does yielding occur before collapse.

- The accuracy of triaxial analysis depends upon the accurate representation of (1) the conditions that exist when the pipe is installed in the well and (2) the subsequent loads of interest.

Connections

Threaded connections are the mechanical means for joining neighboring tubing or casing joints. These threads must hold joints together during axial tension and compression.

CASING DESIGN

Selection of a threaded connection may depend on strength requirements, the ability to re-cut the thread, cost, or leak resistance. For all casing sizes, the threads are not intended to be leak-resistant when made up.

Coupling Internal Yield Pressure

The internal yield pressure is the pressure that will initiate yield at the root of the coupling thread.

$$p = Y_c \left(\frac{W - d_1}{W} \right) \qquad (9\text{-}15)$$

Where,

Y_c is the minimum yield strength of the coupling (psi),

W is the nominal OD of the coupling (in.), and

d_1 is the diameter (in.) at the root of the coupling thread in the power-tight position.

This dimension is based on data given in API Specification 5B and other thread geometry data.

The coupling internal yield pressure is typically greater than the pipe body internal yield pressure. The internal-pressure leak resistance is based on the interface pressure between the pipe and coupling threads as a result of makeup.

$$p = \frac{ETNP_t(W2 - E_s^2)}{2E_s W^2} \qquad (9\text{-}16)$$

Where,

p is the internal-pressure leak resistance,

E is the modulus of elasticity,

T is the thread taper,

N is a function of the number of thread turns from the hand-tight to power-tight position,

P_t is the thread pitch, and

E_s is the pitch diameter at the plane of the seal, as given in API Specification 5B.

Round-Thread Casing-Joint Strength

The round-thread casing-joint strength is given as the lesser of the *pin* fracture strength and the jump-out strength. The pin fracture strength is determined from Eq. 9-17.

$$F_j = 0.95 A_{jp} U_p \tag{9-17}$$

The jump-out strength is determined from Eq. 9-18.

$$F_j = 0.95 A_{jp} L \left[\frac{0.74 D^{-0.59} U_p}{0.5L + 0.14D} + \frac{Y_p}{L + 0.14D} \right] \tag{9-18}$$

Where,

F_j is the minimum joint strength (lbf),

A_{jp} is the cross-sectional area (in.²) of the pipe wall under the last perfect thread, which is equal to $\pi/4[(D - 0.1425)^2 - d^2]$,

L is the engaged thread length given in API Specification 5B, and

U_p is the minimum ultimate tensile strength of pipe (psi).

Buttress-Thread Casing-Joint Strength

The buttress-thread casing-joint strength is given as the lesser of the fracture strength of the pipe body (the pin) and the coupling (the box).

Pipe-Thread Strength

$$F_j = 0.95 A_p U_p \left[1.008 - 0.0396 \left(1.083 - Y_p / U_p \right) D \right] \tag{9-19}$$

Coupling-Thread Strength

$$F_j = 0.95 A_c U_c \tag{9-20}$$

Where,

U_c is the minimum ultimate tensile strength of the coupling,

A_p is the cross-sectional area of the plain-end pipe, and

A_c is the cross-sectional area of the coupling, which is equal to $\pi/4(W^2 - d_1^2)$.

Extreme-Line Casing-Joint Strength

Extreme-line casing-joint strength is calculated as follows:

$$F_j = A_{cr} U_p \tag{9-21}$$

Where,

A_{cr} is the critical section area of the box, pin, or pipe, depending on which area is smallest.

When designing the casing, it is very important to note that the API joint-strength values are a function of the *ultimate tensile strength*. This is a different criterion than that used to define the axial strength of the pipe body, which is based on *yield strength*.

Connection Design Limits

Connection design limits are also a function of operational variables, including:

1. The type of thread compound used,
2. Makeup torque,
3. The use of a resilient seal ring (which is not recommended by many manufacturers and service companies),
4. The type of fluid exposure (drilling fluid, clear brine, or gas),
5. Temperature and pressure cycling, and
6. The presence of large doglegs in medium- or short-radius horizontal wells.

EXTENDED-REACH DRILLING

Radial Safety Factor

Traditionally, the collapse safety factor (*SF*) is the ratio of tubular collapse resistance to collapse load. The collapse resistance is usually calculated using formulas suggested in API 5C3 or ISO 10400. If the collapse load is very small while the tension stress and/or internal pressure are high, the collapse *SF* could be very large, which is unrealistic because the load point is close to the collapse envelope. A radial approach for collapse *SF* calculation provides a new solution. Moreover, the application of this approach can be properly extended to the calculation of both the burst and connection *SFs* for arbitrary load combinations.

The new *SF* is called the "radial safety factor" and must meet the following requirement: when all of the tubular loads (axial force, internal pressure, and external pressure) are scaled by this *SF*, the load point must fall exactly within the failure envelope. Therefore, for collapse, the new *SF* must simultaneously satisfy (1) API 5C3 collapse formulas and (2) the through-load-point radial line equation. Ridders' method is used to solve the *SF* for a specific load case. The algorithm has been implemented in a computer program and integrated with commercial software. This radial approach has been applied to both the pipe body and connectors.

Generalization to Combined Loading

In tubular design, there are always a number of loads and forces acting at the same time, and, therefore, the concept of the safety factor needs to be generalized for combined loading. Let us gather these load/force variables, such as axial force, F_a, internal pressure, p_i, external pressure, p_o, bending moment, M_b, and torque, M_t, into a vector (Eq. 9-22) and pipe parameters, such as the outside diameter, *OD*, wall thickness, *WT*, minimum wall thickness, WT_{min}, ovality, *OV*, eccentricity, *EC*, residual stress, *RS*, yield stress, *YS*, and Young's modulus, *E*, into a vector (Eq. 9-23), while including the notion of a model uncertainty factor, X_m.

$$\vec{x} = \{F_a, p_i, p_o, M_b, M_t, ...\} \qquad (9\text{-}22)$$

$$\vec{\beta} = \{X_m \ ; \ OD, WT, WT_{min}, OV, EC, RS, YS, E, ...\} \qquad (9\text{-}23)$$

CASING DESIGN

Any pipe- or connection-strength envelope (i.e., the "limit state") may then be defined as:

$$G(\vec{x}, \vec{\beta}) = 0 \qquad (9\text{-}24)$$

The value $\vec{x}_r$ gives the load combinations at the limit state satifying the equation 9-24 This is illustrated in **Fig. 9.4** for the situation that there are only two loads.

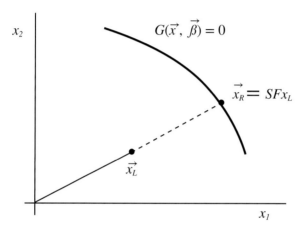

Fig. 9.4 – Definition of the Safety Factor, SF, Scaling the Load Point, $\vec{x}_{R'}$ to the Resistance Point, $\vec{x}_{R'}$ on the Strength Envelope, G = 0.

With the resistance, R, generalized to the strength envelope, $\vec{x}_R$, for which $G = 0$, we can generalize the load, L, to the load point, $\vec{x}_R$. For combined loading, the safety factor is then defined by:

$$\vec{x}_R = SF\,\vec{x}_L \qquad (9\text{-}25)$$

In other words, the safety factor is that factor that would scale the load-point vector to reach the strength envelope. Alternatively, the radial SF can be defined as the factor that would scale the strength envelope to reach the load point. For homogeneous materials, the strength envelope can be scaled down by dividing the material strength properties, such as ultimate tensile strength (UTS), yield strength (YS), and Young's modulus (E), by SF. This equivalency is further verified in the following discussions about triaxial burst and Klever-Tamano (KT) collapse of the pipe body.

Effect of Parameter Derating

Suppose we want to derate the strength envelope for elevated temperatures, what would the effect be on the safety factor? This may be illustrated by an example where the yield strength is derated for temperature.

At room temperature, the strength envelope, $\vec{x}_R$, is determined by Eq. 9-26.

$$\vec{\beta} = \{..., YS, ...\} \quad ; \quad G(\vec{x}, \vec{\beta}) = 0 \rightarrow \vec{x}_R \qquad (9\text{-}26)$$

Whereas, at elevated temperature (**Fig. 9.4**), the strength envelope is reduced, following from:

$$^T\vec{\beta} = \{..., {}^T YS, ...\} \quad ; \quad G(\vec{x}, {}^T\vec{\beta}) = 0 \rightarrow {}^T\vec{x}_R = \lambda \vec{x}_R \qquad (9\text{-}27)$$

thus defining the temperature deration factor, λ.

From Eq. 9-26, we can derive Eq. 9-28, which shows (**Fig. 9.5**) that the safety factor, $^T SF$, between a load point, $\vec{x}_L$, and the derated strength envelope, $^T\vec{x}_R$, is the same as when upscaling the load point to $^T\vec{x}_L = \vec{x}_L / \lambda$ and comparing that to the original strength envelope, $\vec{x}_R$.

$$\lambda \vec{x}_R = {}^T\vec{x}_R = {}^T SF\, \vec{x}_L \quad \text{or} \quad \vec{x}_R = {}^T SF\, \frac{\vec{x}_L}{\lambda} = {}^T SF\, {}^T\vec{x}_L \qquad (9\text{-}28)$$

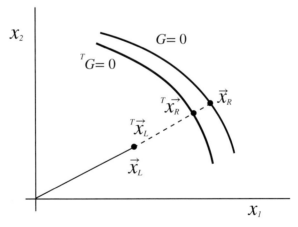

Fig. 9.5 – The Safety Factor Between the Load Point, $\vec{x}_L$, and the Derated Strength, $^T\vec{x}_R$, is the Same as between the Upscaled Load Point, $^T\vec{x}_R$, and the Original-Strength Envelope, $\vec{x}_R$.

Pipe-Body Collapse

The legacy collapse-strength formulas in API 5C3, Chapter 8, or Annex E describe the collapse strength, p_c, as a function of the diameter-over-thickness ratio, yield stress, Young's modulus, and the three load variables (internal pressure, external pressure, and axial stress). For an arbitrary load point $\{p_i, p_o, s_a\}$, the safety factor follows from the equation for the strength envelope.

$$G = p_c \left\{ \frac{OD}{WT}, YS_{ax}\{SF\, \sigma_a\}, E \right\} + \left(1 - 2\frac{WT}{OD}\right) SF\, p_i - SF\, p_o = 0 \quad (9\text{-}29)$$

Where, $f\{x_i\}$ denotes a function of variables, x_i.

In 2015, an addendum to API 5C3 was issued that altered the method of accounting for combined loading in collapse strength (Greenip 2016), which means that the API 5C3 collapse-strength envelope becomes:

$$G = p_c \left\{ \frac{OD}{WT}, YS_{com}\{SF\,(\sigma_a + p_i)\}, E \right\} + SF\,(p_i - p_o) = 0 \quad (9\text{-}30)$$

Connections Burst and Collapse

Given a connection-strength envelope (CSE) of an arbitrary but realistic shape, the radial approach for calculating the safety factor is a suitable method. As shown in **Fig. 9.6**, a casing connection has a closed strength envelope (thick, blue line). For the burst load at point A inside the envelope, the radial line intersects the envelope at point C. Therefore, the safety factor is represented as:

$$SF = |OC| / |OA| \quad (9\text{-}31)$$

The calculation of safety factor avoids the ambiguity that occurs when using different definitions for different load combinations, such as the ratio of tension capacity |OD| to tension load |OS| or the ratio of burst strength |SQ| to burst load |SA|, with:

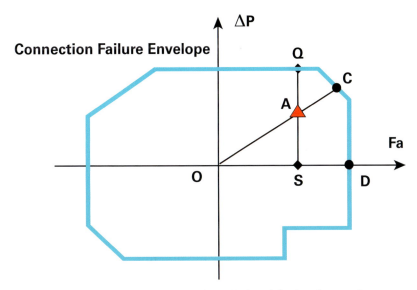

Fig. 9.6 – Radial Safety Factor for a Notional Casing Connection.

Loads on Casing Strings

Casing loads result from running the casing, cementing the casing, subsequent drilling operations, production, and well workover operations.

Casing loads are principally:

- Pressure loads,
- Mechanical loads, and
- Thermal loads.

Pressure loads are produced by:

- Fluids within the casing,
- Cement and fluids outside the casing,
- Pressures imposed at the surface by drilling and workover operations, and
- Pressures imposed by the formation during drilling and production.

Mechanical loads are associated with:

- Casing hanging weight,
- Shock loads during running,
- Packer loads during production and workovers, and
- Hanger loads.

Thermal loads are associated with temperature changes. Temperature changes and resulting *thermal expansion loads* are induced in casing by drilling, production, and workovers, and these loads may cause buckling (bending stress) loads in uncemented intervals.

The following casing loads are typically used in preliminary casing design.

External-Pressure Loads

The following pressure distributions are typically used to model the external pressures in cemented intervals.

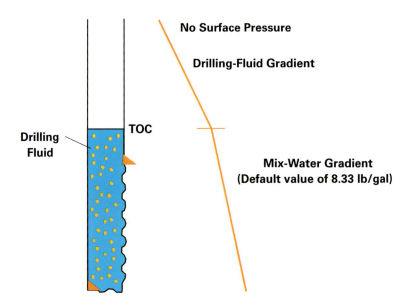

Fig. 9.7 – Mud-Cement Mix-Water External-Pressure Profile.

The external pressure is given at a certain depth ($TVD < TVD_{toc}$) in which:

$$P_{external} = g \times \rho_{mud} \times TVD$$

At depths greater than $TVD > TVD_{toc}$,

$$P_{external} = g \times \rho_{mud} \times TVD_{toc} + g \times \rho_{cem} \times (TVD - TVD_{toc})$$

Where,

ρ_{mud} is the mud gradient,

ρ_{cem} is the cement mix-water gradient (internal pore-fluid pressure gradient), and

TVD_{toc} is the true vertical depth of the top of cement.

This pressure profile is continuous with depth.

Mud and Cement Slurry (Collapse)

From the hanger to the top of cement (TOC), the external-pressure profile is given by:

$$P_{external} = g \times \rho_{mud} \times TVD$$

From the TOC to the top of the tail slurry:

$$P_{toc} = g \times \rho_{mud} \times TVD_{toc}$$

$$P_{external} = P_{toc} + g \times \rho_{lead\ slurry} \times (TVD - TVD_{toc})$$

From the top of the tail slurry to the shoe:

$$P_{tail\ slurry\ top} = P_{toc} + g \times \rho_{lead\ slurry} \times (TVD_{tail\ slurry\ top} - TVD_{toc})$$

$$P_{external} = P_{tail\ slurry\ top} + g \times \rho_{tail\ slurry} \times (TVD - TVD_{tail\ slurry\ top})$$

Hydrostatic Isolation Depth (HID)

The external pressure is given by the following.

From the hanger to the weak formation depth:

$$P_{external} = P_{frac} + g \times \rho_{mud} \times (TVD_{weak\ formation\ depth} - TVD_{toc})$$

From the weak formation depth to the HID:

$$P_{external} = P_{frac} - g \times \rho_{mud} \times (TVD - TVD_{weak\,formation\,depth})$$

From the HID to the current shoe:

$$P_{external} = pore\ pressure\ at\ TVD$$

The collapse-load external-pressure profile is given by the following (where TOC < Prior Shoe Depth or HID Depth < Prior Shoe Depth).

From the hanger to the HID:

$$P_{external} = g \times \rho_{mud} \times TVD$$

From the HID to the prior shoe:

$$P_{external} = g \times \rho_{EMW}\ at\ prior\ shoe \times TVD$$

From the prior shoe to the current shoe:

$$P_{external} = pore\ pressure\ at\ TVD$$

Permeable Zones: (Burst and Collapse)

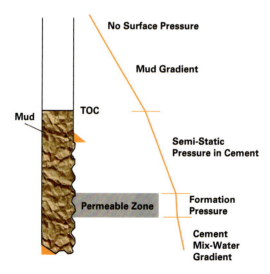

Fig. 9.8 – Permeable Zones – External-Pressure Profile: Good Cement.

The external pressure is given at a certain depth ($TVD < TVD_{toc}$) in which:

$$P_{external} = g \times \rho_{mud} \times TVD$$

For the condition such that $TVD_{toc} < TVD < TVD_{depth}$,

$$P_{external} = g \times \rho_{mud} \times TVD_{toc} + [P_{depth} - \rho_{mud} \times TVD] \times (TVD - TVD_{toc})$$

For the condition in which $TVD_{depth} < TVD < TVD_{fb}$,

$$P_{external} = P_{depth}$$

For depths greater than $TVD > TVD_{fb}$,

$$P_{external} = P_{fb} + \rho_{cem} \times (TVD - TVD_{fb})$$

Where,

$P_{external}$ is the formation pore-pressure profile over the permeable zone interval, TVD_{ft} to TVD_{fb} true vertical depths (ft).

For example, if P_{depth} was a linear distribution, then:

$$P_{depth} = p + (p_{fb} - p)(TVD - TVD_{depth})/(TVD_{fb} - TVD_{depth})$$

Where,

P_{depth} is the pressure at TVD_{ft}, and

P_{fb} is the pressure at TVD_{fb}.

This pressure profile is continuous with depth.

The external pressure is given at a certain depth ($TVD < TVD_{toc}$) in which:

$$P_{external} = P_{tf} + g \times \rho_{cem} \times (TVD_{toc} - TVD_{ft}) + g \times \rho_m \times (TVD - TVD_{toc})$$

For depths greater than $TVD > TVD_{fb}$,

$$P_{external} = P_{fb} + g \times \rho_{cem} \times (TVD - TVDft)$$

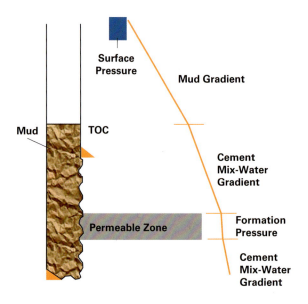

Fig. 9.9 – Permeable Zones – External-Pressure Profile: Poor Cement – High-Pressure Zone.

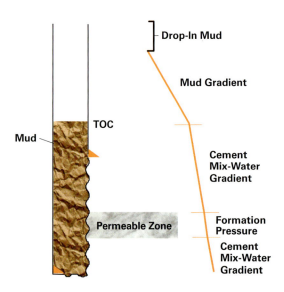

Fig. 9.10 – Permeable Zones – External-Pressure Profile: Poor Cement – Low-Pressure Zone.

For the condition in which $TVD_{ft} < TVD < TVD_{fb}$,

$$P_{external} = P_{ft}$$

For depths greater than $TVD > TVD_{fb}$,

$$P_{external} = P_{fb} + g \times \rho_{cem} \times (TVD - TVD_{fb})$$

In this case, the formation pore pressure is felt at the surface through the poor cement. This pressure profile is continuous with depth.

The external pressure is given at a certain depth ($TVD < TVD_{md}$) such that:

$$P_{external} = 0$$

For the condition in which $TVD_{md} < TVD < TVD_{toc}$,

$$P_{external} = P_{tf} + g \times \rho_{cem} \times (TVD_{toc} - TVD_{ft}) + g \times \rho_m \times (TVD - TVD_{toc})$$

For the condition in which $TVD_{toc} < TVD < TVD_{ft}$,

$$P_{external} = P_{tf} + g \times \rho_{cem} \times (TVD - TVD_{ft})$$

For the condition in which $TVD_{ft} < TVD < TVD_{fb}$,

$$P_{external} = P_f$$

For depths greater than $TVD > TVD_{fb}$,

$$P_{external} = P_{fb} + g \times \rho_{cem} \times (TVD - TVD_{fb})$$

Where, the mud drop TVD_{md} is defined as:

$$TVD_{md} = TVD_{toc} - [P_{tf} + \rho_{cem}(TVD_{toc} - TVD_{ft})]/\rho m$$

This pressure profile is continuous with depth.

Fluid Gradients with Pore Pressure (Burst and Collapse)

The external pressure is given at a certain depth ($TVD < TVD_{toc}$) such that:

$$P_{external} = g \times \rho_{mud} \times TVD$$

CASING DESIGN

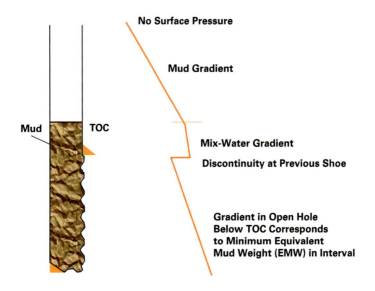

Fig. 9.11 – Openhole Pore Pressure – External-Pressure Profile: TOC Inside Previous Shoe.

For the condition in which $TVD_s < TVD < TVD_{toc}$,

$P_{external} = g \times \rho_{mud} \times TVD_{toc} + g \times \rho_{cem} \times (TVD - TVD_{toc})$

For the condition in which $TVD < TVD_s$,

$P_{external} = g \times \rho_{em} \times TVD$

Where,

TVD_s is the true vertical location of the previous shoe, and

ρ_{em} is the minimum equivalent mud-weight gradient of the open hole below the shoe.

This pressure profile is not continuous with depth; it is discontinuous at the previous shoe.

TOC Below Previous Shoe Without Mud Drop

The external pressure is given at a certain depth ($TVD < TVD_{toc}$) such that:

$$P_{external} = g \times \rho_{mud} \times TVD$$

For the condition in which $TVD < TVD_{toc}$,

$$P_{external} = g \times \rho_{em} \times TVD$$

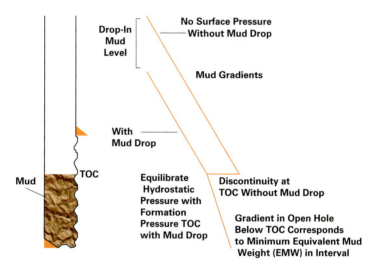

Fig. 9.12 – Open-Hole Pore Pressure – External-Pressure Profile.

This pressure profile is not continuous with depth; it is discontinuous at the top of cement.

TOC Below Previous Shoe with Mud Drop

The external pressure is given at a certain depth ($TVD < TVD_{md}$) such that:

$$P_{external} = 0$$

For the condition in which $TVD_{md} < TVD < TVD_{toc}$,

$$P_{external} = g \times \rho_{em} \times TVD_{toc} + g \times \rho_m \times (TVD - TVD_{toc})$$

For the condition in which $TVD_{toc} < TVD$,

$P_{external} = g \times \rho_{em} \times TVD$

Where, mud-drop TVD_{md} is defined as $TVD_{md} = TVD_{toc} - \rho em\, TVD_{toc}/\rho_m$. This pressure profile is continuous with depth.

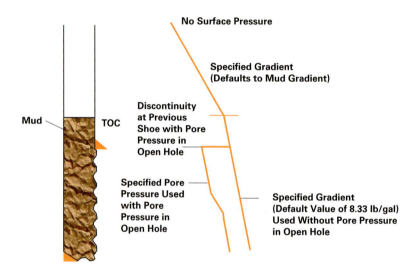

Fig. 9.13 – Above/Below TOC – External-Pressure Profile.

With Specified Pore Pressure in Open Hole

The external pressure is given at a certain depth ($TVD < TVD_{toc}$) such that:

$P_{external} = g \times \rho_{em} \times TVD$

For the condition in which $TVD_s < TVD < TVD_{toc}$,

$P_{external} = g \times \rho_m \times TVD_{toc} + g \times \rho_{cem} \times (TVD - TVD_{toc})$

For the condition in which $TVD > TVD_s$,

$P_{external} = P_{spec}$

Where,

P_{spec} is the specified openhole pore pressure.

This external-pressure distribution may be discontinuous at z_s, depending on $P_{spec}(z)$.

With Specified Pore-Pressure Gradient in Open Hole

The external pressure is given at a certain depth ($TVD < TVD_{toc}$) such that:

$P_{external} = g \times \rho_m \times TVD$

For the condition in which $TVD_s > TVD > TVD_{toc}$,

$P_{external} = g \times \rho_m \times TVD_{toc} + g \times \rho_{pp} \times (TVD - TVD_{toc})$

Where,

ρ_{pp} is the specified openhole pore-pressure gradient.

This pressure distribution is continuous.

For an onshore well, this logic simplifies to the following from mean ground level (MGL) to the shoe.

$P_{external} = [(TVD - TVD_{mgl}) / (TVD_{shoe} - TVD_{mgl})] \times P_{pore}$

Above/Below Prior Shoe (Liners)

From the prior shoe to the hanger:

$P_{prior\ shoe} = g \times EMW_{min} \times TVD_{prior\ shoe}$

$P_{external} = P_{prior\ shoe} - g \times \rho_{mix\text{-}water} \times (TVD_{prior\ shoe} - TVD)$

From the prior shoe to the current shoe:

$P_{external} = g \times EMW_{min} \times TVD$

Minimum Formation Pore Pressure (Burst)

Mud-Drop Option Enabled and TOC in Open Hole

The TVD at the mud level is determined from:

$P_{shoe} = g \times EMW_{min} \times TVD_{shoe}$ or $P_{toc} = g \times EMW_{min} \times TVD_{toc}$

$TVD_{equivalent} = P_{shoe} / (g \times \rho_{mud})$ or $TVD_{equivalent} = P_{toc} / (g \times \rho_{mud})$

$TVD_{mud\ level} = max\{ TVD_{hanger}, TVD_{shoe} - TVD_{equivalent} \}$

Where, the TVD for EMW_{min} is either TVD_{shoe} or TVD_{toc}, depending on whether the minimum EMW in the open hole is applied at the prior-string shoe or at the current-string top of cement.

From the hanger to the prior shoe (if EMW_{min} is applied from the prior shoe):

$P_{external} = max\{ P_{atm}, P_{atm} + P_{shoe} - g \times \rho_{mud} \times (TVD_{shoe} - TVD) \}$

From the prior shoe to the current shoe (if EMW_{min} is applied from the prior shoe):

$P_{external} = g \times EMW_{min} \times TVD$

From the hanger to the TOC (if EMW_{min} is applied from the TOC):

$P_{external} = max\{ P_{atm}, P_{atm} + P_{toc} - g \times \rho_{mud} \times (TVD_{toc} - TVD) \}$

From the TOC to current shoe (if EMW_{min} is applied from the TOC):

$P_{external} = g \times EMW_{min} \times TVD$

Mud-Drop Option Disabled and TOC in Open Hole

From the hanger to the prior shoe:

$P_{external} = g \times \rho_{mud} \times TVD$

From the prior shoe to the current shoe (if EMW_{min} is applied from the previous shoe):

$$P_{external} = g \times EMW_{min} \times TVD$$

From the prior shoe to the TOC (if EMW_{min} is applied from the TOC):

$$P_{external} = g \times \rho_{mud} \times TVD$$

From the TOC to the current shoe (if EMW_{min} is applied from the TOC):

$$P_{external} = g \times EMW_{min} \times TVD$$

TOC in Cased Hole

From the hanger to the TOC:

$$P_{external} = g \times \rho_{mud} \times TVD$$

From the TOC to the prior shoe:

$$P_{toc} = g \times \rho_{mud} \times TVD_{toc}$$

$$P_{external} = P_{toc} + g \times \rho_{mix\text{-}water} \times (TVD - TVD_{toc})$$

From the prior shoe to the current shoe:

$$P_{external} = g \times EMW_{min} \times TVD$$

Green Cement Pressure Test (Collapse – External)

From the hanger to the TOC, the external pressure profile is given by:

$$P_{external} = g \times \rho_{mud} \times TVD$$

From the TOC to the top of the tail slurry:

$$P_{toc} = g \times \rho_{mud} \times TVD_{toc}$$

$$P_{external} = P_{toc} + g \times \rho_{lead\ slurry} \times (TVD - TVD_{toc})$$

From the top of the tail slurry to the shoe:

$$P_{tail\ slurry\ top} = P_{toc} + g \times \rho_{lead\ slurry} \times (TVD_{tail\ slurry\ top} - TVD_{toc})$$

$$P_{external} = P_{tail\ slurry\ top} + g \times \rho_{tail\ slurry} \times (TVD - TVD_{tail\ slurry\ top})$$

Pressure Load Cases

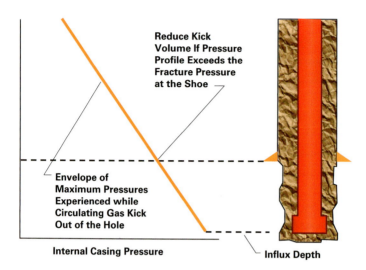

Fig. 9.14 – Burst (Drilling): Gas Kick.

This load case uses an internal-pressure profile, which is the envelope of the maximum pressures that the casing experiences while circulating out a gas kick using the driller's method. It should represent the worst-case kick to which the current casing can be exposed while a deeper interval is drilled. Typically, this means the casing will have to withstand a kick at the target depth (TD) of the next hole section.

If the kick volume causes the pressure to exceed the maximum fracture pressure at the casing shoe, it is reduced to the maximum volume that can be circulated out of the hole without exceeding the fracture pressure at the shoe. The maximum pressure experienced at any casing depth occurs when the top of the gas bubble reaches that depth.

This load case uses an internal-pressure profile consisting of a gas gradient extending upward from a formation pressure in a deeper hole interval or from the fracture pressure at the casing shoe.

$$p(z) = p_f - \gamma_g z \qquad (9\text{-}32)$$

Where,

γ_g is the gas gradient in psi/ft.

This pressure physically represents a well-control situation in which gas from a kick has completely displaced the mud out of the drilling annulus from the surface to the casing shoe. This load is the worst-case drilling-burst load that a casing string could experience. If the fracture pressure at the shoe is used to determine the pressure profile, it ensures that the weak point in the system is at the casing shoe and not at the surface. This precludes a burst failure of the casing near the surface during a severe well-control situation.

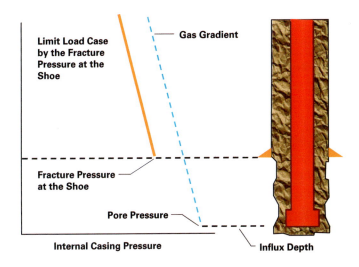

Fig. 9.15 – Burst (Drilling): Displacement to Gas.

This load case is a variation of the displacement-to-gas load case that is widely used in the industry and taught in several popular casing-design schools. Historically, this load case has been used because it results in an adequate, but conservative, design (particularly for wells deeper than 15,000 ft) and is easy to calculate. The load case consists of a gas gradient (typically, 0.1 psi/ft) extending upward from the fracture pressure at the shoe up to a mud/gas interface and then from the mud gradient to the surface, as shown by Eqs. 9.33 and 9.34.

CASING DESIGN

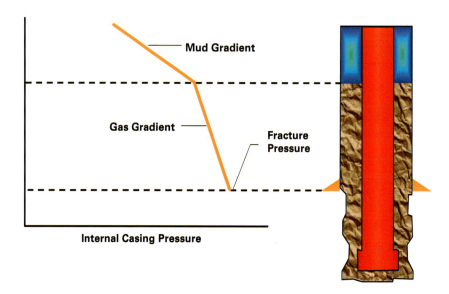

Fig. 9.16 – Burst (Drilling): Maximum Load Concept.

$$p(z) = p_{frac} + \gamma_m (z - z_{int}) + \gamma_g (z_{int} - z_{shoe}) \quad z < z_{int} \quad (9\text{-}33)$$

$$p(z) = p_{frac} + \gamma_g (z - z_{shoe}) \quad\quad\quad z_{int} < z < z_{shoe} \quad (9\text{-}34)$$

Where,

p_{frac} is the frac pressure at the depth of the shoe, z_{shoe}, and

γ_m is the mud gradient above the mud/gas interface depth, z_{int}.

The mud/gas interface is calculated in a number of ways, the most common being the *fixed-endpoint* method. The interface is calculated based on a surface pressure typically equal to the blowout preventer (BOP) rating and the fracture pressure at the shoe, and a continuous pressure profile is assumed. The interface can also be based on a specific gas volume or a percentage of the openhole TD.

This load case models an internal-pressure profile that reflects pumping water down the annulus to reduce the surface pressure during a well-

control situation where lost returns are occurring. The pressure profile represents a freshwater gradient applied upward from the fracture pressure at the shoe depth.

$$P = P_{frac} + \rho_{water}(TVD - TVD_{shoe}) \qquad TVD < TVD_{shoe} \qquad (9\text{-}35)$$

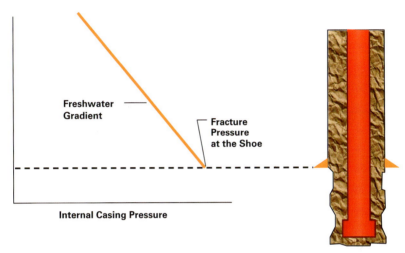

Fig. 9.17 – Burst (Drilling): Lost Returns with Water.

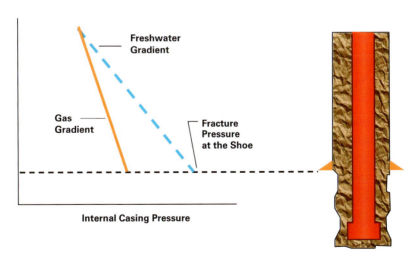

Fig. 9.18 – Burst (Drilling): Surface Protection (BOP).

A water gradient is used, assuming that the rig's barite supply has been depleted during the well-control incident. This load case will typically dominate the burst design when compared to the gas-kick load case, especially for intermediate casing.

This load case is less severe than the displacement-to-gas criteria and represents a moderated approach to preventing a surface blowout during a well-control incident. It is not applicable to liners. In this load, a gas gradient from this surface pressure is used to generate the rest of the pressure profile:

$$p(z) = p_{frac} - \gamma_{water} z_{shoe} + \gamma_g z \qquad z < z_{shoe} \qquad (9\text{-}36)$$

This load case represents no actual physical scenario; however, when used with the gas-kick criterion, it ensures that the casing weak point is not at the surface. Typically, the gas-kick load case will control the deeper portion of the design, and the surface protection load case will control the shallower portion of the design. As a result, the string's weak point is somewhere in the middle.

This load case models an internal-pressure profile that reflects a surface pressure applied to a mud gradient.

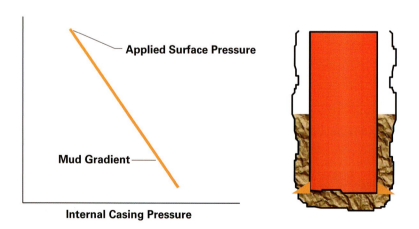

Fig. 9.19 – Burst (Drilling): Pressure Test.

$$P = P_{surface} + g \times \rho_m \times TVD \tag{9-37}$$

The test pressure is typically based on the maximum anticipated surface pressure determined from the other selected burst load cases plus a suitable safety margin (e.g., 500 psi). For production casing, the test pressure is typically based on the anticipated shut-in tubing pressure. This load case may or may not dominate the burst design, depending on the mud weight in the hole at the time the test occurs. The pressure test is normally performed before the float equipment is drilled out.

Burst (Drilling): Green Cement Pressure Test

From the hanger to the float collar, the internal pressure profile is given by:

$$P_{internal} = P_{test} + g \times \rho_{displacement\ fluid} \times TVD$$

From the float collar to the shoe:

$$P_{shoe} = P_{tail\ slurry\ top} + g \times \rho_{tail\ slurry} \times (TVD_{shoe} - TVD_{tail\ slurry\ top})$$

$$P_{internal} = P_{shoe} - g \times \rho_{tail\ slurry} \times (TVD_{shoe} - TVD)$$

Burst (Drilling): Gas Over Mud Ratio

The internal pressure at the shoe above the open-hole target depth (TD), based on the pore pressure at the influx depth and the gas gradient, is given by:

$$P_{shoe\ above\ openhole\ TD} = P_{pore\ influx\ depth} - g \times \rho_{mud} \times (TVD_{influx\ depth} - TVD_{shoe\ above\ openhole\ TD})$$

If this pressure exceeds the fracture pressure at that depth, P_{frac}, and the Limit to Fracture at Shoe option is enabled on the Design Parameters dialog, then the pressure at the gas/mud interface is given by:

$$P_{gas/mud} = P_{frac} - g \times \rho_{mud} \times (TVD_{shoe\ above\ openhole\ TD} - TVD_{gas/mud})$$

If the gas/mud interface is above the depth of the shoe, then:

$$P_{gas/mud} = P_{frac} - g \times \rho_{gas} \times (TVD_{gas/mud} - TVD_{shoe\ above\ openhole\ TD})$$

Otherwise, the pressure at the gas/mud interface is given by:

$$P_{gas/mud} = P_{pore} - g \times \rho_{mud} \times (TVD_{influx\ depth} - TVD_{gas/mud})$$

From the gas/mud interface to the shoe, if the gas/mud interface is less than the shoe depth, then:

$$P_{internal} = P_{gas/mud} + g\ \rho_{mud} \times (TVD - TVD_{gas/mud})$$

From the hanger to the gas/mud interface:

$$P_{internal} = P_{gas/mud} - g \times \rho_{gas} \times (TVD_{gas/mud} - TVD)$$

Burst (Drilling): Drill Ahead

$$P_i = 0.052 * [\ MW\ (next\ hole\ section) + ECD\ ] * TVD$$

How P_i and P_e are Calculated

If onshore, then calculate P_i and P_e at:

- Top of string
- TOC
- Shoe depth

Burst (Drilling): Fracture at Shoe 1/3 Bottom Hole Pressure (BHP) at Wellhead

From the hanger to the shoe:

$$P_{surface} = 1/3 \times P_{pore\ at\ openhole\ td}$$

$$P_{internal} = P_{surface} + [(TVD) / (TVD_{shoe\ above\ openhole\ td})] \times (P_{frac} - P_{surface})$$

Burst (Drilling): Fracture at Shoe with Gas Gradient Above

From the hanger to the prior shoe:

$$P_{external} = P_{frac}\ @\ _{prior\ shoe} - g \times \rho_{gas} \times (TVD_{prior\ shoe} - TVD)$$

From the prior shoe to the current shoe:

$$P_{external} = P_{frac} @_{prior\ shoe} + g \times \rho_{mud} \times (TVD - TVD_{prior\ shoe})$$

Maximum Anticipated Surface Pressure (MASP Frac Method)

$$MASP_{frac} = P_{frac} - (TVD_{shoe} - TVD_{ref}) \times \rho_{gas\ gradient}$$

Where,

P_{frac} is the fracture pressure (psi) at the shoe of the current string,

TVD_{shoe} is the true vertical depth (ft) at the shoe for the current string, and

TVD_{ref} is the true vertical depth (ft) of the reference depth point.

Maximum Anticipated Surface Pressure (MASP) BHP Method

$$MASP_{bhp} = BHP - F_{mud} \times (TVD_{openhole\ td} - TVD_{ref}) \times \rho_{mud} - (1 - F_{mud}) \times (TVD_{openhole\ TD} - TVD_{ref}) \times \rho_{gas\ gradient}$$

Where,

$TVD_{openhole}$ TD is the greatest openhole TVD to which the string is exposed to drilling loads,

BHP is the pore pressure (psi) at the greatest open-hole TVD to which the string is exposed to drilling loads,

F_{mud} is the wellbore fluid column occupied by the drilling fluid, expressed as a fraction of the greatest openhole TVD to which the string is exposed to drilling loads, and

ρ_{mud} is the mud weight at $TVD_{open\ hole\ TD}$ (expressed in psi/ft).

This load case models an internal- and external-pressure profile that reflects the collapse load imparted on the casing after the plug has been bumped during the cement job and the pump pressure has been bled off. The external pressure considers the mud hydrostatic column and different densities of the lead and tail cement slurries. The internal pressure is based on the gradient of the displacement fluid. If a light displacement fluid is used, the cementing collapse load can be significant.

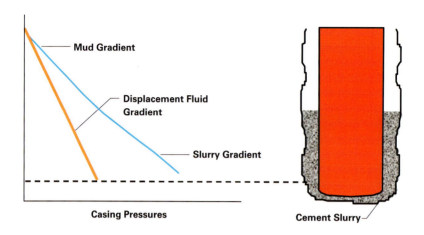

Fig. 9.20 – Collapse (Drilling): Cementing.

Collapse (Drilling): Full/Partial Evacuation

From the hanger to the mud level:

$P_{internal} = P_{atm}$

From the mud level to the shoe of the current string:

$P_{internal} = P_{atm} + g \times \rho_{mud} \times (TVD - TVD_{mud\ level})$

Collapse (Drilling): Drill Ahead

$P_i = g \times [\rho_{mud}\ (next\ hole\ section) + \rho_{ECD}\ ] \times TVD$

How P_i and P_e are Calculated

If onshore, then calculate P_i and P_e at:

- Top of string
- TOC
- Shoe depth

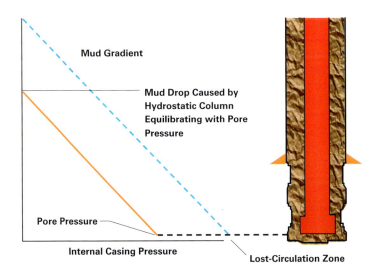

Fig. 9.21 – Collapse (Drilling): Lost Returns with Mud Drop.

This load case models an internal-pressure profile that reflects a partial evacuation or a drop in the mud level caused by the mud hydrostatic column equilibrating with the pore pressure in a lost-circulation zone.

From the depth to the mud-drop depth:

$P_{internal} = 0$

From the mud-drop depth to the lost-circulation depth:

$P_{internal} = P_f + g \times \rho_m \times (TVD - TVD_{lc})$

Where,

P_f is the pore pressure at the lost-circulation zone depth, TVD_{lc}.

The mud-drop depth is given by:

$$TVD_{md} = TVD_{lc} - P_f/\rho_m \quad (9\text{-}38)$$

The heaviest mud weight used to drill the next hole section should be used, along with a pore pressure and depth that result in the largest mud drop. Many operators conservatively assume that the lost-circulation zone is at

the TD of the next hole section and that it will be normally pressured (a 0.465-psi/ft gradient). A partial evacuation of more than 5,000 ft caused by lost circulation during drilling will normally not be seen. Many operators use a partial evacuation criterion in which the mud level is assumed to be a percentage of the openhole TD.

Collapse (Drilling): Other Load Cases

Full Evacuation

The full-evacuation load case should be considered if drilling with air or foam. It may also be considered for conductor or surface casing where shallow gas is encountered. This load case would represent all of the mud being displaced out of the wellbore (through the diverter) before the formation bridges off.

Water Gradient

For wells with a sufficient water supply, an internal-pressure profile consisting of a freshwater or seawater gradient is sometimes used as a collapse criterion. This load case assumes a lost-circulation zone that can only withstand a water gradient.

This load case applies to both production and injection operations, and represents a high surface pressure on top of the completion fluid caused

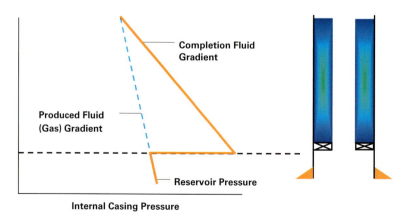

Fig. 9.22 – Burst (Production): Tubing Leak.

by a tubing leak near the hanger. A worst-case surface pressure is usually based on a gas gradient extending upward from reservoir pressure at the perforations.

$$P(z) = P_{res} - \rho_g z_{res} + \rho_m z \qquad (9\text{-}39)$$

Where,

P_{res} is the reservoir pressure at reservoir depth, z_{res}.

If the proposed packer location was determined during the casing design, the casing below the packer can be assumed to experience a pressure based solely on the produced fluid gradient and reservoir pressure.

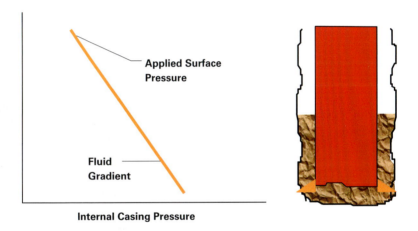

Fig. 9.23 – Burst (Production): Injection Down Casing.

This load case applies to wells that experience high-pressure annular injection operations, such as a casing fracture-stimulation job. The load case models a surface pressure applied to a static fluid column, as follows:

$$P(z) = P_s + \rho_m z \qquad (9\text{-}40)$$

Where,

P_s is the applied surface pressure.

This load case is analogous to a screenout during a fracturing job.

Burst (Production): Stimulation Surface Casing

From the hanger to minimum of {packer, shoe}:

$P_{hanger} = P_{injection} + g \times \rho_{injection\ fluid} \times TVD_{prod\ casing\ hanger}$

$P_{internal} = P_{hanger} + g \times \rho_{packer\ fluid} \times (TVD - TVD_{prod\ casing\ hanger})$

If the shoe is deeper than the packer, then from the packer to the shoe:

$P_{internal} = P_{injection} + g \times \rho_{injection\ fluid} \times TVD$

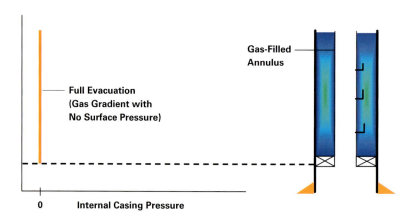

Fig. 9.24 – Collapse Above Packer (Production): Full Evacuation.

This severe load case has the most application in gas-lift wells and represents a gas-filled annulus that loses injection pressure.

$$P(z) = \rho_g\, z \qquad (9\text{-}41)$$

Many operators use the full-evacuation criterion for all production casing strings, regardless of the completion type or reservoir characteristics.

This load case is based on a hydrostatic column of completion fluid equilibrating with depleted reservoir pressure during a workover operation:

$$P(z) = 0 \qquad z < z_{drop} \qquad (9\text{-}42)$$

$$P(z) = P_{res} + \rho_c\,(z - z_{res}) \qquad z_{drop} < z < z_{res} \qquad (9\text{-}43)$$

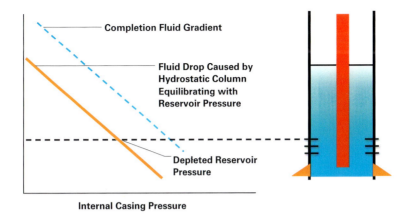

Fig. 9.25 – Collapse Above Packer (Production): Partial Evacuation.

With,

$$z_{drop} = z_{res} - P_{res}/\rho_c \qquad (9\text{-}44)$$

Where,

P_{res} is the depleted reservoir pressure,

z_{res} is the depth of the reservoir, and

z_{drop} is the depth of the fluid top of completion fluid, γ_c.

Some operators do not consider a fluid drop, but just a fluid gradient in the annulus above the packer. This practice is acceptable if the final depleted pressure of the formation will be greater than the hydrostatic column of a lightweight packer fluid.

Collapse Below Packer (Production): Common Load Cases

Full Evacuation

This load case applies to severely depleted reservoirs, plugged perforations, or a large drawdown of a low-permeability reservoir and represents the most commonly used collapse criterion.

Fluid Gradient

This load case assumes zero surface pressure applied to a fluid gradient. A common application is the underbalanced fluid gradient in the tubing before perforating (or after perforating if the perforations are plugged). It is a less conservative criterion for formations that will never be drawn down to zero.

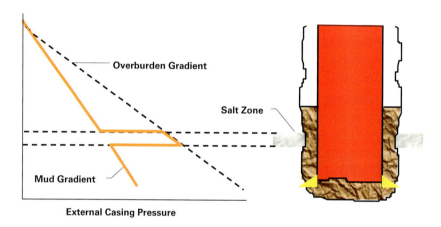

Fig. 9.26 – Collapse: Salt Loads.

Creep behavior results from the instability of the salt formation, which causes a slow flow and results in permanent deformations. Creep and deformation occur over time and are initiated once the salt formation has been penetrated. Completion of the wellbore does not stop formation creep. The constant creep of the formation causes excess stress on the well completions, which will eventually cause the casing to collapse (Wang and Samuel 2014). The creep rate in the salt formation can be defined by two components, as described above: one is known as the primary creep rate, $\dot{\bar{\varepsilon}}_p$, and the second is known as the secondary creep rate, $\dot{\bar{\varepsilon}}_s$. The additive decomposition is given by Eq. 9-45.

$$\dot{\bar{\varepsilon}} = \dot{\bar{\varepsilon}}_p + \dot{\bar{\varepsilon}}_s \tag{9-45}$$

If a formation that exhibits plastic behavior, such as a salt zone, will be isolated by the current string, an equivalent external collapse load (typically

assumed to be the overburden pressure) should be superimposed upon all of the collapse load cases (except cementing) from the top to the base of the salt zone.

$$P(z) = \rho_{ob} z \tag{9-46}$$

Where,

ρ_{ob} is the overburden gradient (typically 1 psi/ft).

Mechanical Loads

Changes in Axial Load

In tubing and over the free length of the casing above the top of cement, changes in temperatures and pressures will have the largest effect on the ballooning and temperature load components. The incremental forces caused by these effects are given by Eq. 9-47.

$$\Delta F_{bal} = 2\upsilon\left(\Delta p_i A_i - \Delta p_o A_o\right) + \upsilon L\left(\Delta \rho_i A_i - \Delta \rho_o A_o\right) \tag{9-47}$$

Where,

ΔF_{bal} is the incremental force (lbf) caused by ballooning,

υ is Poisson's ratio (0.30 for steel),

Δp_i is the change in internal pressure at the surface,

Δp_o is the change in external pressure at the surface,

A_i is the cross-sectional area associated with the casing ID,

A_o is the cross-sectional area associated with the casing OD,

L is the free length of the casing,

$\Delta \rho_i$ is the change in internal fluid density, and

$\Delta \rho_o$ is the change in external fluid density.

$$\Delta F_{temp} = -\alpha E A_s \Delta T \tag{9-48}$$

CASING DESIGN

Where:

ΔF_{temp} is the incremental force (lbf) resulting from temperature change,

α is the thermal expansion coefficient (6.9 × 10^{-6} °F^{-1} for steel),

E is Young's modulus (3.0 × 10^7 psi for steel),

A_s is the cross-sectional area of pipe, and

ΔT is the average change in temperature over the free length (°F).

Axial Load: Running in Hole

This installation load case represents the maximum axial load that any portion of the casing string experiences as it is run into the hole. This load case can include the effects of:

1. Self-weight

2. Buoyancy forces at the end of the pipe and at each cross-sectional area change

3. Wellbore deviation

4. Bending loads superimposed in dogleg regions

5. Frictional drag

6. Shock loads based on an instantaneous deceleration from a maximum velocity.

This velocity is often assumed to be 50% greater than the average running speed, which is typically 2 ft/sec to 3 ft/sec. Typically, the maximum axial load experienced by any joint in the casing string is the load that occurs when the joint is picked up out of the slips after it is made up.

Axial Load: Overpull During Running

This installation load case models an incremental axial load applied at the surface while the pipe is run into the hole. Casing that is designed on the basis of this load case should be able to withstand an overpull force

applied with the shoe at any depth if the casing becomes stuck as it is run in the hole. This load case includes the effects of:

1. Self-weight

2. Buoyancy forces at the end of the pipe and at each cross-sectional area change

3. Wellbore deviation

4. Bending loads superimposed in dogleg regions

5. Frictional drag

6. The applied overpull force.

Axial Load: Green Cement Pressure Test

This installation load case models the application of surface pressure after the plug is bumped during the primary cement job. Since the cement is still in its fluid state, the applied pressure will result in a large piston force at the float collar, which often results in the worst-case surface axial load. This load case includes the effects of:

1. Self-weight

2. Buoyancy forces at the end of the pipe and at each cross-sectional area change

3. Wellbore deviation

4. Bending loads superimposed in dogleg regions

5. Frictional drag

6. Piston force caused by differential pressure across the float collar.

Other Axial Load Cases

Two other load cases involve examining the *air weight of casing* and the *buoyed weight plus overpull*. Both of these criteria have calculations

that are easy to perform and normally result in adequate designs. Both load cases are still frequently used in the industry today, but, since many factors are not considered, they are typically used with a high-axial design factor (1.6+).

Axial Load: Shock Loads

Shock loads can occur if the pipe hits an obstruction or the slips close while the pipe is moving. The maximum additional axial force caused by a sudden deceleration to zero velocity is given by Eq. 9-49.

$$F_{shock} = VA_s\sqrt{E\rho_s} \qquad (9\text{-}49)$$

Where,

F_{shock} is the axial force caused by shock loading,

V is the instantaneous running speed,

A_s is the cross-sectional area of the pipe,

E is the elastic modulus, and

ρ_s is the density of steel.

The shock-load equation is often expressed as:

$$F_{shock} = Vw_{nom}\sqrt{E/\rho_s} \qquad (9\text{-}50)$$

Where,

w_{nom} is the nominal casing weight per unit length $\approx A_s r_s$, and

$\sqrt{E/\rho_s}$ is the speed of sound in steel (16,800 ft/sec).

For practical purposes, some operators specify an average velocity in this equation and multiply the result by a factor (typically 1.5) that represents the ratio between the peak and average velocities.

Axial Load: Service Loads

For most wells, installation loads will control axial design. However, in wells with uncemented sections of casing and where large pressure or temperature changes will occur after the casing is cemented in place, changes in the axial load distribution can be significant. These changes are the result of self-weight, buoyancy forces, wellbore deviation, bending loads, changes in internal or external pressure (ballooning), temperature changes, and buckling.

Axial Load: Bending Loads

Stress at the pipe's outer diameter caused by bending can be expressed as:

$$\sigma_b = \frac{ED}{2R} \qquad (9\text{-}51)$$

Where,

σ_b is the stress at the pipe's outer surface, and

R is the radius of curvature.

This bending stress can be expressed as an equivalent axial force, such that:

$$F_b = \frac{E\pi}{360} D(\alpha/L) A_s \qquad (9\text{-}52)$$

Where,

F_b is the axial force caused by bending, and

α/L is the dogleg severity (in degrees per unit length).

The bending load is superimposed on the axial load distribution as a local effect.

Thermal Loads and Temperature Effects

In shallow, normally pressured wells, temperature will typically have a secondary effect on tubular design. In other situations, loads induced by temperature can be the governing criteria in the design.

Temperature increases that occur after the casing is landed can cause thermal expansion of fluids in sealed annuli, which results in significant pressure loads. Usually, these loads do not need to be included in the design because the pressures can be bled off. Changes in temperature will increase or decrease tension in the casing string as a result of thermal contraction and expansion, respectively. The increased axial load caused by the pumping of cool fluid into the wellbore during a stimulation job can be the critical axial design criterion. In contrast, the reduction in tension during production caused by thermal expansion can increase buckling and possibly result in compression at the wellhead.

Changes in temperature not only affect axial loads but also influence the load resistance. Since the material's yield strength is a function of temperature, higher wellbore temperatures will reduce the burst, collapse, axial, and triaxial ratings of the casing.

In sour environments, operating temperatures can influence the types of equipment that can be used at different depths in the wellbore. Produced temperatures in gas wells will also influence the gas gradient inside the tubing, since gas density is a function of temperature and pressure.

References

Adams, A.J. and MacEachran, A. 1994. Impact on Casing Design of Thermal Expansion of Fluids in Confined Annuli. *SPEDE*, **9** (03): 210.

API 5C2, *Bulletin on Performance Properties of Casing, Tubing, and Drill Pipe*, 18th edition. 1982. API, Dallas, Texas (March 1982).

API 5C3 Addendum, *Addendum to the Technical Report on Equations and Calculations for Casing, Tubing, and Line Pipe Used as Casing or Tubing; and Performance Properties Tables for Casing and Tubing*, first edition. 2008. API, Washington, DC (October 2015).

API 5C3, *Bulletin on Formulas and Calculations for Casing, Tubing, Drill Pipe, and Line Pipe Properties*, fourth edition. 1985. API, Dallas, Texas (February 1985).

API TR 5C3, *Technical Report on Equations and Calculations for Casing, Tubing, and Line Pipe Used as Casing or Tubing*; and *Performance Properties Tables for Casing and Tubing*, first edition. 2008. API, Washington, DC (December 2008).

Crandall, S.H. and Dahl, N.C. 1959. *An Introduction to the Mechanics of Solids*, 199. New York: McGraw-Hill Book Co.

Greenip, J.F. 2016. Collapse Strength of Casing Subjected to Combined Load. Paper SPE 178806 presented at the IADC/SPE Drilling Conference and Exhibition, Fort Worth, Texas, 1–3 March.

ISO TR 10400, Petroleum and Natural Gas Industries – Equations and Calculations for the Properties of Casing, Tubing, Drill Pipe and Line Pipe Used as Casing or Tubing, first edition. 2007. ISO, Geneva, Switzerland (December 2007).

Klever, F.J. and Tamano, T. 2006. A New OCTG Strength Equation for Collapse Under Combined Loads. *SPEDC*, **21**(03).

Liu, Z., Klever, F., Samuel, R., Gonzales, A., and Kang, Y. 2016. The Radial Approach to Safety Factors for Tubular Design. Paper SPE 181459 presented at the SPE Annual Technical Conference and Exhibition, Dubai, UAE, 26–28 September.

Samuel, R., Kumar, A., and Chaudhari, N. 2013. Method and Analysis for Holistic Casing Design for Planning and Real-Time. 025320.0219PTWO.

Samuel, R. and Gonzales, A. 1999. Minimum Cost Casing Design. Paper SPE 36448 presented at the SPE Annual Technical Conference, Houston, Texas, 3–6 October.

Samuel, R. and Gonzales, A. 2000. Wellhead growth index aids multistring casing design. *Oil & Gas Journal*.

Timoshenko, S.P. and Goodier, J.N. 1961. *Theory of Elasticity*, third edition. New York: McGraw-Hill Book Co.

CHAPTER **TEN**

Casing Wear

The last couple of decades have seen the development of complex wells, including long horizontal wells for shale development, extended-reach wells for onshore and offshore development, and multilateral wells to maximize reservoir productivity. Complex wells require advanced casing programs in order to maintain good wellbore integrity. One problem that needs to be accurately addressed pertaining to different casing sections installed during the drilling of such complex wells is casing wear.

Casing Wear and Hole Erosion

Casing wear usually results from contact between the drillpipe tool joints and the casing due to rotation of the drillstring. The wear rate depends primarily on the contact force, the length of contact time under rotating conditions, and the surface condition of the contacting surfaces (e.g., tool joints). Exxon's work in the 1980s showed that higher-grade casing wears slightly faster than lower-grade casing. Therefore, it may be desirable

to use lower-grade/higher-weight casing instead of higher-grade/lower-weight casing if casing wear is a prime consideration.

The contact force mainly depends on the drillstring tension and the dogleg severity in the wellbore at the contact point. As either drillstring tension or dogleg severity increases, the contact force will increase. The worst combination is high tension or doglegs at a point where extensive rotation occurs. A generally accepted criterion for limiting casing wear to an acceptable level is to limit the contact force to a maximum of 2,000 lbf (8,896 N).

To minimize casing wear, drillstring rotation should be avoided with any drillstring component that has rough surface conditions or that could otherwise be expected to cause more rapid casing wear. For example, newly hard-faced tool joints and stabilizers (e.g., while drilling out the float equipment) have been known to cause rapid casing wear when significant drillstring rotation has occurred. If drillstring rotation cannot be completely avoided, then the rotary speed should be minimized.

A drillstring simulation (also known as torque/drag) program should be used to predict the expected contact forces on the casing. If the analysis indicates that casing wear could be significant, then consider the following steps:

- Ensure that wall thickness is included in the casing inspection.
- Run a base-casing caliper log before drilling out. These logs provide accurate change estimates for the inner diameter of the casing, but not in the absolute value of it.
- Place ditch magnets in the flow line to measure the amount of metal being worn off the casing.
- Track rotary speed and rotating hours. Use this information with the estimated contact force to estimate casing wear.
- Use drillpipe protectors.
- Analyze casing design to account for the effects of casing wear on burst, collapse, and combined bending and tension.

In some cases, the deep build section will not be completely cased while drilling the lateral section. If the formations are sufficiently competent, the last casing shoe may be set at approximately 75° inclination. Then, the final build to horizontal will remain as open hole. This uncased section will have the potential for hole erosion, which could lead to key seating due to long rotation time and relatively high contact forces. This has not been a problem to date. However, one explanation is that formations prone to such erosion are usually cased off before drilling the lateral section.

Estimation

Casing wear continues to be a challenge faced by the industry, as accurate estimation of downhole wear remains an unaccomplished goal. Various casing-wear estimation techniques have been investigated and developed through research and joint-industry projects; however, the accuracy of all the models developed is still in question. Even though some of the models have proven to be accurate for some test wells, the intrinsic drawback of the developed techniques is that their application could not be accurately extended to wells in different fields having different well profiles.

Typically, during any complex drilling program, the downhole casing wear is measured using caliper logs or sonic/ultra-sonic imaging tools, and the actual depth of the casing wear groove is estimated using these log measurements. Based on these measurements and other drilling operation parameters, the casing-wear models are used to back-calculate the casing-wear factor for the well section that was logged. However, when the same wear factors are applied for the next drilling operation in that well or while drilling another similar well, the predictions have been way off. It is because of these disparities from actual measurements and the large uncertainties involved in casing-wear estimation that most operators largely apply excess safety factors in their casing designs and overdesign their casing to prevent failures. However, overdesigning the casing results in an increase in costs to drill and complete each well and, therefore, it should be minimized.

Studies

Bradley et al. (1975) have presented one of the foremost efforts undertaken by the industry to understand and effectively model different casing-wear scenarios. They developed procedures to estimate casing wear caused by rotating, tripping, and running wireline and by derived empirical wear coefficients from laboratory wear measurements. They concluded that the drillstring rotation was the major cause of casing wear as compared to the wear caused during tripping and running wireline, and that drillpipe rubbers could be effectively used in places where contact loads were high.

White et al. (1987) investigated the casing wear caused by rotation of non-hard-banded tool joints with a full-sized test machine. They performed their study using three grades of casing (K55, N80, and P110), both oil-based and water-based muds, and contact forces of 1,000 lbf and 2,000 lbf. By measuring both the casing wear and friction forces, they proposed a linear wear-efficiency model that related the casing metal removal to the amount of energy dissipated as friction in the wear process.

Schoenmakers (1987) presented four case studies to prove that the laboratory simulations of casing wear caused by tool-joint hardfacings corresponded well to field-measured casing wear. He concluded that the prediction of casing wear is possible with laboratory simulations and that casing wear could be effectively controlled by sufficiently smooth hardfacings, weighted mud, and moderate tool joint/casing contact forces. Hall et al. (1994) developed and verified a mathematical model that described casing wear in terms of hole geometry, casing/tool-joint material, mud system, and drilling program. They performed over 300 laboratory wear tests to estimate wear factors that formed an integral part of the casing-wear model, and allowed the model to be implemented in a wide range of well geometries and drilling programs. They also incorporated the model into a computer program "CWEAR" to be used as both a planning and operational tool.

Hall et al. (2005) then extended this study to more than 475 eight-hour casing- and riser-wear tests and analyzed this extensive database to develop the contact-pressure threshold concept. They measured the depth

of the wear groove at various time intervals and normalized the dataset to propose a new relation that now used three different variables to describe the wear history of the system, in contrast to the single wear factor customarily used to characterize the casing/tool joint drilling fluid system. They conclude that there exists only a very loose correlation between wear factors and contact-pressure thresholds, and that larger values of contact-pressure threshold are more likely to be associated with smaller values of wear factor.

Gao et al. (2009) presented a new method to estimate the depth of the wear groove on the intermediate casing and also discussed the change of casing-wear groove depth vs. drilling footage under different-sized drillstrings. They proposed a mechanical model for predicting casing-wear locations based on well trajectory and drillstring movement, and have also predicted the casing-wear groove depth of a planned well with inversion of the casing-wear factor from the drilled well. Calhoun et al. (2010) have presented the casing-wear monitoring standard-operating practice developed by Chevron to proactively manage and mitigate casing wear during drilling operations, and have demonstrated that casing wear can be predicted, managed, and/or mitigated with proper planning and execution. Using a casing-wear event from a Chevron well, they have presented the different aspects involved in casing-wear analysis and have provided recommendations to more accurately predict casing wear.

Mitchell et al. (2012) have investigated this problem from a different perspective and have presented an improved casing-wear prediction and mitigation method using a statistically based model. They created an extensive database from a wide variety of wells with measured depths greater than 13,000 ft and analyzed the dataset to generate the probabilities for dogleg severities in common well types and correlated them to the actual back-modeled wear factors. They concluded that the type of well, build rate, use of rotary steerable systems, and survey frequency significantly influence the dogleg severity, and the statistically based tortuosity model presented by them was able to predict the actual dogleg severity more accurately for the purposes of modeling casing wear. However, due to a relative scarcity of casing-wear logs, they were unable to determine a statistical distribution of casing-wear factors.

A thorough review of the various investigations conducted over the years suggests that a comprehensive solution to this complex problem of accurately predicting downhole casing wear is still elusive and that the large number of uncertainties involved in casing-wear estimation has led to a lot of misinterpretations of the existing casing-wear modeling techniques. Hence, this study was undertaken to analyze in detail the fundamentals behind the casing-wear prediction models, the limitations of the modeling methods, the various uncertainties and complexities involved in wear estimation, and the possible methods to improve casing-wear prediction.

In addition, the direct influence of the casing-wear factors on the collapse and burst pressure ratings of the worn-out casing strings has also been investigated to help improve the overall well-integrity analyses and reduce failures due to casing wear. A new visualization and interpretation technique using casing-wear maps has also been presented to help better model the wear and provide future predictions.

Casing-Wear Model

This modeling approach for ERD wells has been slightly modified while being applied to address the different kinds of operations that are performed to successfully drill a well. Five major operations are considered in this analysis–drilling, backreaming, rotating off-bottom, sliding, and reciprocation. This study focuses on wear caused only by these above operations, which can be performed in different sequences to reach the target depth. Other possible reasons for downhole wear – such as erosion while fracking, corrosion, or any other mechanical wear during production – are not considered in this analysis.

For the drilling and backreaming operations, Eq. 10-1 has been applied for analysis. The drilling or backreaming operation starts from a given measured depth, and the drill bit progresses farther down (drilling) or up (backreaming) the hole to reach the target end depth for that operation. As a result, the tool-joint contact with the inner casing wall varies as the drillstring moves down or up the hole. The last factor in Eq. 10-1, the ratio of tool-joint length over drillpipe length, is applied to account for this contact resulting from tool joints only. The average side

force supported by the tool joints is calculated using Eq. 10-2, assuming that the entire load is taken solely by the tool joints and there is no pipe-body contact.

$$WV = W_f \times SF_{tj} \times \pi \times D_{tj} \times RPM \times 60 \times t \times \frac{L_{tj}}{L_p} \qquad (10\text{-}1)$$

$$SF_{tj} = SF_{ft} \times \frac{L_p}{L_{tj}} \qquad (10\text{-}2)$$

The wear volume for the sliding operation that has no rotations is estimated using Eq. 10-4. The total sliding distance, d_{sld}, under this scenario is given by Eq. 10-5. The wear analysis for sliding is segmented into operational steps using Eq. 10-3, just as in drilling or backreaming. In case the drillstring is rotated at very low rotary speeds while sliding, Eq. 10-1 is used to estimate wear volume, and this operation becomes similar to drilling for wear-volume calculation purposes.

$$WV = W_f \times SF_{tj} \times d_{sld} \times 12 \times \frac{L_{tj}}{L_p} \qquad (10\text{-}3)$$

$$d_{sld} = MD_{end} - MD_{srt} \qquad (10\text{-}4)$$

To clean the wellbore and to ensure that the openhole section is gauged, it is a common practice in the field to reciprocate the drillstring after drilling each stand. In other scenarios, the drillstring may be reciprocated just while circulating for better hole cleaning. The wear resulting from this drillstring reciprocation is estimated using Eq. 10-5. The total reciprocation distance, d_{rcp}, is estimated using Eqs. 10-6 through 10-8. The reciprocation operation is also divided into separate operational steps, as shown in Eq. 10-4, for each of the up or down strokes, and each stroke may further be segmented in case the stroke length is in excess of 30 ft.

$$WV = W_f \times SF_{tj} \times d_{rcp} \times \frac{L_{tj}}{L_p} \qquad (10\text{-}5)$$

$$d_{rcp} = \sqrt{d_{ax}^2 + d_{rot}^2} \qquad (10\text{-}6)$$

$$d_{ax} = L_{stk} \times 12 \qquad (10\text{-}7)$$

$$d_{rot} = \pi \times D_{tj} \times RPM_r \times t_{stk} \qquad (10\text{-}8)$$

Torque-and-Drag Model – Soft String vs. Stiff String

The earlier-stated equations for wear modeling clearly suggest that the key to successfully predicting the downhole casing wear lies in being able to accurately estimate the normal contact load or side forces acting between the tool joints and the inner casing wall.

The soft-string torque-and-drag model, which is often considered as the industry standard, has been conventionally used for all wear-modeling purposes. This soft-string model is considered to represent the real drillstring behavior by neglecting the bending stiffness of the string components so that the entire length of the string behaves as a cable or chain. This model also assumes that the drillstring trajectory is the same as the wellbore trajectory to solve the wellbore contact problem, and the contact is further assumed to be continuous along the wellbore.

Even though these assumptions work well for conventional torque-and-drag analysis, they fail to fulfill the underlying requirements for accurately modeling casing wear. The wear groove predicted by using the soft-string model is assumed to be concentrated only at one particular location on the low side for any casing cross-section, which does not corroborate the field observations of worn-out casings. Hence, to overcome these existing challenges, a more comprehensive stiff-string model has been applied for wear analysis in this study.

Mitchell and Samuel (2009) have presented a detailed background on the drawbacks of the soft-string model, and have developed a more comprehensive stiff-string model that accounts for the bending stiffness of the components and accurately estimates drillstring contact points in the wellbore rather than assuming continuous contact. This model is considered more appropriate for advanced wear analysis. The stiff-string model estimates more accurate side forces, particularly for high dogleg wells, as the soft-string model has limitations in such scenarios. Estimating multiple wear groove locations using stiff-string modeling is also expected to reduce the over-prediction of wear, which has been one of the major drawbacks of the soft-string model. The detailed method of modeling multiple wear grooves can be referred to in the SPE paper 178833.

Casing-Wear Factors

The concept of casing-wear factors was introduced by the study conducted by Hall et al. (1994) from Maurer Engineering Inc. as part of the joint-industry project, DEA-42. The wear factors formed an integral part of the casing-wear model proposed by this study, which was based on the phenomenon that when a rotating tool joint impinges against the inner wall of the casing, a crescent-shaped groove is worn into the inner wall. The fundamental assumption of this model was that "the volume of steel removed from each unit length of casing at a point on the inside surface of the casing is proportional to frictional work done at that point by the tool joint rotating in contact with the casing."

The following equations explain the basic relation between the casing-wear factor and its underlying variables.

Volume removed per foot = Frictional work done per foot / Specific energy (10-9)

Specific energy is the energy required to remove one cubic inch of steel.

Frictional work done per foot = Normal force per foot * Friction factor * Sliding distance (10-10)

Combining friction factor and the specific energy, the wear factor is defined and the new casing-wear model is derived.

Wear factor = Friction factor / Specific energy (10-11)

Volume removed per foot = Wear factor * Normal force per foot * Sliding distance (10-12)

This study conducted more than 300 laboratory tests to compute the values of wear factors under various drilling conditions by repeating the experiments for different sets of materials and scenarios. For each test done, the "volume removed per foot," "normal force per foot," and the "sliding distance" were determined at fixed intervals of time, and then

the value of the wear factor was computed. The wear factor calculated by using this procedure is a very small number and is conventionally reported in units of E-10/psi. Hence, a wear factor of 2 actually refers to a value of 2×E-10/psi.

In order to apply the model proposed by this study, the normal force per foot was computed based on the well path, drillstring design, and the drilling parameters, and the sliding distance was estimated based on the drilling program. This, combined with the appropriate wear factor for the drilling scenario, helped estimate the wear volume per foot and, subsequently, the depth of the wear groove on the inner wall of the casing.

Influencing Parameters

A thorough understanding of the underlying parameters involved in casing-wear estimation and a comprehensive step-by-step modeling approach will help to reduce these uncertainties and help us to more accurately calculate the correct wear factors and predict casing wear. Some of the key parameters that influence casing-wear modeling and wear estimation have been listed below along with further details on each one of them (Kumar and Samuel 2015):

- Contact force
- Calculation steps in monitoring
- Friction factor
- Well path and survey
- Nonlinearity
- Multiple wear factors
- Wear-groove location
- Rig operations
- Downhole conditions
- Variations in parameters
- Other modeling uncertainities
- Casing-wear logs

1. Estimation of Normal Contact Force

Hall et al. (1994) pointed out that the key to successful prediction of casing wear is to accurately compute the normal contact force acting between the drillpipe tool joints and the inner wall of the casing. The normal contact force forms an integral part of the casing-wear equation, and inaccuracies in computing contact forces will lead to accumulating error in wear estimation. In order to calculate the normal contact force, the conventional soft-string model has been used in most of the applications. However, various torque-and-drag analyses presented in the industry prove that the more advanced stiff-string analysis, which includes the bending stiffness of the drillstring, should be performed for higher accuracy. In particular, the stiff-string model should be used in cases that have high doglegs, as the soft-string model has limitations in such scenarios.

Casing-wear peaks are more often encountered in areas of such high doglegs, so performing a more advanced computation of normal contact force using the stiff-string model or a comprehensive finite-element model will help us improve the accuracy of casing-wear estimation. Another drawback of the conventional soft-string model is that it assumes contact between the tool joints and the casing at all the points along the wellbore and leads to an overestimation of the wear. The stiff-string model helps to depict a more realistic scenario and computes a value of normal contact force acting between the tool joint and the casing inner wall only if there is any contact between them. This will prevent overestimating the contact forces and help in computing a more accurate wear factor for a given drilling operation. In addition, changes in normal contact force due to drillstring buckling should also be incorporated.

2. Detailed Calculation Steps and Monitoring

Casing wear is estimated as a consequence of all the operations that the well has undergone. Hence, it becomes very critical to capture and simulate all the operational steps in greater detail to improve the accuracy of wear estimation. For the drilling of a given hole section starting from a particular measured depth, the normal contact force between the tool joints and the casing inner wall varies as the drill bit progresses farther down the hole to drill the formation. This variation in contact forces at any

depth along the casing needs to be correctly captured and accounted for in wear calculations. For example, in this drilling scenario, the calculation of normal contact forces and the resulting wear as the drill bit penetrates each 30-ft section of the formation will represent more accurate wear-calculation results as compared to a case when these calculations are performed every 500 ft of the drilled section.

The length along the casing over which the average casing wear is estimated and monitored also needs to be small enough to effectively capture the effect of all the detailed calculation steps. For example, calculating and monitoring casing wear for every 10-ft section along the casing will prove to be more accurate in representing the field scenario as compared to a case where the average casing wear is reported every 100 ft of the casing section. The objective of casing-wear analysis is to correctly predict the peaks of casing-wear logs, and it is important to independently track smaller casing lengths for all the conducted operations to achieve this objective. Coarse calculation steps and reporting average wear over a long section along the casing will cause inaccuracies in wear calculation and result in an erroneous value of the back-modeled wear factor.

3. Friction Factor

As explained in Eq. 10-3, the friction factor forms an integral part of the casing-wear factor. Samuel (2010) has provided a comprehensive treatise on friction factors and explains the fundamentals of the coefficient of friction and the underlying complexities. He suggests that the friction factor is used as a proxy for the coefficient of friction or the Coulomb friction because of large uncertainties in the modeling of long drillstrings, including cuttings bed, tortuosity, mud properties, and fluid viscous effects. In addition, the friction factor also varies with the type of operation, rotational speed, and the temperature of the surfaces in contact. Hence, in order to account for all the uncertainties, the friction factor is calibrated in much the same way as the casing-wear factor by using measured hookload and torque data from the surface.

The casing-wear factors, as measured under the laboratory conditions, were not able to account for all these complexities associated with the friction factor. The experimental conditions corresponded to lower friction

factors as compared to that expected in the field, and, hence, the measured values of wear factors were underpredicted. It is for this reason that a multiplier greater than one is required to be used with the laboratory-determined casing-wear factors to match actual field scenarios.

4. Well Path and Wellbore Survey

All the studies conducted on casing-wear modeling agree that the accuracy of wear estimation depends tremendously on the accuracy of the well path and wellbore survey points. Wellbore surveys directly influence the calculation of normal contact forces, and coarse survey spacing will result in omissions of high dogleg points that cause maximum wear. Calhoun et al. (2010) suggested that definitive surveys may be supplemented with "synthetic" surveys using appropriate tortuosity factors to account for uncertainties in survey measurement and for better representation of the well path for casing-wear modeling. Mitchell et al. (2012) proposed a new statistically based tortuosity model to supplement wellbore surveys for improving casing-wear prediction.

The effect of wellbore torsion should also be accounted for to have a more realistic representation of the well path. Kumar et al. (2013) presented a casing-wear model using the wellbore profile energy by accounting for the wellbore torsion. In addition, the wellbore survey measured before running in the casing should be updated using a stiff-string model after the casing is cemented in place to address any misalignments of the casing with the initially drilled open-hole section. Calhoun et al. (2010) also suggested that a gyro survey be run at a casing point if there is excessive uncertainty in the actual well path. The updated casing locations along the wellbore will help improve wear estimation and reduce suspicions about the back-modeled wear factors.

5. Nonlinear Behavior

Hall et al. (2005) explained that the wear-groove formation on the inner wall of the casing due to tool joint contact does not vary directly with the test duration and displays a nonlinear behavior based on the groove depth. The wear factors estimated decrease with increasing wear depth for a given set of test conditions and approach an asymptotic value as wear

exceeds about 40%. The laboratory-reported wear factors are based on these asymptotic values of wear percent. However, if, for a given drilling situation, the wear on the casing is below this asymptotic value, then an empirically derived correlation should be used to account for this nonlinear behavior and correct the wear-factor values.

Hence, the experimental wear factors would result in underpredicting the wear if this non-linear characteristic is not accounted for in case of small values of wear percent, while the back-modeled wear factors would erroneously be higher than the actual value. These inaccurate back-modeled wear factors subsequently result in a loss of confidence in the casing-wear modeling techniques.

6. Multiple Wear Factors

The advent of complex drilling programs has resulted in significant advancements in the drillpipe and casing material now being used for operations. Different drillstring and casing-string configurations are used to cater to different drilling programs, and assuming that casing wear along the entire wellbore can be simulated using a single wear factor will be erroneous. For example, to drill multilateral wells, special aluminum-casing pipes are used in the main borehole from where a lateral is to be initiated, as it is easier to drill through aluminum as compared to steel. Hence, in this case, separate wear factors should be used in the casing-wear analysis for the aluminum and steel-casing pipes.

Casing-friendly tool joints are also repeatedly used at certain critical portions along the drillstring. Using a single wear factor to represent the more aggressive and more friendly types of drillpipe tool joints in a single drillstring will lead to erroneous casing-wear estimation. A limited number of drillpipe protectors may also be used for a given operation; thus, the downhole drilling scenario cannot be correctly represented for the entire string using a single wear factor. In addition, using multiple wear factors is especially useful while back-modeling wear factors from casing-wear logs, as different values of wear factors may be required for different casing sections to accurately match the field data.

7. Wear-Groove Locations

As mentioned previously,, the side force estimated using the stiff-string model is considered to be more accurate than the soft-string model. This calculated value of side force per foot of drillstring can be used to predict the side force acting on the inner casing wall owing to tool-joint contact. In addition, the contact location between the drillstring and the casing can also be estimated for any casing cross-section, which can be used to model the development of multiple wear grooves.

The high-position and right-position estimates for the drillstring location at any cross-section obtained from the stiff-string model can be used to predict the contact points of the drillstring with the inner casing wall, and wear resulting from this contact can be modeled. As any operation conducted through the casing progresses, the contact points of the drillstring vary, and, hence, wear grooves at different locations of a casing cross-section are formed for any given depth. The estimation of multiple wear grooves for any given operation becomes a very complex process because of the sheer number of variables and parameters involved in the modeling technique.

An example calculation for a drilling operation has been described here. From the start depth of the operation, the bit position is moved by the incremental operation step of 30 ft, and the new drillstring configuration inside the wellbore is estimated using stiff-string modeling. Based on this new bit position, side forces along the drillstring are calculated. Time taken for this incremental step is estimated based on the total drilling time and the total number of steps involved. Using the calculated side force, along with the time taken for the step and other operating parameters (such as the rotary speed, wear factor, and drillstring properties), the amount of casing-wear volume is calculated using Eq. 10-1 for this small incremental step of 30 ft.

For this bit depth, the high and right positions are estimated for each of the drillstring segments along the wellbore using the stiff-string model. The high and right positions are then used to estimate the contact point along the casing cross-section for each of the drillstring segments. This contact point would result in wear only at that particular location of the casing

cross-section. The incremental wear volume calculated above is assigned to the slice present at this contact point. The next incremental step in the drilling operation is then processed by moving the bit depth by another 30 ft, and this analysis is performed again. Wear volume from each of these incremental steps is assigned to slices for each casing section in a cumulative manner. The drilling steps are increased in this manner until the target end depth of the operation.

Reaching the operation end depth by following this process results in an accumulated distribution of wear volumes assigned to each of the slices for each 10-ft casing section. These wear volumes are then used to calculate wear grooves at those respective locations. The conventionally used crescent-shaped wear-groove model is used to calculate grooves based on wear volume, as presented by Hall et al. (2005). A total of 72 slices spanning 5° each are considered in this method. The method consists of analyzing all the 72 slices to select the slice that has the maximum assigned wear volume, and then calculating a wear groove based on this wear volume. If the calculated groove encompasses more than 50% of the area of the adjacent slices, the wear volume from the three slices are combined together, and one larger groove depth is calculated. If the initially calculated groove encompasses less than 50% of the area of the adjacent slices, then the method moves forward to analyze the next largest slice based on assigned wear volume.

Fig. 10.1 shows an example scenario of when the calculated groove spans less than 50% of the adjacent slices, while **Fig. 10.2** illustrates when the groove encompasses more than 50% of the adjacent slices. In the case of **Fig. 10-2**, the wear volume of the two adjacent slices 1 and 3 are added to the wear volume from slice 2, and these three slices are treated together as one large slice for further analysis. Using the above explained algorithm, multiple wear grooves for each of the 10-ft casing sections along the wellbore are estimated.

8. Rigsite Operations

As already pointed out, the total wear on the casing is a consequence of all the operations that are conducted through that casing string. Hence,

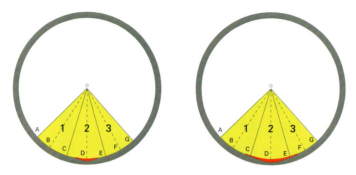

Fig. 10.1 – Calculated Groove Spans Less Than 50% of the Adjacent Grooves.

Fig. 10.2 – Calculated Groove Encompasses More Than 50% of Adjacent Grooves.

it becomes critically important to keep vigilant track of each and every operation carried out that may have contributed to wear. For example, a conventional drilling operation may comprise a short reaming of the hole section after drilling every stand. In this case, it is important to account for the additional wear due to this small reaming operation, as, over the course of the entire drilling program, this additional wear would accumulate. Field observations suggest that casing has also been worn out, even in situations when the drillstring is not rotating but just reciprocating inside the casing shoe due to wave heave in an offshore environment. Hence, it is critical to capture all the downhole scenarios that may contribute to wear.

The sequence in which the operations are conducted is also important, as it affects the nonlinear wear-groove formation. The wear factors may

also vary based on the type of operation being conducted, and different wear factors may be used for estimating wear from different operations. Additionally, during rigsite operations, the values of the drilling parameters, like weight on bit and rotational speed, vary during any operation. Accounting for variations in these parameters to estimate normal contact force and the resulting wear will help improve the accuracies of the back-modeled wear factors.

9. Downhole Conditions

Casing-wear estimation should account for changes in downhole conditions to improve accuracy of wear predictions. Calhoun et al. (2010) investigated a casing-failure event due to excessive wear and suggested that one of the root causes was thermally induced buckling of the casing while drilling at deeper depths. Buckling was observed in the area above the top of the cement because of increases in temperature and/or mud weight while drilling, and, combined with the doglegs, created a condition for excessive casing wear. Hence, buckling analysis of the casing should be performed for a more accurate calculation of back-modeled wear factors.

High casing wear may also result from excessive downhole vibrations while drilling if the vibrating portion of the drillstring is still inside the casing. This wear due to the vibrational impacts of the drillstring on the inner wall of the casing should not be modeled using the same wear factors as used for the other operations, because this wear is a consequence of a different wear mechanism. Kumar et al. (2013) have presented a modeling method to predict casing wear as a result of drillstring vibrations inside the casing. Jianchun et al. (2008) have also presented some experimental results on fatigue wear due to large lateral vibrations of the drillstring. In addition, high-pressure/high-temperature (HPHT) downhole drilling conditions may also influence wear factors, and, as a result, back-modeled wear factors for a conventional well cannot be accurately applied for an HPHT well.

10. Variation with Parameters

The casing-wear experiments performed as a part of the DEA-42 project to estimate values of wear factors for different combinations of casing material, tool-joint material, and mud type were all carried out for the same

set of lateral load, rotary speed, and reciprocation rate. However, with complex drilling programs, all these parameters vary significantly from the laboratory testing conditions, and wear factors may vary for different rotary and load conditions. The testing conditions did not account for any influence of mud flow rate, which may also significantly affect the wear factors.

In addition, advancements have also been made on the materials used for casing and tool joints, along with improvements in the drilling mud that is now being used in operations. A new set of experimental wear factors should be determined for these new operating conditions.

11. Casing-Wear Logs

The importance of having accurate casing-wear measurement logs is crucial when trying to estimate casing wear using back-modeled wear factors. Multi-finger caliper logs are generally considered to be more accurate as compared to a sonic or ultra-sonic log, as the estimation of casing-wall inner diameter is a direct physical measurement for caliper logs as compared to ultra-sonic logs that have the casing-wall thickness as an indirect estimation derived from other parameters. All proper precautions should be taken while running these logs to be as accurate as possible when associating a particular casing depth with a certain value of measured casing-wear-groove depth. Inaccurate casing-wear logs will certainly result in erroneous back-modeled wear factors and incorrect wear predictions.

All these parameters and uncertainties listed for casing-wear estimation play a significant role in governing the accuracy of the wear-prediction models. An improper analysis done by discounting any of these parameters will result in incorrect back-modeled wear factors and cause inaccurate casing-wear estimation for the next set of operations when these wear factors are used. In addition, other uncertainties may also exist, like the wearing out of the casing inner wall from other downhole-wear mechanisms, which may not require a tool joint and casing-wall contact and may be very difficult to model using this technique. Additional casing wear due to drillpipe-body contact apart from the tool joints may also be observed in certain operating conditions.

Well Log Comparison and Validation

The results of the modeling simulation were compared with the ultrasonic wear log run in an offshore deviated well from the North Sea. Only the 9-5/8-in. casing section was logged between the depths of 9,445 ft and 16,540 ft. The values of the minimum remaining wall thickness from the ultrasonic log have been compared with the minimum remaining wall thickness estimated from the modeling approach proposed by this study.

Investigation of this wear log comparison with the model was divided into two parts – the high-wear zone between the depths of 9,445 ft and 11,400 ft and the low-wear zone between 11,400 ft and 16,540 ft, which was the bottom of the logged section. The wear log comparison of the high-wear zone has been more closely highlighted in **Fig. 10.3**. Here, the peaks of the ultrasonic wear log lying outside the manufacturing tolerance limit correspond well with the wear distribution for this zone predicted using the model. Estimated wear percent for the worst groove at any casing cross-section falling in the high-wear zone varied from a minimum of 10% wear to a maximum of 26% wear.

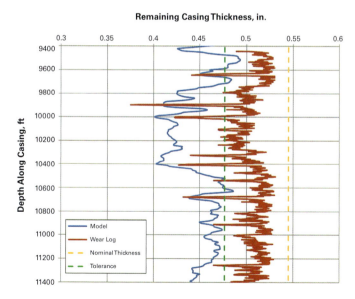

Fig. 10.3 – Remaining Casing Wall Thickness Comparison with Ultrasonic Log for the High-Wear Zone.

The slight variations in wear between the measured log values and the estimated values using the model are attributed to some of the underlying uncertainties in the input parameters that we used for modeling. As suggested by Kumar and Samuel (2015), total wear predictions are heavily influenced by parameters like wellpath, survey frequency, multiple wear factor distribution along the casing or the drillstring, operation parameters like weight on bit or rpm, and the downhole wellbore conditions. Variation or inaccuracies in any of these input parameters would, in turn, influence the final predicted wear.

The model over-predicted the amount of wear when compared with the wear log in the low-wear zone between the depths of 11,400 ft and 16,540 ft. This zone was further examined to investigate any possible underlying causes that may have contributed to this over-prediction. After careful analysis, it was considered that the comparison between the model and the wear log had limitations when the measured and calculated wear was below the pipe tolerance limit. This may have resulted from a lack of a base log to identify the actual casing ID to run the wear simulations or some limitations on the logging tool.

The other important parameter that has been used for validation and comparison between the wear log and the model is the azimuthal location of the worst wear groove at any casing cross-section in the logged zone. Such comparisons between the measured azimuthal location of wear grooves and the modeled location of wear grooves have not been performed before for casing-wear analysis in the industry and will help to further understand the accuracy of the underlying modeling method.

Fig. 10.4 shows the wear groove position comparison between the modeled wear grooves and the ultrasonic wear log. Out of the multiple wear grooves modeled using the proposed method, the azimuthal location of the worst groove having the maximum groove depth has been compared with the log. The high side of the wellbore is considered to be 0° in the used convention, and the casing cross-section is traversed in a clockwise direction to model multiple grooves. Using the ultrasonic log again, the logged location of the wear grooves correlates very well with the location of the worst groove, as estimated by the model. It should be noted that the entire

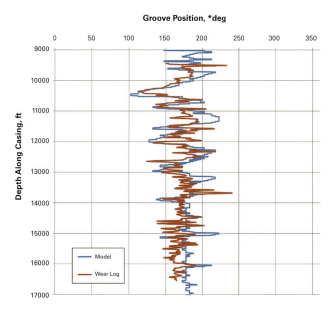

Fig. 10.4 – Wear Groove Position Comparison with Ultrasonic Log.

logging depth lies in the deviated section of the wellbore; hence, maximum wear was caused on the low side of the casing. Both the measured and the predicted values in Fig. 2 further confirm this observation, as most of the groove locations fell on either side of 180°, which represented the low side.

Fig. 10.5 shows the multiple wear grooves estimated at a particular depth of the casing section – at the depth of 10,400 ft, where we observe one of the peaks of the logged casing section. This depth lies in the deviated section of the well, and, conventionally, one single wear groove should have been expected in the low side. However, the azimuthal contact locations predicted by using the stiff-string model show that the wear was distributed between multiple wear grooves lying between 90° and 180° of the casing cross-section based on the clockwise convention specified above. This location of the maximum wear groove has been marked here with an orange pointer. The location of the worst wear groove predicted by the model at this depth correlates very well with the azimuthal location of the groove as measured by the ultrasonic log at the depth of 10,400 ft. This comparison can be clearly drawn from **Fig. 10.4**.

CASING WEAR

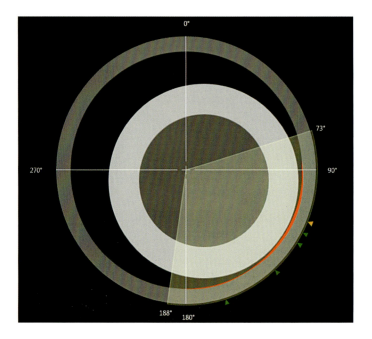

Fig. 10.5 – Casing Cross-Section Looking Down Hole, Showing Multiple Wear Groove Prediction at Depth of 10,400 Ft.

12. Other Modeling Uncertainties

Some of these influencing variables include nonlinear behavior of wear factors, variation of wear factors along the casing, application of hardbandings or drillpipe protectors on the drillstring, and the effect of uncertainty in dogleg severity along the wellbore. These underlying parameters are coupled with this proposed modeling method to further improve the accuracy of wear prediction.

The suggested method of segmenting the entire casing section in small intervals of 10 ft each helps to capture any minor variations in wear factors along the casing. Hardbandings or drillpipe protectors applied on the drillstring are analyzed using the stiff-string model to incorporate their influence on side forces and contact locations at any casing cross-section. Additionally, the variation in the wear factors owing to the use of hardbandings or drillpipe protectors along the string is very effectively

captured by performing small incremental operation steps of 30 ft, each as just described. For any given operation, the 10-ft section of the casing that experiences maximum wear can be further analyzed to understand which segments of the drillstring had maximum contact with that casing section and contributed to wear. Hence, this information can be used to mitigate wear by either intelligently applying drillpipe protectors on those high-wear-causing segments of the drillstring or modifying those segments to reduce their underlying wear factors.

Well Integrity

Wearing out of the inner casing wall results in degradation of the casing strength and causes a reduction in the burst and collapse pressure ratings, thus compromising well integrity. Several models, apart from the most commonly used API equations for burst and collapse, have been presented that address the calculation of degraded casing strength based on the reduction in wall thickness of the casing due to wear. Shen et al. (2012) have proposed an analytical solution for hoop-stress estimation in the worn-out casing based on the boundary-superposition principle, which also accounts for the contribution of thermal stresses. Samuel et al. (2014) have suggested corrections to the standard API equations to account for the stress concentration around the casing-wear grooves by quantifying it with a stress multiplier known as the stress concentration factor.

Casing-wear factors play a significant role in determining the remaining wall thickness after casing wear and, thus, have a great influence on estimating the overall well integrity. Inaccurate back-modeled wear factors may cause underestimation of the groove depth, compromising the wellbore integrity and resulting in catastrophic repercussions.

Casing-Wear Maps

A new visualization and interpretation method to accurately plan for the downhole casing wear has been proposed using "casing-wear maps." These casing-wear maps are 2-D or 3-D graphs that have the underlying parameters to estimate casing wear as the axes of the graphs. The wear maps can be applied in different ways to plan for expected casing wear

by monitoring it over the entire drilling program. The variation of wear percent, normal contact forces, and wear factors for all the planned operations can be put together simultaneously to help provide good insight into the causes of wear, along with ways to mitigate it. One such example of a casing-wear map for estimating wear percent with operation time along the entire casing depth has been shown in **Fig. 10.6**.

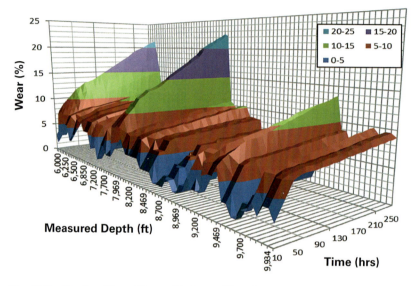

Fig. 10.6 – Casing-Wear Map to Estimate Wear Percent with Operation Along the Entire Casing Section.

Lubricity

Torque-and-drag problems are particularly severe in high-angle and horizontal wells. The pipe lies naturally on the low side of the hole, resulting in a large contact area with the formation and casing. Using a highly lubricating fluid can be a significant benefit in these situations, provided other mud properties are optimized and good drilling practices are adopted. Accepted friction factors for open hole are generally between 0.14 and 0.22 for oil-based mud (OBM) and between 0.2 and 0.40 for water-based mud (WBM). For cased hole, the friction factors are around 0.18 for OBM and 0.25 for WBM, depending on the mud being used. The friction factors

of field muds span a broad range, and the OBM and WBM values may overlap, depending on the mud formation and software used.

The torque-and-drag software must not be used in isolation. Emphasis must also be placed on field experience. If previous high-angle wells required the use of lubricants, and it is felt that all other drilling variables were optimized, then lubricants should be programmed for future wells. Field experience should take priority under these circumstances. Where possible, post-well evaluations should include calculating friction factors based on the actual hookloads and torque valves observed on the well. These friction factors can then be used for the prediction of torque and drag on the next well. In laboratory tests, WBM and OBM were used to evaluate the lubricity of the muds at varying densities and by using various concentrations of lubricants. The test comprised a 165-mm (6-1/2-in.) OD smooth tool joint rotating with varying loads against the internal diameter of 244-mm (9-5/8-in.) casing. The load varied between 4 kN and 8 kN (0.9 Kips and 1.8 Kips). It corresponds to the contact force in a build sector of a well with a hookload of 1,000 kN (225 Kips) and a build rate of 3°/30 m (3°/l00 ft). The "string" was rotated at 112 rpm while immersed in various mud systems.

No difference was found between the various commercially available lubricants for unweighted muds, as they all reduced casing wear to some degree (**Fig. 10.7**).

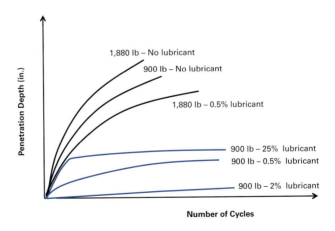

Fig. 10.7 – Results of Wear Experiments.

CASING WEAR

The addition of glass beads or diesel had no effect at all. The size of the glass beads prevented them from getting between the steels of the casing and the tool joint. Diesel did not form any chemical bond to cause a friction-reducing film on the steel.

Salt and polymer addition had some effect in reducing wear (torque), though the effects were lower than that of the lubricants.

No effect on wear of either lubricants or mud addition was found for weighted muds. The greatest effect was by the type of weighting material (**Fig. 10.8**).

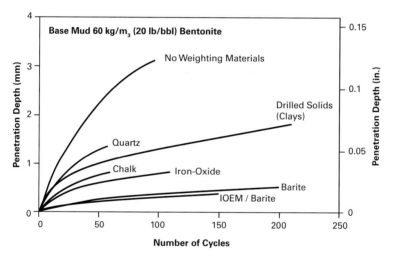

Fig. 10.8 – Results of Casing Experiments.

Software Use

Halliburton CasingWear™ software results can be analyzed incrementally or cumulative, i.e., incremental analyses are useful to perform operational comparisons with respect to the impact of a variable on casing-wear results, and cumulative analyses historically track the progression of wear in time across all operations, including the associated overall total revolutions and maximum wear limit. Cumulative wear can be defined between operations as long as they have the same analysis settings (torque-and-

drag model and linear or nonlinear wear factor correction) within the same case or across prior cases (as in prior wellbore cases, such as sidetrack scenarios).

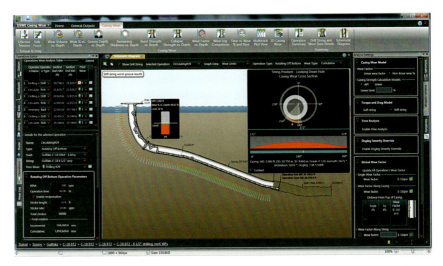

Fig 10.9 – CasingWear™ Analysis Options Include Linear Wear Factors, API Casing Strength, and Soft-String Torque-and-Drag Modeling.

References

An Engineering Approach to Horizontal Drilling – Halliburton Manual, 1992.

Bol, G.M. 1986. Effect of Mud Composition On Wear and Function of Casing and Tool Joints. *SPEDC*, **1**(05).

Bradley, W.B. and Fontenot, J.E. 1975. The Prediction and Control of Casing Wear. *JPT*, **27**(2): 233–245. http://dx.doi.org/10.2118/5122-PA.

Calhoun, B., Langdon, S., Wu, J., Hogan, P., and Rutledge, K. 2010. Casing Wear Prediction and Management in Deepwater Wells. Paper SPE 137223 presented at the SPE Deepwater Drilling and Completions Conference, Galveston, Texas, 5–6 October. http://dx.doi.org/10.2118/137223-MS.

Gao, D., Sun, L., and Lian, J. 2010. Prediction of Casing Wear in Extended-Reach Drilling. *Petroleum Science*, **7**(4): 494–501.

Hall, R.W. Jr. and Malloy, K.P. 2005. Contact Pressure Threshold: An Important New Aspect of Casing Wear. Paper SPE-94300-MS presented at the SPE Production and Operations Symposium, Oklahoma City, Oklahoma, 17–19 April. http://dx.doi.org/10.2118/94300-MS.

Hall, R.W. Jr. and Malloy, K.P. 2005. Contact Pressure Threshold: An Important New Aspect of Casing Wear. Paper SPE 94300 presented at the SPE Production and Operations Symposium, Oklahoma City, Oklahoma, 17–19 April. http://dx.doi.org/10.2118/94300-MS.

Hall, R.W. Jr., Garkasi, A., and Deskins, G., et al. 1994. Recent Advances in Casing Wear Technology. Paper SPE-27532-MS presented at the IADC/SPE Drilling Conference, Dallas, Texas, 15–18 February. http://dx.doi.org/10.2118/27532-MS.

Hall, R.W. Jr., Garkasi, A., Deskins, G., and Vozniak, J. 1994. Recent Advances in Casing Wear Technology. Paper IADC/SPE 27532 presented at the IADC/SPE Drilling Conference, Dallas, Texas, 15–18 February. http://dx.doi.org/10.2118/27532-MS.

Jianchun, F., Shengli, C., Laibin, Z., and Huiyuan, Y. 2008. Research on Mechanism of Casing Wear in Sliding-Impact Wear Condition. Proceedings of CIST2008 & ITS-IFToMM2008, Beijing, China.

Kumar, A. and Samuel, R. 2014. Modeling Method to Estimate the Casing Wear Caused by Vibrational Impacts of the Drillstring. Paper IADC/SPE 167999 presented at the IADC/SPE Drilling Conference and Exhibition, Fort Worth, Texas, 4–6 March. http://dx.doi.org/10.2118/167999-MS.

Kumar, A. and Samuel, R. 2015. Casing Wear Factors: How Do They Improve Well Integrity Analyses? Paper SPE-173053-MS presented at the SPE/IADC Drilling Conference & Exhibition, London, UK, 17–19 March.

Kumar, A., Nwachukwu, J., and Samuel, R. 2013. Analytical Model to Estimate the Downhole Casing Wear Using the Total Wellbore Energy. *Journal of Energy Resources Technology*, 135: 1–8.

Mitchell, R. and Samuel, R. 2009. How Good is the Torque/Drag Model? SPEDC, **24**(1): 62–71.

Mitchell, S. and Xiang, Y. 2012. Improving Casing Wear Prediction and Mitigation Using a Statistically Based Model. Paper IADC/SPE 151448 presented at the IADC/SPE Drilling Conference and Exhibition, San Diego, California, 6–8 March. http://dx.doi.org/10.2118/151448-MS.

Samuel, R., Kumar, A., Gonzales, A., Marcou, S., Mette Rød, A. 2016. Solving the Casing Wear Puzzle Using Stiff-String Model, SPE 178833, IADC/SPE Drilling Conference and Exhibition held in Fort Worth, Texas, 1–3 March.

Samuel, R. 2010. Friction Factors: What Are They For? Torque, Drag, Vibration, Bottomhole Assembly and Transient Surge/Swab Analysis. Paper IADC/SPE 128059 presented at the IADC/SPE Drilling Conference and Exhibition, New Orleans, Louisiana, 2–4 February. http://dx.doi.org/10.2118/128059-MS.

Samuel, R. and Gao, D. 2014. *Horizontal Drilling Engineering: Theory, Methods and Applications*. Houston: SigmaQuadrant Publishers.

Samuel, R. and Gao, D. 2015. *501 Solved Problems and Calculations for Drilling Operations*. Houston: SigmaQuadrant Publishers.

Schoenmakers, J.M. 1987. Casing Wear During Drilling: Simulation, Prediction and Control. *SPEDC*, 2(04): 375–381. http://dx.doi.org/10.2118/14761-PA.

Shen, Z. and Beck, F.E. 2012. Intermediate Casing Collapse Induced by Casing Wear in High-Temperature and High-Pressure Wells. Paper SPE 155973 presented at the SPE International Production and Operations Conference and Exhibition, Doha, Qatar, 14–16 May. http://dx.doi.org/10.2118/155973-MS.

White, J.P. and Dawson, R. 1987. Casing Wear: Laboratory Measurements and Field Predictions. *SPEDC*, 2(01): 56–62. http://dx.doi.org/10.2118/14325-PA.

EXTENDED-REACH DRILLING

Index

Aquathermal Pressuring – 49

Axial Load – 246, 247, 248, 249

Axial Strength – 204

Axial Vibrations or "Bit Bounce" – 165

Azimuth – 72

Background Gas – 51

Barite Sag – 146

Basic 1-D Pore-Pressure Estimation Process – 60

Basic Well Path Designs – 91

BHA and Drillstring Design – 84

BHA Modeling – 158

BHA Response – 151

Bit Whirl – 166

Bowers' Method – 64

Build Rates – 74

Buildup Rate – 73

Burst (Production) – 243

Burst Strength – 198

Buttress-Thread Casing-Joint Strength – 212

Casing Loads – 218

Casing Program – 75

Casing Wear and Hole Erosion – 253

Casing-Wear Factors – 261

Casing-Wear Logs – 262

Casing-Wear Maps – 276

Casing-Wear Model – 258

Catenary Design – 95

Cementation Deterioration – 33

Chemical Effects – 33

Clay Swelling (Hydration) and Migration – 33

Clothoid Curve – 105

Completion and Reservoir Drainage – 74

Collapse Below Packer (Production) – 244

Collapse (Drilling) – 239

Collapse Strength – 199

Combined Burst and Compression Loading – 208

Combined Burst and Tension Loading – 208

Combined Collapse and Tension – 207

Connections – 210

Connections Burst and Collapse – 217

Connection Design Limits – 213

Connection/Trip Gas – 51

Coupling Internal Yield Pressure – 211

Critical Inclination Angle – 99

Curvature and Torsion – 112

Curvature Bridging – 109

Curved-Compaction Trend – 63

Departure – 74

Design Control – 86

Designer Wells – 7

Drainage of Reservoir – 74

Drill-ahead Models – 159

Drillstring Considerations – 163

Drillstring Design – 152

Drillstring Dynamics – 164

Drilling-Fluid Weight – 34

Drilling Tangent Sections – 86

Drillpipe Eccentricity – 142

Drillstring Buckling – 174

Drucker-Prager Criterion – 28

Eaton's Method – 57

Effect of Parameter Derating – 216

Equilibrium Models – 159

Estimation – 255

Expected Influx Volume – 183

Extended-Reach Drilling – 2

Extended-Reach Drilling Envelope – 7

External-Pressure Loads – 219

Extreme-Extended-Reach Wells – 9

Extreme-Line Casing-Joint Strength – 213

Failure Criteria – 25

Faults and Folding – 75

Fluid Gradient – 245

Fluid Gradients with Pore Pressure – 224

Formation Anisotropy – 160

Formation Pressure – 43

Formation Temperature – 52

Fracture Gradient and Pore Pressure – 180

Fracture-Gradient Prediction – 55

Fracture Pressure – 46

Fracture Toughness – 19

Friction Factor – 261

Full Evacuation – 241, 244

Helical Method – 120

Hoek-Brown Criterion – 27

Hole Cleaning – 139

INDEX

Hole-Cleaning Management – 143

Hubert and Willis Method – 56

Hydraulics and Wellbore-Pressure Management – 128

Hydraulics Management – 84

Hydrostatic Isolation Depth (HID) – 220

Inclination – 72

Ion Exchanging – 33

Kick After Pump Shutdown – 186

Kick Classification – 182

Kick Detection – 182

Kicks While Drilling – 183

Kick-Off Point – 73

Kick Tolerance – 193

Killing the Well – 188

Lateral vibrations of the BHA – 166

Lift Factors – 142

Long-Radius Wells – 76

Lost Circulation – 137, 187

Lubricity – 277

Mathews and Kelly Method – 57

Mechanical Effects – 34

Mechanical Loads – 219, 246

Medium-Radius Wells – 77

Miller's Method – 65

Minimum Formation Pore Pressure – 229

Mohr-Coulomb Failure Criterion – 26

Mud and Cement Slurry (Collapse) – 220

Mud Consideration – 130

Mud Properties – 52

Near-Wellbore Damage – 33

Near-Wellbore Stress Field – 20

Nonlinear Behavior – 265

Overburden Pressure – 42

Pipe-Body Collapse – 217

Pipe Strength – 198

Pore-Pressure Calculation – 58

Pore Pressure Estimation – 54

Poroelasticity – 14

Pressure Loads – 218

Pressure Load Cases – 231

Primary Control – 177

Projected Pore Pressures – 59

Quantification of Borehole Complexity – 112

Radial Safety Factor – 214

Random Inclination and Azimuth Method – 120

Random Inclination-Dependent Azimuth Method – 120

Rate of Penetration (ROP) – 52

Relative Strain Energy – 117

Rig Capabilities – 161

Risk Management Process – 82

Round-Thread Casing-Joint Strength – 212

Samuel's Wellbore Energy Index – 116

Secondary Control – 177

Shear Failure – 34

Short-Radius Wells – 79

Sine-Wave Method – 119

Steel Grades – 198

Stuck Pipe – 136

Surging – 182

Survey Management – 83

Survey Stations – 72

Swabbing – 181

Tangent Section – 74

Tensile Failure – 34

Tertiary Control – 177

Thermal Loads – 219

Thermal Expansion Loads – 219, 250

Thermoviscoelasticity – 15

Tool-Failure Prediction – 173

Torque and Drag – 154

Torque and Drag Management – 84

Torsional Vibrations of the Drillstring – 166

Tortuosity – 118

Total Strain Energy Change – 116

Trajectory Calculations – 110

Transition Curves – 104

Trapped Gas – 192

Trip Speed and Pipe Rotation – 156

Troublesome Zones – 75

True Vertical Depth – 73

Ultra-Extended-Reach Wells – 8

Ultra-Short-Radius Wells – 80

Undercompaction – 49

Vibration Management – 85

Viscoelasticity – 15

Wang and Samuel Approach – 28

Water Gradient – 241

Wellbore Indices – 114

Wellbore Instability – 32, 138

Well Integrity – 276

Well Path – 141

Well-Path Planning – 82

Other resources written by Dr. Judy Davidson, published by the RENEW Center, PO BOX 125, Berea, Ky 40403 859-986-7878. www.renew.net   E-mail: renew@mis.net

Adult Grief Process Video   **$39.95**
Dr. Judy Davidson narrates this 23 minute educational video filled with practical information applicable to understanding adult grief following deaths that were unexpected or due to terminal illnesses. The experience of loss is described as healing a deep wound, with pangs of grief or waves of pain that you think may overwhelm you. She provides a road map to recovery.

The Child's Grief Process Video   **$39.95**
Excellent educational video for parents, teachers, and counselors. In this 18 minute video, Dr. Davidson incorporates clinical research, her experience with two small children after their father's death, a teenager after her son's death and the families she has counseled.

Grieving Well   A personal journal about loss for adults   **$14.95**
A personal journal for adults that guides them through the grief process. The writer is prompted by leading statements to write about his or her personal experiences.

**My Own Grief Journal   A personal journal
about loss for the young child, ages 7-12**   **$11.95**
A personal journal for anticipated deaths that guides the young child through the grief process. The child is prompted by leading statements to write or draw about his or her experiences. Illustrated characters may also be colored.

**My Own Grief Journal   A personal journal
about loss for the young child, ages 4-6**   **$11.95**
A personal journal for anticipated deaths that guides the young child through the grief process. The child is prompted by leading statements to write or draw about his or her experiences. Illustrated characters may also be colored.

Each day is a new beginning. I will ...

When I think about the meaning of life, itself, I realize...

In my life, the most important thing is ...

Nobody is perfect.
Because all human beings make mistakes, there are probably a few things your loved one did that they should not have done. Maybe he or she hurt another person, or you. Perhaps they said hurtful things, or were inconsiderate.

Writing about these behaviors is not disrespectful.

These may be the kinds of things that need to be forgiven. How was your loved one LESS THAN PERFECT? How are YOU LESS THAN PERFECT?

The most important lesson I have learned since the death of my loved one is...

_____
_____
_____
_____
_____
_____

Sad Days

Some days are more difficult than others when you are grieving... it may be your first Christmas or birthday... or it could be the anniversary of the death.

Write about these difficult, sad days.

_____
_____
_____
_____
_____
_____
_____
_____
_____
_____
_____
_____
_____
_____
_____
_____

The things I miss most are . . .

_____
_____
_____
_____
_____

If you could write the person who died, how would you finish this sentence? I know your death is not my fault, but sometimes I feel bad because . . .

_____
_____
_____
_____
_____
_____
_____
_____

Different DIFFERENT

I sometimes feel very different from other people.

Write about how you see yourself now, following this loss and how you are different from before the death.

_____
_____
_____
_____
_____
_____
_____
_____
_____
_____
_____
_____
_____
_____
_____
_____

If I could see my loved one again, I would say...

Sometimes we regret things... and it helps to write about them. I wish I had...

_____
_____
_____
_____
_____
_____
_____
_____
_____
_____
_____
_____

I wish I had not . . .

_____
_____
_____
_____
_____
_____
_____
_____
_____
_____
_____
_____
_____

Releasing Unfinished Business

When death happens and we didn't expect it . . . or it happens in such a way as to leave us angry with others, we may find ourselves seeking justice against those we feel are to blame. When we hold onto anger, resentment, or blame, we are filled with negative thoughts and feelings that keep us from healing. Forgiveness is important, especially if nothing can be changed now. Is there anything that you are still holding onto that upsets you? Are you angry with someone? Do you blame someone? What other unfinished business or feeling could you list?

_____
_____
_____

Life changes and adjustments must be made...

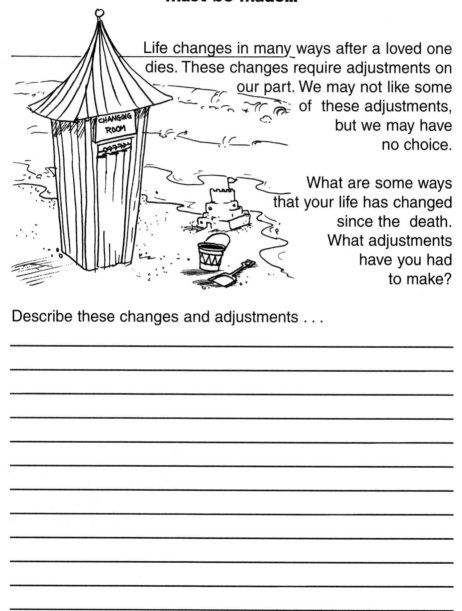

Life changes in many ways after a loved one dies. These changes require adjustments on our part. We may not like some of these adjustments, but we may have no choice.

What are some ways that your life has changed since the death. What adjustments have you had to make?

Describe these changes and adjustments . . .

_____
_____
_____
_____
_____
_____
_____
_____
_____
_____
_____
_____
_____

Sometimes I daydream about things being different. When I daydream, I think about . . .

What I wish other people understood...

Need a friend   Be a friend

Think about the best friend you have who allows you to talk about your feelings. Write a letter to your best friend telling him or her what you really like and appreciate about him/her. Share in your letter how he/she
has helped you to
deal with your loss . . .

_____
_____
_____
_____
_____

One of the funniest things I remember was...

Picture Your Family's Grief.

Draw a picture of your family grieving . . . and describe how each member of your family is grieving. Who is angry? Who does the things in the family that the person who died used to do? Who is pretending it didn't happen? Who has taken on new roles in the family and how do you feel about them? Who is staying so busy that they appear not to be grieving?

_____
_____
_____
_____
_____
_____
_____
_____

Family Losses

Not only do individuals in a family grieve when a death occurs, but the family has to grieve as a group the things they have lost.

What are some" things" your family has lost because of the death? Make a list of each member in your family and the kinds of "things" they have lost. For example, you may have a younger sibling . . . who will never go fishing with Dad. . . or Mom won't ever get to see graduate... or Dad won't be there to give you or your sister away at your weddings.

_____
_____
_____
_____
_____
_____
_____
_____

Worry?

Sometimes people worry about other bad things that might happen after they lose a love one.

What have you, or what are you worrying about?

_____
_____
_____
_____
_____
_____
_____
_____
_____
_____
_____
_____
_____
_____
_____
_____

Regrets   Everybody has some

When a person dies, we look back over our lives and sometimes we have regrets. Are there things you wish you had done? Or done differently? Do you sometimes think about "what if . . ." or "if onlys?" Write about your thoughts, fears and feelings.

_____
_____
_____
_____
_____

The last time I saw or talked to the person who died was...

Describe the things you enjoyed doing most with the person who died.

Describe the special qualities of the person who died. While it is important that you remember the good qualities, it is O.K. to write about negative qualities you may have experienced. . .

Describe your relationship with the person who died. What can you recall about your relationship?

Remind yourself that you can come back to this part of the journal any time.

_____
_____
_____
_____
_____
_____
_____
_____
_____
_____
_____
_____
_____
_____
_____
_____
_____
_____
_____
_____
_____
_____
_____
_____
_____
_____

How people at school reacted when I returned to classes...

How I felt about going back to school.

Who was there to give you support?

_____
_____
_____
_____
_____
_____
_____
_____

Some days I feel angry. When I am upset, my anger is about . .

_____
_____
_____
_____
_____

Some days I feel sad. When I am sad, my sadness is about...

_____
_____
_____
_____
_____
_____
_____

However, sometimes we also have things happen at the funeral that we wish had not happened, or regrets about things we wish had been done. Nothing can be changed that has already occurred, but we can release our feelings, fears and thoughts about it.

What happened at the funeral visitation, or memorial service that you thought was helpful?

_____
_____
_____
_____
_____
_____

What happened that you didn't like?

_____
_____
_____
_____
_____
_____

Is there something you wish you had done, or that you wish someone else had done?

_____
_____
_____
_____

Remembering and releasing during the funeral, visitation, or memorial service.

The last time you saw your loved one's remains may have been very painful, so painful that you may not want to remember what happened.

Questions Without Answers

Do you have any unanswered questions about death? Are you thinking about how the person died, the circumstances surrounding the death, or any thing that has been done since they died? Are there any questions you or others close to you have, which have not yet been answered? Are there any "pieces" of the "puzzle" missing?

Write about them.

_____
_____
_____
_____
_____
_____
_____
_____
_____

Picture Your Grief

Think about what this death means to you and then draw a picture that describes or symbolizes it. After you have drawn the picture, write words that describe your feelings, fears, or thoughts regarding this death.

How I Heard About The News

What were your thoughts when you heard the sad news about your loved one's death?

What do you remember hearing, seeing, or what did you do?

How did others who were important to you respond to the sad news?

_____
_____
_____
_____
_____
_____
_____
_____
_____
_____
_____
_____

My name is_____

The name of the person who died is_____

He/she was my _____

What thoughts would best summarize how you would like your loved one remembered?

_____
_____
_____
_____
_____
_____
_____
_____
_____
_____
_____
_____
_____
_____
_____
_____
_____
_____
_____
_____
_____

The Grief Process

To complete the grief process you will do "grief work." In your grief work, you will complete four tasks of mourning, described by Dr. William Worden.

The first task of mourning is to accept the reality that the person you love is dead. This is hard to believe and our minds will drift into disbelief even after we have been told the truth. Acceptance of the truth can usually be accomplished through viewing the body and attending closing rituals, such as a wake, funeral, or memorial service. However, your mind may drift into denial for brief periods of time even after you have experienced these services.

You may search for understanding by asking yourself questions that have no acceptable answers, such as "Why?" "If only," "What if?" The search for understanding is part of your acceptance process.

The second task of mourning involves a review of your life experiences with the person who died. As you do this, you may recall experiences you regret as well as enjoyed. Making peace with the experiences you regret, "righting wrongs," working through forgiveness, may result in changes in the way you relate to others. During this time, you learn important "life lessons" about what you value and how you will live in the future.

The third task of mourning involves adjusting to the changes in your life and the lives of your family members without the roles, responsibilities, and family rituals fulfilled by the person who died. Someone else in the family may assume these roles, tasks, or responsibilities, or you must learn to live without them. You may assume some of these responsibilities and as you do, you will learn new skills. Family holidays will also change, because someone you shared these events with is now gone.

The fourth task of mourning occurs when you RENEW life. When you do so, you have completed your grief work, clarified what you value, adjusted to life without the loved one, and you are now ready to reinvest your energies in living in a joyful and productive way. Know that the grief process may take you several years to complete.

Listen to your thoughts and feelings. Pay attention to your body and nurture yourself in healthy ways. Do not avoid the pain. Rather work your way through the pain. You suffer because an important bond has been broken. Continue to hold the person who died lovingly in your heart and your heart will mend.

Dear Fellow Travelers

This journal is for you to use as a tool for processing and recording your life and loss experiences. Writing in it will help you to understand as well as give you a way to release painful emotions.

There is no right or wrong way to feel when a death occurs. All feelings are normal and good. How, when, and with whom you share these feelings is an important issue. Not all people you know will be comfortable with your pain. If not, they probably have not yet had a loss, so they may not understand how to be helpful and supportive. When there is no one around to talk with, use the time to write in your journal. The journal does not have to be completed quickly. Your journal is private and does not have to be shared with others, unless you choose to do so.

You may want to date each entry so that you can read through your journal entries later. You will gain many insights as you work through your grief. You will learn some important lessons about life, love, family, and friends. Your journal will help you remember what is most important so that you can RENEW your commitment to life again.

The Center for Personal Recovery is within you. Becoming aware of your thoughts, feelings and memories, will help you use your "grieving time" to heal.

Judy Davidson, Ed. D.

Table of Contents   **Page No.**

Dear Fellow Travelers   1
The Grief Process   2
Introduction   3
How You Heard the News   5
Picture Your Grief   7
Questions Without Answers   8
The Funeral   9
Going Back to School   12
How People at School Treat Me   13
Your Relationship   14
Special Qualities   17
What You Enjoyed   18
Last Visit   19
Regrets   20
Worry   22
Family Losses   23
Family Grief   24
Funniest Memory   25
Need a Friend   31
I Wish   28
Daydream   29
How Life Has Changed   31
Releasing   34
Regrets   36
See Again   37
Different   38
Not My Fault, But I Feel Bad   39
Miss Most   40
Sad Days   41
Life Lessons   42
Nobody's Perfect   43
What's Important   44
Meaning in Life   45
Each Day   46

Grief Skills For Life
A personal journal for teenagers about loss

Judy Davidson, Ed. D.

Copyright 1997-2002
    All rights reserved. This book may not be reproduced or quoted in whole or in part by any means whatsoever without written permission from:

    RENEW: Center for Personal Recovery
    PO BOX 125, Berea, Ky 40403
    859-986-7878
    www.renew.net
    renew@mis.net

    Permission is never granted for commercial purposes.
    First printing 1997
    Printed in the United States.
    ISBN: 0-9719569-1-X

Graphic Artist: Ken Venton
Electronic Design: Sharon Romine

Grief Skills for Life

A personal journal for teenagers about loss

Judy Davidson, Ed. D.